SOCIETAL REFORM

TAKING THE KINGDOM TO THE SYSTEMS

PATRICK ISAAC

Societal Reform
Taking the Kingdom to the Systems

Unless otherwise indicated, scriptural quotations of the Bible are from:

Holy Bible
with commentary of C.I. Scofield (9th edition)

The New King James Version of the Bible (NKJV)

Dépôt Légal - Bibliothèque nationale du Québec, 2014
Legal Deposit - Library and Archives du Canada, 2014

iUniverse books may be ordered through booksellers or by contacting:

iUniverse
1663 Liberty Drive
Bloomington, IN 47403
www.iuniverse.com
1-800-Authors (1-800-288-4677)

ISBN: 978-1-4917-6431-2 (sc)
ISBN: 978-1-4917-6432-9 (e)

Print information available on the last page.

iUniverse rev. date: 10/19/2016

Table of Contents

Foreword

Societal Reform is a mandate from heaven, and Patrick Isaac has written a comprehensive book on this mandate. God loves society because he loves people. The condition of our society will affect people either positively or negatively. Reform is necessary when society has become corrupted by ungodly influences, and in need of change.

It is with excitement and joy that I recommend this book. We live in an exciting age with many breakthroughs occurring at an unprecedented rate. The rate of change is astounding. The Church must also keep pace with this change, and remove outmoded ways of thinking if we are to be relevant. This book is a catalyst to help the Church accelerate, and meet the challenges of a fast changing world.

The Church is the agent of the kingdom of God. The advance of the kingdom should be the primary goal of the Church. This advance will affect society, and bring reformation.

The Church must be challenged to influence the systems of the world. This challenge must be bold, and come from apostolic voices. Patrick Isaac is a voice that challenges the Church to get involved in society, and affect the systems. The

Church cannot afford to only have a vision for heaven, while abandoning God's plan for the earth.

The principles and power of the Kingdom bring transformation. The Church has often emphasized individual transformation, while neglecting societal transformation. This book confronts the prevailing mindset of many churches of individual emphasis, rather than societal emphasis.

Societal reformation is possible, but it will require a new vision and a new faith. It will also require a new breed of Christians who have been changed by the truths taught in this book. The wisdom in this book needs to be received worldwide by leaders, and implemented globally. The systems of this world can be blessed, but only if the Church gets involved, and reforms them.

Reformation is work. Reformation requires boldness. This book is bold in its approach and style. Patrick Isaac is courageous in teaching these principles. Many things taught may be contrary and different from what has been commonly taught. Truth is often confrontational, but necessary to liberate us from errors that have kept us from fulfilling God's mandate and plan for the earth.

Where there is no vision, the people perish (Prov. 29:18). This book gives a vision that is seldom seen. The vision for societal reformation is larger than just having a local church. The vision of this book is larger than what has been commonly taught. We are not abandoning the world, and relinquishing it to darkness. We are getting a vision to bring light to the systems of this world, and bring change and reform where needed.

I have seen Patrick Isaac's passion for societal reform. I know him personally. I have heard his message, and I know his heart. This passion and message are written throughout the pages of this book. I believe you will not only receive information and revelation, but also an impartation. The anointing upon his life will flow through the pages of this book into your life. You will be activated and mobilized. You will be stretched and challenged.

I encourage those who read this book to not only read it, but get involved in this current reformation. This book is a call to action. It is not for those who want to do nothing, but for those who want to be world changers. The systems of this world can be a blessing for generations to come. What we do today in our nations can bring world transformation in ways we have never seen. Let's do it for our children, and our children's children.

Apostle John Eckhardt
OCTOBER, 2014

Preface

There is a soul searching question that seems to be resonating in every nation on the face of the earth. That question is, "Why with all the churches, prayers, Christians, conferences and conventions does it seem that our world is getting worse instead of better?" Why do we have more crime, criminals, corruption, prostitution, murder and mayhem like never before? What in the world is going on? I believe that the answer is in the question. The problem is that God's Church is not going to the world. Yes, we are evangelizing trying to save sinners, but what we are missing is that we have not focused on shifting societies.

I come with good news that there, I believe, is a paradigm shift that is taking place with the revelation of the new initiative that is going on worldwide of a focus on the seven mind molders of society. These seven mind molders are Media, Arts and Entertainment, Business, Education, Government, Family and yes, Religion. These seven mind molders are called different things in different places, such as systems, mountains, but the clearest definition has to be the kingdoms of this world. And one of the giants and generals of this new move of God is my friend and covenant brother, Apostle Patrick Isaac,

Spiritual Authority of the PQL Ministries in Montreal Canada, author of the book "Societal Reform, Taking the Kingdom to the Systems." Without question this book will not only be a standard, but a working manual for a generation in the shifting of societies.

What gives this publication credence and credibility is that Apostle Isaac is not only teaching it, but he is doing it. PQL Ministries in Montreal is a map and model ministry as to the what, the why and the way to bring about invading and infecting these seven vital systems that are found in every nation on the face of the earth. This book is a must read, not only for those who have caught the revelation of the seven kingdoms, but those that need to catch the revelation of the how to do Matthew 28:20, which is the mandate from the Master. Not only should you read this awesome book, but recommend it to every believer you know. For this is not a revelation for just church leaders, but for the activation of all of the called of Christ.

I have been blessed and motivated, as never before, by the study and reading of this anointed book to do all in my power to bring the prophetic proclamation of Revelation 11:15 to pass — "And the kingdoms of this world have become the kingdoms of our Lord and His Christ and He shall reign forever."

Apostle H. Daniel Wilson

Introduction

THE CHURCH'S MANDATE: ADVANCE THE KINGDOM OF GOD ON EARTH

Jesus Christ died, resurrected and is seated at the right hand of God and from there oversees the kingdom he has established over 2,000 years ago. Everyone who receives Jesus as Lord and Savior needs to understand that he is not just preparing for heaven but has received the glorious call to advance the kingdom of our King Jesus on earth. It is imperative for every child of God to know that the Lord God has called him to be positioned to make an impact. Ephesians 2:10 says: "For we are His workmanship, created in Christ Jesus for good works, which God prepared beforehand that we should walk in them." As children of the King of Kings, Jesus has a call on our lives. He has prepared good works beforehand so that we should walk in them. Although the religious church has swayed us in believing that only the Pastor has a call on his life; every saint has a call on his life. In fact the reason why some saints are having a hard time getting up in the morning to step out into their workplace is because they have not taken their rightful place.

When somebody is exactly positioned where God has called him to be, he won't need to have anybody to wake him up in the morning because he is always ready to go. If you are counting the hours until your 15 minute break, praying to God for your lunch break and your 15 minute break at 3 o'clock, and dreaming of when 5 o'clock hits for you to jump on the bus or your car to go home, something is wrong. You are definitely not in your divine position; this cannot be God's desire for your life. He wants you to be positioned to make an impact. Until you are accurately positioned, there is a dimension and a level of breakthrough that you will never see in your life. Your breakthrough comes when you are seated where God desires for you to occupy. When you are sitting in that proper position, every grace, every anointing, every breakthrough, every opening is able to come to you. That is why some goodwill Christians have certain things that they have not even put their hands on, because they are out of place. In some cases it might be that they are being processed but for some people, it is the result of being out of place. This is why it is important to know that this book is not just a book to have.

In this season God is creating order out of disorder. The trumpet is being blown in Zion through His apostolic and prophetic voices to set proper foundations to propel His people in their divine destiny. Therefore you need to be positioned to have an impact. You need to refuse to be irrelevant, refuse to die in anonymity. You should die leaving a legacy of having changed the world. But I believe there is a reason why you are breathing air right now. You are alive because you are called to have an impact. You are called to do something, to shift something, to leave your name, your mark in your sphere of influence. You need to reach that level of determination of having such an impact that even if people around you wanted to, they couldn't forget you, for you have stepped into your realm of influence and taken over. This book is about someone desiring to be positioned to impact and wanting to leave his footprints on earth for Jesus Christ. Impacting one's society, impacting one's nation, impacting the world for Jesus Christ such is the call on your life.

I received Jesus Christ as my Lord and Savior at 25 years old. I believe the mediocrity of the churches in my area is one of the main reasons it took me so long to be attracted to God. I felt that church was good for my mother and that her prayers for me were good enough. That mindset was due to what I had seen in the lives of churchgoers. I had not encountered anyone of them who had any type of impact on me.

I believe that God is raising a new generation of churchgoers, an apostolic generation of people making a difference in the world, affecting it with the gospel of the kingdom. It is imperative to know that we will not have any type of significant and substantial influence in advancing the kingdom of God on earth without the establishment of the apostolic church.

1

The Church of Jesus Christ is Called to be Apostolic

The only church that is born of Jesus Christ is the apostolic church. Before you declare me a heretic, I will biblically prove that the church of Jesus Christ is nothing else but apostolic.

> MARK 3: 13-15
> *"And He went up on the mountain and called to Him those He Himself wanted. And they came to Him. Then He appointed twelve, that they might be with Him and that He might send them out to preach and to have power to heal the sicknesses and to cast out demons."*

This Scripture depicts the election of the twelve apostles of the Lord Jesus Christ. The Lord went up on the mountain to spend some time with the Father to get clear direction for the choice of his first twelve apostles. After this time of consecration, he called those he wanted and appointed them that they might be with him. Why did he appoint them to be with him? Was our Lord suffering from loneliness? Not at all. There was a specific purpose for having the twelve with Him. Understand that Jesus could have fulfilled his ministry on earth without the help of anyone, but our Lord was strategic. Being the Chief Apostle and the Supreme Visionary of the plan of God to advance his kingdom on earth He knew He had to train and equip the first apostles to ensure that God's plan was fulfilled on earth.

Therefore verses 14-15 say,

> "They might be with Him and that He might SEND them out to preach".

The word "send" in verse 15 comes from the Greek verb *"apostello"* which literally means "He who is sent out". Jesus knew that he had just three years to train and equip those men to follow through the divine purpose of salvation and kingdom advancement of our God on earth. The disciples received an intensive training, walking with Jesus, eating with Jesus, witnessing the Lord's ministry and then practicing for one strategic purpose: "so they could be sent out by Him". They were called, trained to be apostolic, to be sent out to preach the Good News of the kingdom of God. My question for you is: "Is there a saint or a local church member of the Body of Christ who is not sent out to preach the Good News of the kingdom of God? If you are theologically and doctrinally sound, the only answer that you can have is: "No." Therefore, every saint, every local church member, every minister is sent out to preach the Good News of the kingdom of God. Henceforth every saint, every local church and every ministry, part of the Body of Christ is *apostolic, sent out* to preach the Good News of the kingdom of God. The church of Jesus Christ can therefore be nothing but apostolic, for it is sent out to preach the word of God and advance the kingdom of our Lord and King Jesus on earth. Henceforth the purpose of the apostolic restoration and reformation is to bring the church through proper apostolic structure, to the level of being able to be sent out to advance the kingdom of God on earth. Apostolic restoration and reformation is literally the instrument of God to raise an apostolic church.

APOSTOLIC RESTORATION AND REFORMATION

MATTHEW 16: 18

"And I say to you that you are Peter, and on this rock I will build My church, and the gates of Hades shall not prevail against it."

The first century church began with authority and power; demonstrated without a shadow of doubt the works of Jesus Christ. Unfortunately, men started putting their faith in their ideas and opinions and the church started losing its effectiveness. Since the 16th century, God has been restoring biblical truths that men had polluted or taken out of the church. For the last 10 to 15 years, the church has been experiencing apostolic restoration and reformation. Understand that apostolic restoration and reformation is not a spooky movement initiated by men of God seeking for upgraded titles but is the order that God, through revelation and insight, has given to his apostles and prophets to bring the church back to its place of authority and power to enforce and advance his kingdom on earth. Apostolic restoration is the return to the fullness of the apostolic office, apostolic structure and apostolic anointing in the church of Jesus Christ for the fulfillment of the church's destiny on this earth.

§

Peter preached one message and about 3,000 souls were added to the kingdom of God. Surely the people of God want to see the church flow in great power in its quest to enforce the kingdom. There is no doubt that the Body of Christ desires apostolic restoration and the level of impact of the first century church manifested in our generation. But in order to see apostolic restoration we need reformation.

What is Reformation?

"Reformation is an administrative term that speaks of form anew, reorganization, modification brought because of persistent lacks, inefficacy and non-productivity."

Truly, the church needs reorganization and modification because of persistent lack of productivity. When we look in a region of the world like North America, the United States have so many churches and so many people call themselves Christians; nevertheless, sin is rampant and Christian values are depleting in a rapid rate in that society. If what we were doing were good, we would have seen more fruits. Reformation brings change and reorganization for greater breakthrough and fruit. To have restoration, the church has to pay the price of reformation. It will cost a church reformation to have restoration. There is no reformation without deformation. Deformation will cost. For it is not easy to change form. Man in his nature does not like change. How easy it is for man to always eat in the same restaurants, buy the same type of clothes and shoes, take the same route to work and back to his house and sit in the same chair or same row or same area in the congregation. Human beings do not like change. Therefore, reform is not a popular setting for many churches and many ministries although they clearly suffer from inefficacy and non-productivity. The Church will have to pay the price of reformation to have apostolic restoration. What is henceforth the price of reformation? What are the reformation stoppers?

THE REVELATION OF THE WORD OF GOD IS PROGRESSIVE

In order for a church to experience reformation, it will have to understand that the revelation of God's word is progressive. Not accepting that the revelation of the Word of God is progressive will stop reformation in the church. One of the church's biggest pitfalls is its propensity to put God in a box. Too many saints tend to restrict God to what they know of Him and somewhat forget that God is greater than the revelation they have of Him. God supersedes our revelation of Him. We need to know that we can function for a season at a certain level, but if we don't remain open to revelation that comes out of the Word of God, we will not progress in our spiritual walk. For it takes new revelation to reach new levels in God. So if you are not open to the progression of the revelation of the Word of God, you will be stuck with what you know.

1 Corinthians 13:9, declares,

"We know in part..."

Notice the Word says we know in part, therefore what we know today is nothing but a drop of the infinite ocean of revelation of the fullness of who God is. Understanding that the revelation of the word of God is progressive becomes a prerequisite to added knowledge and revelation of God and in God.

In Exodus 6: 2-3, God speaks to Moses and says,

> "And God spake unto Moses and said unto him, I am the Lord: and I appeared unto Abraham unto Isaac, and unto Jacob, by the name of God Almighty, but by my name Jehovah was I not known to them." (KJV)

Here God is speaking to Moses concerning the knowledge that His people have of Him. Three generations received and had knowledge of a certain dimension of God but were ignorant of another dimension of God that only the subsequent generation received. They received illumination for a new dimension of God. The Lord reveals Himself in a progressive way.

Notice that 2 Peter 3: 18 speaks of "...growing in the knowledge of the Lord."

> "But grow in the grace and knowledge of our Lord and Saviour Jesus Christ. To him be glory both now and forever!"

It is our responsibility to grow in the knowledge of God. Apostolic restoration and reformation are neither a fad nor a new trend but the Spirit of God shedding light in the revelation of His Church. This enlightenment of the Holy Spirit is being released all over the body of Christ, positioning the Church for its greatest breakthrough and penetration of the world with the gospel of the kingdom.

THE REFORMATION STOPPERS

Religion

Religion is certainly a reformation stopper, because it does not like change. It is for this cause that in every season, we need to guard ourselves from religion and religious mindsets. Religion stops the move of God. It will stop the growth of revelation in a local house. It boxes the revelation of the Word of God in the confinements of its rituals. Religion has an understanding and knowledge of God and it puts God in that box. Religion becomes god and the religious person says, "God you must function but only within my parameters. If you move away from my prescription then I know it is not you at work."

If God wants to be worshipped in a different way that is not acceptable. If He moves another way, that is not Him. Even if there is no fruit, the religious will still continue to do things the same way. God is boxed in a religious set up: Sunday School then worship service for example. That may be the format for years, and although nobody or very few show up for Sunday School, the religious church would relentlessly keep that fruitless structure. Denominationalism says, "Do this because it is the rule of the denomination; fruitless but still in place. You do it out of faithfulness to religion.

Jesus spoke to the Scribes and Pharisees and said in Matthew 15: 6,

> *"Thus you have made the commandment of God of no effect by your tradition."*

And in Mark 7: 13,

> *"Making the Word of God of no effect through your*
> *tradition which you have handed down. And many such*
> *things you do."*

A lot of things done in church have been passed down but are neither the intent nor the will of the Holy Spirit. The order of services, the way church is done are Christian traditions or transmissions from fathers in the Lord or come from denominations. But it is not necessarily the will of the Holy Ghost for this generation. 'They did it and I grew up in that church so I still do it.' But that is what Jesus said to the Pharisees: you do it although the Holy Spirit is not in it; it has been passed down. Therefore it is done because the denominational creed and format say so, even though it is not effective and does not bring forth fruit. Ask yourself if everything you do comes from the Holy Spirit, or has it been passed down? If it's fruitless and you still do it, it's religious! If you vehemently continue to do it although it's not led by the Holy Spirit you are religious! We need to know that the spirit of religion is a major tool of the devil, sent to block reformation and henceforth apostolic restoration for kingdom advancement.

§

Let me give you some examples of religion. Fruitless spiritual activities are fruitless activities that the church continues to do. The assemblies live through annual religious rituals that do not produce fruit. The same crusades, the same conferences, the same old revival services that revive but a few, the same retreats that only seem to retreat the flesh of some for a short period of time and, above all, let us not forget the monthly, quarterly and yearly guest speakers who are club members for life in certain local churches to a point that their messages can be remotely controlled and that their voices have become elevator music.

Spiritual Exercises Without Spiritual Growth

You have tongue talking, public abasement, fasting experts but there is no fruit. There is no sign of any significant spiritual growth. You have the right terminology but no fruit, the right moves and the right spiritual rhythms but no anointing and no demonstration of the power of God: it's religious. I still remember a minister sharing his experience going in a church where the preacher preached on the "red jacket" with no biblical base nor biblical truths brought forth but still people were shouting and some in emotional delirium nevertheless started running in the aisle of the church: it's religious! We need to know that if the Holy Spirit is not in it, it's religious. The demon of religion will have to fall for restoration and reformation to take place in the Body of Christ.

Spirit of pride

JOB 41: 1, 34
"Can you draw out Leviathan with a hook or snare his tongue with a line which you lower?... He is king over all the children of pride."

As we examine Job 41: 1, 34; we are enlightened about Leviathan, a demon who is king over all the children of pride. The Leviathan spirit inflicts pride or enhances pride that is already a strong carnal attribute in some people. That spirit of pride is another reformation stopper. Why? Because pride will stop you from changing, you will not receive the reformation of the Word of God. Pride stops revelation from entering in one's spiritual process. When you are over-indulged in pride, you cannot talk about God the Father, but Leviathan your father. You see a prideful person is a stubborn person, hard to change, hard to submit to the illumination of the word of God.

Proverbs 16: 18 says,

> *"Pride goes before destruction, a haughty spirit before a fall."*

God wants to change you in order to bless you but you are haughty. Know that the ultimate result of pride is destruction. Pride will make you think you are excellent, when in fact you are mediocre. You are irrelevant, but pride will make you think you are relevant. Pride will make you think you are learned when in fact you're ignorant. No use trying to counsel or impart wisdom to the prideful. He can even give you a hug and thank you for the word of wisdom and turn around and still continue in his irrelevant and mediocre ways.

Humility will permit you to accept change that brings growth and expansion in your life, when it comes with love. But for the prideful, even if one begs him to change, he will not change. When the revelation comes, you will say "glory to God", but still wish that you'd be left alone. Pride opens you up to the spirit of witchcraft. It gives lead to the spirit of competition and jealousy in the church. But humility will permit you to receive and accept the changes that the Lord is bringing in your life and his body.

Job 34: 23, 24 are verses that we need to take heed to,

"For God has no need to examine men further
that they should come before him in judgment.
Without inquiry he shatters the mighty and sets
up others in their place." (ESV)

God is good and God is patient, but there comes a time when God will break the one who is prideful and haughty. Now when that happens, He puts someone after you so appointed and anointed that people will not even remember you. Notice that the Word says 'without inquiry'. The Lord will not inquire of you if He should break you. After He has been talking and talking, warning and warning, there comes a time when He will come without inquiry and shatter the prideful. God is reforming His Church and the prideful will not be able to stop Him; humility will permit us to receive and accept the changes He is bringing in His Body. He is raising His apostolic church for this time and age to radically advance His kingdom on earth. Now when apostolic reformation takes place, it will bring the establishment of apostolic structure in the local church and bring forth the apostolic model church.

2

The Apostolic Model Church

As I am endeavoring to shed light on the apostolic model church, it is important to understand that my goal is not to disregard, crush or put down the churches in the format that they are in. The purpose is not to destroy or cast down the structures that we have in the local churches, it is rather to bring insight to improve or strengthen them.

APOSTOLIC LEADERSHIP

An apostolic model church is one with apostolic leadership, whether that leader is an apostle as the spiritual authority of the local church or an apostle spiritually covering a church with any other of the ascension gifts leading it.

A local church can only be at the level of its leadership. If the leadership is anointed, the church will be anointed. If the leadership has depth and revelation in the Word, the church will have depth and revelation in the Word of God. If the leadership has no power then the church will have no power. If the leadership lacks revelation and depth then the church will lack it also. You see this is what we call the 'lid' theory.

The leadership is the lid of a church; the saints will plateau at the level of their leaders.

Now the word says in 1 Corinthians 12: 28,

"And God hath set some in the church, first apostles, secondarily prophets, third teachers." (KJV).

Notice that the Word says that God has set 'in the church'. It means that the apostles are in the local house. The word 'first' is from the Greek word "Proton" and speaks of first in rank, in honor and authority. As this revelation is being released to the Body of Christ, many leaders are shifting title from pastor to apostle. True apostolic leadership though is not just a change of title from pastor to apostle. But the apostolic leadership must be able to raise an apostolic people and establish an apostolic house. It is not just a title. The Church of Jesus Christ needs to be raised up. If the people of God do not reach their destiny something is wrong in the leadership. A presiding apostle is recognized by his capacity to release the people of God in their destiny. Apostolic leadership has the ability to give the saints of God the means to reach their destiny. The apostleship is shown by the people and not the title one has. It is about the fruit and not about the title. It is about the people of God being perfected for the work of the ministry and the advancement of the kingdom of God. Now there is nothing wrong with putting titles on cards, but the fruit of the title needs to be seen. Today, everybody can have a beautiful website and have a card; and there is nothing wrong with that, it is needed to impact this digital generation, but one needs to show forth the fruit and give relevancy to the well designed website and cards. The heart of God is His people and they have to be raised up in order to penetrate the world and have impact and influence in the different societal systems to fulfill the great commission. An apostolic leadership is called to raise an apostolic structured house for apostolic results of kingdom expansion.

APOSTOLIC STRUCTURED HOUSE

What is an apostolic structured house? It is not a beautiful building. It is not a one-man show. Have you ever been on the Internet and seen the website of a mega-church featuring a super-hero? Nobody else but that minister and his wife are seen on the website. Everybody else is cheerleading this man or woman. And if he travels, the local ministry is on hold. Have you ever seen these types of churches? Just one man and his wife who are able to minister, lay hands on the sick, prophesy or preach. In such a case, apostolic grace has not yet been established in their structure. The ministry of the sons and daughters of an apostolic leader shows apostolic anointing. If a leader cannot sit down and have the church minister with mature fruit, that church is not yet apostolic. A church is not yet apostolic when the saints take some time off in the absence of their senior leader ministering on the road because of the superficiality of the anointing and grace of the other ministers of the church.

Philippians 1: 1 gives us insight into the structure of the apostolic house. Paul speaks and greets the saints of the church of Philippi.

"Paul and Timothy, bondservants of Jesus Christ, to all the saints in Christ Jesus who are in Philippi, with the bishops and deacons."

This verse gives us insight on the order of authority in the church. Hierarchy in spiritual authority is set this way: Bishops, Deacons and saints.

Now the Greek word *"episkopois"* is in some versions translated overseer. We therefore see that in one church, they had deacons, bishops (overseers) and saints. Now bishops and elders speak of the same office. "Elders" is the Greek word *"presbuteros"*, a title given to the persons. Bishops, *"episcopos"*, guardian, protector, overseer therefore speaks to the title of the elders in the church. Elder is the title and bishop is his function. The Elder has the function of bishop. Elder and bishop speak of the same person.

Acts 20: 17-28 gives us more insight on this truth. In these verses, Apostle Paul calls the elders of the church of Ephesus to possibly encourage them for a last time.

VERSE 17
"And from Miletus he sent to Ephesus, and called the elders of the church."

As it is written, we can observe that there were many elders in the church of Ephesus. Paul called them and told them in verse 28;

> *"Take care and be on guard for yourselves and the whole flock over which the Holy Spirit has appointed you bishops and guardians, to shepherd (tend, feed and guide) the church of the Lord..." (Amplified Version).*

Apostle Paul told the multiple elders of the church of Ephesus to take heed to themselves and the whole flock that they received the mandate of God "to bishop". Here again the word elder and bishop are connected to the same person.

TITUS 1: 5-7

"For this reason I left you in Crete, that you should set in order the things that are lacking, and appoint elders in every city as I commanded you. If any man is blameless, the husband of one wife, having faithful children not accused of dissipation or insubordination, for a bishop must be blameless as a steward of God, not self willed, not quick tempered, not given to wine, not violent; not greedy for money."

Once more in the book of Titus, the word elder and bishop are intertwined. Bishops and elders speak of the same person. In every church in the first century, there was a plurality of elders established to bishop the saints of that church. An elder is established by spiritual maturity and not by the age of a saint or the number of years he has been in that particular ministry. A minister can be 20 years old and be an elder in a church and another believer can be 50 years old and still be a baby in the faith.

PLURALITY OF ELDERS

Ephesians 4: 8, 11-13 says,

"When He ascended on high, He led captivity captive, and gave gifts to men. And He Himself gave some to be apostles, some prophets, some evangelists, and some pastors and teachers, for the equipping of the saints for the work of ministry, for the edifying of the Body of

Christ, till we all come to the unity of the faith and of the knowledge of the Son of God, to a perfect man, to the measure of the stature of the fullness of Christ."

The ascension gifts of Ephesians 4:11 are the elders in the church. Apostles, prophets, evangelists, pastors and teachers are commonly called the ascension gifts, since the Lord released them as He ascended on high, as explained in verse 8. Verse 12 tells us that they are there for the perfecting of the saints for the work of ministry. Notice that the word bishop in Greek speaks of guarding, overseeing, taking care and edifying which is exactly the function of the ascension gifts explained in verse 12. The ascension gifts have the function of bishop.

1 PETER 5: 1

"The elders who are among you I exhort, I who am a fellow elder and a witness of the sufferings of Christ, and also a partaker of the glory that will be revealed."

Peter, an apostle of Jesus Christ, declares himself an elder. In fact, it is because he is a seasoned elder that he is able to exhort them on the function of an elder in verse 1 of 1 Peter. He therefore encourages the elders to have a heart for the flock, to feed them and to give them the proper oversight. The elders are the ascension gifts of Ephesians 4: 11.

ACTS 13: 1

"Now in the church that was at Antioch there were certain prophets and teachers."

The word says here that they were prophets and teachers in the church of Antioch. So what were these ascensions gifts doing? They were taking care of the flock. We therefore see once more ascension gifts of Ephesians 4:11; elders of a local church doing the function of bishop. It is also interesting to see that in every case there is a plurality of elders in every church.

DOES PLURALITY MEAN DEMOCRACY?

ACTS 14: 23
"Paul and Barnabas appointed elders for them in each church and, with prayer and fasting, committed them to the Lord, in whom they had put their trust."

Does plurality of elders in a church's leadership mean democracy? Does the majority win in the decisional process of a plural elders' church? The elaboration and answer to this question will bring insight and peace in the heart of many ministers who are challenged with the transition of a pastoral lead church to an apostolic structured church. Because one of the inner struggles of the vision holder of a pastoral lead church that has not implemented the establishment of ascension gifts in his church is: What will happen to my authority and leadership when other ascension gifts are established? Will my authority be challenged? Will I lose the vision or the grip of the vision the Lord gave me? Well the answer to the question whether plurality means democracy is definitely "no!". God does not function by democracy but by theocracy. The theocracy of God is seen through spiritual authority. Even if the church has 50 elders, there is but one spiritual authority. There will always be one set man over the house. When you have two heads in one place, you have a demon. If there are 20 apostles and 15 prophets, in that college there will always be one spiritual authority. Unfortunately, a lot of churches have demons. They have one called leader, but have many active carnal leaders giving direction and henceforth division in the midst of the church. You see, a vision must have one visionary, two visionaries is division (di: two and vision). Division in a church is simply two or more vision enforcers in the midst of the vision. God never establishes a church without putting a leader in place to lead it. Some churches name a senior pastor and an assistant pastor, but in a properly structured church, there is no need for the assistant pastor title. According to Scripture, in the church in Jerusalem, they had apostles — not a chief or Senior Apostle.

Matthew 10: 1-2 gives us insight on this,

> "He called his twelve disciples to him and gave them authority to drive out evil spirits and to heal every disease and sickness. These are the names of the twelve apostles: first, Simon (who is called Peter) and his brother Andrew; James, son of Zebedee and his brother John; Philip and Bartholomew; Thomas and Matthew, the tax collector; James, son of Alphaeus and Thaddeus; Simon the zealot and Judas Iscariot, who betrayed him."

The word "first" in the second verse is the Greek word "proton" that speaks about first in rank, in honor and in authority. Simon Peter was initially the apostle in authority in the church of Jerusalem. Notice after the mention of "first Simon" there is no mention of second or third indicating that the word first is there to establish Peter's leadership over the twelve apostles. Throughout the New Testament, there is no mention of assistant-pastor or assistant-any of the other ascension gifts. You are either an ascension gift or you're not. There is no such thing as assistant-ascension gift. The gift that was giving assistance to the ascension gifts will be studied later in this book and that is the office of the deacon.

Numbers 27: 16 also shed light on the establishment of an authority over the people of God. It says this,

"Let the Lord, the God of the spirits of all flesh, set a man over the congregation."

"May the Lord, the God of the spirits of all mankind, appoint a man over this community." (NIV)

How can you have a community and have more than one set man? In order to have a properly functional and led community, it needs a leader. Understand that I am not speaking of only one person being active in the implementation of the vision but of one leader who gives direction. Our God is a God of order and He will always set one person to give direction to His local church. Notice that it is also said that this set man is placed 'over the community'. When we speak of spiritual authority in a congregation, the leader is not alongside but over the community he is giving leadership to.

REVELATION 2: 1
"To the angel of the church in Ephesus write: These are the words of him who holds the seven stars in his right hand and walks among the seven golden lampstands."
(NIV)

In Chapters 2 and 3 of the book of Revelation the word "Angel" is mentioned 7 times pertaining to the prophetic word given by our Lord to seven churches of the first century era. In fact he addresses the letter to the Angel of each church on behalf of their churches. The word "Angel" is not speaking about a spiritual being, a spiritual protective being for these churches but of the leader of each one of those churches. Notice that although Acts 20:17 shows us that the church of Ephesus had many elders, only one of these elders had the spiritual leadership of the group and of the church. The prophetic word was given to Apostle John for the set man of every church, pertaining to the state of the church that they had spiritual authority over.

There are different ways in the Bible to depict authority. Sometimes the authority is mentioned first in Acts 3: 1,

> *"One day, Peter and John were going up to the temple at the time of prayer." (NIV)*

The one who speaks in the name of the group sometimes shows authority. In Acts 2: 14, Apostle Peter spoke on behalf of the twelve,

> *"But Peter, standing up with the eleven, raised his voice and said to them."*

Therefore, although every church is called to have a plurality of elders yet the Lord will set only one over the group and congregation. Plurality is truly not a means for democracy in the local churches of God.

APPOINTED ORDINATION AND PROPER POSITIONING OF ELDERS

Before speaking of the specific functions of the different elders, we need to understand the seriousness of the establishment of an elder. Too many elders are released prematurely. Some truly have the gifts but have not gone through the proper process and some others have gone through a process but were not called to be elders. We also see elders being ordained in the wrong office. The ordination of an elder should not be done lightly; there should be truly a high standard for the eldership in the local house. The Spiritual Authorities in local houses must stop releasing them before their time. If an elder is premature and immature, the church will suffer the consequences. The spiritual weakness of some churches is the resultant effect of a weak eldership. We do not have to hear the elders speak to know their level. We just have to look at the church. If the elders are not trained and do not have depth in the Word, it will be reflected in the level of the saints in the church. We just cannot take the ordination and positioning of elders in a local house lightly.

Every local house has ascension gifts in its midst, however these gifts need to be identified and trained. Ministers have started their ministry on the basis of one prophetic word. No wonder some senior leaders are stuck with 20 people for 20 years. In such cases there is obviously something wrong. God will not anoint you to carry a vision without making provision for the vision to grow. God cannot be the author of stagnation and fruitlessness, for everything He ordains and anoints will flourish and bring forth fruit. It is very hard for an elder to perfect saints when he is not himself perfected and properly trained. It is tragic to see ascension gifts positioned in the wrong office or persons bearing titles without the requisite grace. There are critical keys which ministries and potential elders must understand, lest they fall in the trap of prematurely ordaining or wrongly positioning gifts. These keys are also relevant for any minister aspiring to any call and ministry of God.

IMPORTANCE OF AFFIRMATION AND CONFIRMATION

God will give affirmation and confirmation for every call or ministry given to a saint. Affirmation is defined as the assertion that something exists or is true, thus God would affirm the existence or veracity of a call. After receiving affirmation from God, we may then receive confirmation of the call from someone else. I will speak of the personal affirmation and three different confirmations, which though not exhaustive, would help reduce mistakes in positioning elders in ministry.

PERSONAL AFFIRMATION FROM GOD

Before assuming that any word is a word from God, for your ordination or to start any type of ministry for this matter, you need to have a personal affirmation from God. You cannot step into a calling based on what people tell you. You need to have an encounter with God. It is not that receiving prophetic words from others is wrong, but you need to have your own encounter with God affirming your call or ministry before ever thinking of moving forward. The problem in the church is that many, after that personal affirmation, think they are ready to start ministry. Because God spoke to you doesn't mean you are ready to start your ministry. We need to remember that we function in a body. If God speaks to you, he will also speak to others to confirm what you receive from Him. It is important to know that there are three different voices that can speak to us: God, the flesh, and the devil. Henceforth we should not minimize the importance of receiving sound confirmation for our affirmation from God.

In my personal experience, I still remember vividly the first affirmation I received from the Lord for the call for ministry. I was in my living room praying when the Lord appeared and pointed at me. I looked at my left and right and behold the vision of two ministers of my local church on both of my sides. When the Lord pointed, I looked to my left and right, thinking that the Lord was probably pointing to them since they were ministering in our church before me but with a nod He signified to me that He was pointing to me and said that He called me to ministry of His gospel and asked me if I was ready to pay the price? I answered yes and all of a sudden He disappeared. Although I had many affirmations from the Lord for the mandate He gave me, I just cannot forget the first affirmation that is still so vivid in my spirit.

CONFIRMATION FROM THE ELDERS OF THE CHURCH

Please understand that you cannot be the only one in the Body of Christ who receives a word from God concerning your call as an elder. The Lord, respecting authority, will speak to the authorities of a local house concerning the call of a saint under their covering. Therefore the spiritual authority of the local house and the other elders will receive clear direction concerning the call of a saint in the local church. The words they receive concerning your life and ministry are very important in your process as a Christian, since the Lord has set them bishops over your life.

CONFIRMATION FROM BRETHREN IN THE LOCAL HOUSE

The elders will not be the only ones to see the call and the grace on an elder who is called by God. As you continue to minister not only the elders but also brethren in the church will begin to see the grace on your life. Our gifts are given to us for the edifying of the Body of Christ. We have not received gifts from God to minister to ourselves but to His body and the world. Therefore it is understandable that the saints in our local house, being part of the Body of Christ and having proximity to us, will be witnesses and first partakers of the blessings of the grace on our life. They will also receive from God confirmation of our call and ministry in the Body of Christ.

CONFIRMATION FROM THE BODY OF CHRIST

The strength behind a confirmation is its objectivity. A prophetic word of confirmation cannot be called so if it is not objective. The word needs to come from a source that truly hears it from God. In that perspective adding to the fact of not being familiar and known to another saint, the confirmation from a minister or brethren in the Body of Christ who are not in our local house and who do not know us is another way of validating and solidly strengthening the affirmation we receive from God concerning our call and ministry. A week after my wedding, a prophet from the USA spoke to me while I was translating for him in a church in my hometown. He prophesied the teaching and apostolic office on my life. In fact, that was the first time that I heard about the apostolic call on my life. Sure enough, although at that time I was a youth leader in my local church, seven years later, I was commissioned as an apostle in PQL Center, the local house that I oversee. Although the Lord has His way of affirming and confirming the calls of every saint in His Body, the fact is that we should never believe it sound to start any type of ministry without them. Since our Lord is a Lord of order, He will speak to us through the authorities of our lives and the brethren in His Body. He can even use an unbeliever to confirm the call on our lives.

TRAINING

Now although we have received affirmation and confirmation from God, this is still not enough to start a ministry. After we receive affirmation and confirmation, ordination does not follow but training. Let it be known that, a saint cannot and should not step into ministry only after a prophetic word. Many frivolous, immature and ignorant saints have done that bringing hurt to themselves, and sometimes innocent saints in the body of Christ.

That is why some are crashing down, because they did not go through the proper process: the Call, the Training, the Mandate and the Commissioning. Many saints know the call that is on their life, but still are not ready. You are not called and released right after, the next step is training. I received my call in 1995, but I was not released until 2002. So what is your process?

The training period is the grooming period in the life of a saint. It is the time of rooting out, destroying and then planting and building. Some saints have the gift, but lack the character; some have the character but lack the understanding of their gifts. Training is used to break our flesh from bonds of competition, bad habits, cultural flaws, etc. and put it under subjection. This is especially relevant for the ascension gifts because they are exposed, leaders who are called to equip the saints. Therefore the saints see them as examples to imitate and to minister in their likeness. You see although a minister is called to grow in every season of his life, there is a level of growth, of maturity and spirituality that an ascension gift needs to have before being released and being exposed to all. Imagine a pastor who has not conquered pride and refuses to be counseled, who can help him when he walks astray? If there is something that can puff someone up, it is a title. A title can even change the way one speaks. Sometimes pride can be so much of an issue that ministers even have difficulty receiving from the ministry of the word of their peers. They expect every saint to receive but as for them, they just find a way to fine-tune their next sermon. The training is where we work the person, his life experience, his level of humility and his depth in the word. It is also where the character, the spirituality and the maturity in the gifts are dealt with.

MANDATE

Mandate will very often come in the course of our training and ministering in our local house. It is not enough to have a general training and start ministry, but a leader needs to have specificities in the call of God in his or her life. Paul was not only called to minister but he was specifically called to minister to the Gentiles. Peter had a special assignment of God to the Jews. What is your mandate as an ascension gift? I have often encountered ministers changing titles and ministries so often that we, the rest of the Body of Christ, have difficulty knowing where they are in the plan of God. Every season they have a new call: "God has given me a new call and direction." How different from the ministers in the word of God who clearly received specific calls from God that they used a lifetime to carry out. It is not to say that the Lord cannot bring variants, add strategies or some new assignments to the call He already gave us, but going through the musical chair with the different callings of God is questionable for a leader. A minister should have a clear and precise mandate from God.

COMMISSIONING

ACTS 13: 1

"Now in the church that was at Antioch there were certain prophets and teachers: Barnabas, Simeon who was called Niger, Lucius of Cyrene, Manaen who had been brought up with Herod the tetrarch, and Saul. As they ministered to the Lord and fasted, the Holy Spirit said, now separate to Me Barnabas and Saul for the work to which I have called them." Then, having fasted and prayed, and laid hands on them, they sent them away."

After receiving the mandate from God, there is yet another step that should not be undermined in the full establishment of an elder in ministry. The mandate needs to be followed by the commissioning by the authorities in the local house. Unfortunately, some ministers for various reasons miss out on this important step and attract the onslaught of the devil and also experience sterility in their ministry.

In the starting verses of Acts 13, the commissioning of Barnabas and Saul in the apostolic office is depicted. Those two men of God were already ministering in the church of Antioch in either the office of prophet or teacher. They were therefore ordained already in these offices. Knowing the profound revelation of Paul in writing the epistles, he was most probably a teacher in the local house. Certainly, Paul must have received insight from God concerning his future apostolic ministry in the nations, but nowhere is it mentioned that he approached the elders of the church about his calling or revelation. Nowadays a minister can approach the spiritual authority of his local house, say what the next move that God wants him to make, forgetting that God respects His principles. How can someone be called to be released in the Lord's ministry with God bypassing His principle of authority? But in fact, the Scripture says that as the elders were in fellowship with the Lord and fasted, the Holy Spirit spoke to the eldership concerning the apostolic call he had placed on Barnabas and Saul. It is after they fasted and prayed for some clarity and confirmation that they laid hands on them and commissioned them to the apostolic mandate of God for the nations. How different from what we see in the Body of Christ nowadays!

We can see that example of carnal ministers recommending and laying on themselves their stamp of approval in Acts 15: 34,

> *"Since we have heard that some who went out from us have troubled you with words, unsettling your souls, saying, "You must be circumcised and keep the law" to whom we gave no such commandment."*

2 Corinthians 10: 18 states,

> *"For not he who commends himself is approved, but whom the Lord commends."*

The commissioning through the laying on of hands confers spiritual authority to the minister being released and gives him the stamp of approval from recognized authorities, who should normally be in his own local house. How tragic that many carnal ministers, as in the example of these brothers who troubled the saints of Antioch, trouble local ministries, because they are not recommended by their local house. This situation is unfortunately rampant in the Body of Christ in these times and ages where the principle of authority is so misunderstood and disobeyed.

ACTS 13: 4
"So being sent out by the Holy Spirit, they went down to Seleucia."

Now the carnal minister can so easily misinterpret this verse. Notice that it says that the Holy Spirit sent out Barnabas and Saul. Understand that was not done independently from the elders of the local house. The Holy Spirit spoke through the leadership of the local house to send out Apostle Barnabas and Paul. So many ministers recommend themselves to ministry but the word says that the Holy Spirit sent out Barnabas and Saul. Literally meaning that the Holy Spirit directed their 'sending out' by the eldership of the church of Antioch. The principle behind that decision is the commissioning. We are not called to recommend ourselves but the Holy Spirit needs to speak to our authorities in place concerning our being placed in authority. There is something very powerful in the laying on of hands and recommendation. When you are properly released in the ministry, you eliminate certain unwanted and unneeded attacks of darkness, which come about as a result of being in a position of authority without the mantle and heaven's backing for your assignment. I have seen so many peers in ministry who do not have a relationship with their spiritual father or the spiritual leaders of their local house where they grew up in grace and stature for ministry. In fact one of the greatest blessing I have in ministry is the fact that I was clearly recommended and have the support of my pastor for the apostolic task that the Lord has given me. You see there is a level of attack that can never hit and affect a minister who has been properly commissioned and recommended because he ministers with heaven's approval.

The laying on of hands should not be undermined. The royal anointing was given to David with a new level of ministry through the anointing of oil, which represents the Spirit of God approving and commissioning David for his ministry as king.

1 SAMUEL 16: 13
"Then Samuel took the horn of oil and anointed him in the midst of his brothers: and the Spirit of the Lord came upon David from that day forward."

Notice it is said that the Spirit of the Lord came upon David from the day of the commissioning forward. He had the call before the commissioning but the mantle for the ministry came on him from the day of the commissioning onward.

1 SAMUEL 10: 6, 7
"Then the Spirit of the Lord will come upon you, and you will prophesy with them and be turned into another man."

1 SAMUEL 10: 10, 11
"When they came there to the hill, there was a group of prophets to meet him; then, the Spirit of God came upon him, and he prophesied among them. And it happened, when all who knew him formerly saw that he indeed prophesied among the prophets, that the people said to

*one another, "What is this that has come upon the son of
Kish? Is Saul also among the prophets?"*

In the case of Saul, after the anointing fell on him, he was
able to minister the gift of prophecy. There is a new level of
the spiritual gifts that is manifested in minister's life after he
is commissioned.

DEUTERONOMY 34: 9
*"Now Joshua the son of Nun was full of the spirit of
wisdom; for Moses had laid his hands upon him: so
the children of Israel heeded him, and did as the Lord
commanded Moses."*

After receiving the laying on of hands from Moses, the spirit
of wisdom came upon Joshua and because of that the children
of Israel heeded him. Authority for ministry is seen once more
by the commissioning of Joshua in the leadership of the people
of Israel. The Old and the New Testament demonstrate the
application of the principle of commissioning. A true apostolic
house should therefore make it their responsibility to apply
this important principle of God, especially since one of the
prevalent graces of an apostolic house is the capacity to release
saints into their destiny.

GOVERNMENTAL ASCENSION GIFTS

1 CORINTHIANS 12: 28
*"And God had appointed these in the church: first
apostles, second prophets, third teachers, after that,
miracles, then gifts of healing, helps, administrations,
varieties of tongues."*

This Scripture introduces us to an important key to the apostolic structured house. The Lord sheds light on certain ascension gifts He has positioned in the local house. Although many denominations are dodging the call and ministry of apostles and prophets, it is still very peculiar that the Word is giving them a place of predominance in the church's structure. Notice that the Word says apostles; prophets and teachers are set in the church. Therefore, if we believe in the revelation of church establishment we cannot omit the ones the Lord has set first, second and third in His church structure. Their predominance establishes a leadership role in the revealed plan of God for His church. It is imperative to know that the setting apart of these ascension gifts does not undermine the importance of others but rather emphasize their role in the government of the church. They are called the governmental gifts because they are the elders with the gifts and grace to govern, give leadership, direction and doctrine to the local house. We see their leadership in the apostolic centers of Jerusalem and Antioch; apostolic centers from the first century that the Holy Spirit gives detail about.

GALATIANS 2: 9
"And when James, Cephas, and John, who seemed to be
pillars, perceived the grace that had been given to me,
they gave me and Barnabas the right hand of fellowship."

Apostles James, Cephas and John were the pillars in the church of Jerusalem. They were giving direction and leadership to that apostolic center. It is for this reason that their approval of Apostle Paul and Barnabas' ministry was considered by them divine confirmation and recommendation.

We can also see the governmental gifts in position of authority in the church of Antioch.

Acts 13:1 tells us,

> *"Now in the church that was at Antioch, there were certain prophets and teachers."*

Prophets and teachers are mentioned here in the government of the church of Antioch with respect to their order of authority since there were not yet any apostles commissioned in that church. Notice that out of that eldership, two Apostles, Barnabas and Saul, were released. They were actually the ministers initially used to establish that church. The Lord has set in the church: first apostles, second prophets and thirdly teachers. Knowing the care taken by God to edify His church for it to be structured, strategic and effective, our question should be: What is the function of these ascension gifts in the apostolic church?

APOSTLES

The apostle is the governmental gift mentioned first in Ephesians 4: 11 and 1 Corinthians 12: 28. What is therefore the function and characteristics of the Apostle? The apostolic office in an apostolic structured house is the one that carries the spiritual authority. The Word in 1 Corinthians 12: 28 says that the Lord had set in the church first apostles. Now the word first here is the Greek translation of "proton", which Zodiates dictionary translates as "first in position". These verses literally signify that apostles are first in rank, position and authority in the apostolic center. The apostle is the preeminent ascension gift who gives leadership to the elders of an apostolic structured church. In the case of the church of Jerusalem, there were many apostles in the same apostolic house. In such particular case, one of them will carry the spiritual leadership and authority of the house. Apostle Peter was the authority in the establishment of the Apostolic Center of Jerusalem. Notice his pre-eminence in the naming of the disciples in Mathew 10: 2; "Now the name of the twelve apostles are these; the first *"proton"* Simon, who is called Peter..." Apostle Peter in the Church of Jerusalem among the apostles was first in rank, position and authority.

Now it is important in this season of apostolic reformation and restoration for ministers who are leading a church not to fall into the trap of just switching title from pastor to apostle. This would be a devastating mistake because behind the leader's title comes character and the gift of Christ, as well as fruit that should follow a ministry. Unfortunately in this generation many carry the title of apostle without manifesting neither the gifts nor the fruit. Being set first is utterly strategic from the Lord, because the apostle is called to raise an apostolic church. It is truly not enough to be titled apostle but one must be able to release an apostolic church sent out to affect, influence and take over every societal system in the community in order to advance the kingdom of God on earth. Therefore it is much more than a switching of title.

SIGNS OF A TRUE APOSTLE

True biblical restoration can only be validated through the veracity of the Word of God. The apostolic office is certainly not exempted from this principle. In this season where we see more and more spiritual authority of churches stepping into the apostolic office, we need to realize that the apostolic office is not just a change of title. "I was a pastor before, and since it's a trend now, I'll call myself apostle." Great grace accompanies an apostle, but great opposition does too. It is throwing yourself into the mouth of affliction and demonic persecution, when you take a position for which the grace was not granted to you by the Lord. Having the title apostle, having the tag apostle, reading the books on the apostle, dreaming of being an apostle will not cut it. There are definite signs that legitimize and authenticate true apostolic ministry.

> 2 CORINTHIANS 12: 12 (ESV)
> *"The SIGNS of a true apostle were performed among you with utmost patience, with signs and wonders and mighty works."*

As I studied this Scripture, the Lord brought the word "true" to my attention. I understood if there are true apostles, there are also false apostles who aspire to be, but fall short of true apostleship. Fortunately, the Scriptures clearly describe to us the signs that will help us recognize true apostolic ministry without having to enter long fruitless debates. This is truly pertinent in this hour, for there is much prophetic identification in the ministry and not enough demonstration. It is important to understand that the identification of a gifting is connected with its demonstration. In fact, it is the demonstration of the apostolic gifting that should bring confirmation of its identification.

Presently, in the Body of Christ, there is a race for titles and the accumulation of them, thinking maybe that the more you have the more qualified you are. We frequently see ministers with business cards with many titles, believing that the more titles they have the more anointed and solid their ministry is. What a deception! Biblically, signs that follow you rather than the title on your card or nametag qualify you. Please saints, do not be seduced and deceived by these promotional maneuverings. The church will not be built, and the kingdom will not advance on prophetic identification or impartation alone. Prophetic identification and impartation need to produce concrete signs, fruit and demonstration.

The spiritual body functions in a similar manner as the human body, which has many parts and varying functions. There are different gifts and different operations of these gifts in the Body of Christ. The apostolic office is certainly not exempted. A wide variety of mandates and differences in grace can be seen in the apostolic ministry. Nevertheless, in our desire to see depth in the apostolic ministry, I do believe that these following signs need to be looked upon in identifying a true apostle.

Revelatory Word

EPHESIANS 3: 1-5

"For this cause I Paul, the prisoner of Jesus Christ for you Gentiles, if ye have heard of the dispensation of the grace of God which is GIVEN ME to you: How that BY REVELATION he made known unto me the mystery; (as I wrote afore in few words, whereby, when ye read, ye may understand MY KNOWLEDGE IN THE MYSTERY OF CHRIST.) Which in other ages was not made known unto the sons of men, as it is now REVEALED unto his holy apostles and prophets BY THE SPIRIT".

In this portion of Scripture, the Apostle Paul is writing to the church concerning his revelation of the mysteries of Christ. He indicates that there is a certain grace given by God attached to his apostleship. This particular grace gives him understanding in the mysteries of Christ. Notice that this grace was granted by revelation of the Holy Spirit. The Apostle Paul had personal encounters with the Spirit of God, who gave him knowledge in the mysteries of Christ. How remotely different from the shallowness of certain apostolic ministries!

Nowadays, depth in the mystery of Christ is mistaken with tying together information received through books and conferences by ministers who have a personal relationship with the Spirit, who leads in all truths. I say 'tying together information' since repeating or declaring what another minister has said is not revelatory. A minister can have information but still lack revelation. We absolutely cannot counterfeit revelation.

You see, we can copy and repeat what a minister says, but we cannot duplicate the revelation that a certain minister has received at the feet of the Lord. This is not to say that we can't receive through another minister's literary work or sermons. The information received from others should challenge us to seek the Holy Spirit for increased personal insight, in order for the information received to become revelation through the enlightenment of the Holy Spirit.

Psalms 119: 130 says in the French Louis Segond Version,

"The revelation of your word enlightens."

Daniel 11: 32 says,

"But the people that do KNOW their God shall be strong, and do exploits."

The only source of true revelation is our personal knowledge of God. We need to know our God. Although receiving a fresh word from another man of God can open the door to the deep things of God, our personal meditation and encounter in the Word with the Holy Spirit is the way to solidify our depth in God's truth.

ISAIAH 34: 16

"Search from the book of the Lord, and read: Not one of these shall fail; Not one shall lack her mate."

There is a seeking, a searching through the guidance of the Holy Spirit that releases knowledge in the mysteries of Christ.

GALATIANS 1: 15-18

"But when it pleased God, who separated me from my mother's womb, and called me by his grace, to reveal his Son in me, that I might preach him among the heathen; immediately I conferred not with the flesh and blood: Neither went I up to Jerusalem to them which were apostles before me; but I went into Arabia, and returned again unto Damascus. Then after three years I went up to Jerusalem."

Although the first twelve apostles of Jerusalem received insight and revelation at the feet of Jesus Christ himself, the Lord did not send Paul to Jerusalem to know about him after his conversion experience on the Damascus road. Rather, He led him to Arabia for a time in consecration for personal study and meditation to receive explicit revelation from Him before preaching the gospel. The logical thing for Paul to have done was to have gone down to Jerusalem to receive teaching from the church of Jerusalem, but I believe the Lord did not permit this for He wanted that personal fellowship with Paul. This precious time at the feet of the Lord gave the Apostle Paul in-depth revelation of Him, and a special bond with the Savior necessary for the apostolic mandate that he had. I believe the uniqueness of the apostolic calling and responsibility will require its subjects to seek personal revelatory teachings from the Lord through His Holy Spirit. It is very hard to bring to others the knowledge of someone that you have heard of from others, but whom you do not personally know. The Apostle John declared,

> 1 JOHN 1: 1, 3A
> *"That which was from the beginning, WHICH WE HAVE HEARD, which WE HAVE SEEN with our eyes, which we have LOOKED UPON, and our hand HAVE HANDLED, of the Word of life That which we have SEEN AND HEARD DECLARE WE unto you."*

Here again, we understand through the writings and teachings of the Apostle John that apostolic ministry does not stem out of theoretical facts, preaching and teaching, but from personal relationship with the King of kings and Lord of lords. I do reiterate the fact that books and other ministers' preaching and teachings should be complementary, but not be one's primary source of apostolic knowledge and revelation.

You know or have heard of the preaching and teachings of forerunner apostolic and prophetic ministers such as Apostle John Kelly, Apostle John Eckhardt and Bishop Bill Hamon, whom I believe to be major figures in unfolding present apostolic truth in late 20th century and early 21st century, but my question to every emerging apostle and ministering apostle is, "What was revealed to you, personally regarding the apostolic?"

It is not enough to pile up books and have readings. It is not enough to highlight books and duplicate sayings of prominent apostles of our time. It is not enough to re-teach and re-preach their sermons, but the time has come for apostolic depth in our present day apostles. And this means having received a revelatory word straight from the apostolic oven of God, to give a fresh apostolic word to a starving Church of Jesus Christ.

Authority and Demonstration of Power

1 CORINTHIANS 2: 4-5
"And my speech and my preaching was not with enticing words of man's wisdom, but in demonstration of the Spirit and of power: That your faith should not stand in the wisdom of men, but in the power of God." (KJV)

1 CORINTHIANS 4: 19, 20
"But I will come to you shortly, if the Lord will, and will know, not the speech of them which are puffed up, but the power. For the kingdom of God is not in word, but in power."

We have entered a time and season where many are preaching and teaching their truths. The Muslims are preaching the sayings of their prophet Mohammed, the Jehovah Witnesses are preaching the heresies of Russell and Rutherford, and the Mormons are preaching the confusions of Joseph Smith. What will therefore make a difference? Saints of God, we will not be able to make a difference in this action-centered society with enticing words of wisdom. For there are already all kinds of enticing words being released in society in this era. The apostle Paul was encountering the wisdom of Greek philosophers in

Corinth. He realized one thing, "I am not there to try to beat them at their game, but to preach the demonstrative Word of Jesus Christ". We are faced with the same reality today. The Church of Jesus Christ needs to have apostolic leadership that will not only preach and teach the truth of Jesus Christ, but also show the authority and the demonstration of power in Jesus Christ. How can we take cities, regions and countries without the authority and the demonstration of the Spirit and the power? We need authority and power to outmuscle the principalities and powers that rule and reign over our cities, regions and countries. No authority, no power and there will be no kingdom takeover. Where are the apostles who can come into a region and dismantle the work of the enemy in that area?

LUKE 9: 1-2, 6
"Then he called his twelve disciples together, and gave them POWER and AUTHORITY over all devils, and to cure diseases. And he SENT THEM to PREACH the kingdom of God, and to HEAL sick... And they departed and went through the towns, PREACHING the gospel, and HEALING everywhere."

There are certain elements that the Lord gave the disciples that propelled them into the apostolic status. The Word says the Lord gave them power and authority. Knowing the demonic forces that the apostles were going to encounter, the Lord knew their mission would be fruitless, and even life threatening, if they went out without power and authority. But why power and authority, is it not enough to have the power?

The Greek word for power is *"dunamis"*, which means: to be able. All the words derived from the stem *"duna"*, carry the connotation of being able, capable, spoken of intrinsic power.

Power therefore speaks of a residing virtue given by the Lord that enables one to do the work. The disciples received spiritual capability. They received potentiality to do, to minister. Although this potentiality may or may not be active, it is there.

Now they did not only receive power, but they also received authority. Authority in Greek is *"exousia"*. It means: permissible, allowed, permission, authority, right, liberty and power to do something.

"Exousia" in Greek is a legal word. In giving the apostles authority and power, the Lord literally gave them the legal right to exercise the power of God. One cannot be an apostle without the legal right to exercise the power of God, or else the devil will simply tame and make of no incidence that so called "sent one". And unfortunately, too many are called apostle with no prevailing incidence in their city, region, or country. They go in an area unknown, and they leave incognito from the natural and the spiritual realm. In verse 6 of the above Scripture, we observe the apostles delivering after receiving. If you've received impartation, been prophetically identified as an apostle and been ordained, you need to also deliver the fruits of the authority and power you've received. The apostles put declaration into action, for they went through the towns preaching and demonstrating the power of the kingdom.

Apostolic Word of Authority and Power

PROVERBS 18: 21

"Death and life are in the power of the tongue: and they that love it shall eat the fruit thereof."

PROVERBS 16: 10
"A Divine sentence is in the lips of the King: his mouth transgresseth not in judgement." (KJV);

ECCLESIASTES 8: 4
"Where the word of the king is, there is power: and who may say unto him, what doest thou?" (KJV)

Apostles are recipient of kingly anointing due to their pre-eminence and leadership in the body of Christ. You see the office of the king in the Old Testament is a prototype of the apostolic office in the New Testament. New Testament apostles, as the kings of the Old Testament, exerted power and authority in their words. Apostles are called to exercise divine sentence, for where the word of the apostle is, there should be exercised enablement. As we take a close look at apostolic churches today, we see a lack of power and authority in the word of many apostles. There is a level of the fear of the Lord that will come on the saint in the Body of Christ only when they see the power in the word of the apostles.

ACTS 5: 1-5, 7, 9-14
"But a certain man named Ananias, with Sapphira his wife, sold a possession and keptback part of the price, his wife also being privy to it and brought a certain part and laid it at the apostles' feet. But Peter said, Ananias, why hath Satan filled thine heart to lie to the Holy Ghost, and to keep back part of the price thou has not lied unto men, but unto God. And Ananias hearing these words fell down, and gave up the ghost: and GREAT FEAR came on all them that heard these things. And it was about the space of three hours after,

when his wife, not knowing what was done, came in.
Then Peter SAID unto her, how is it that ye have agreed
together to tempt the Spirit of the Lord? Behold, the feet
of them which have buried thy husband are at the door,
and SHALL CARRY THEE OUT. THEN FELL SHE
DOWN STRAIGHTWAY at his feet, and YIELDED
UP THE GHOST AND GREAT FEAR came UPON
all the CHURCH and UPON AS MANY AS HEARD
THESE THINGS. And by the hands of the apostles
were MANY SIGNS AND WONDERS WROUGHT
among the people; (and they were all with one accord in
Solomon's porch. And of the rest durst NO MAN JOIN
HIMSELF TO THEM: but people magnified them. And
believers were the more added to the Lord, multitudes
both men and women." (KJV)

We see in the episode of Ananias and Sapphira, the power
in the word of the apostle. This couple had agreed together to
lie to the apostles of God, thinking that they were mere men,
forgetting they were carriers of the Holy God. This lie cost
them dearly, for they died before their time. We can see in this
segment the authority and power that the word of the apostle
carries. Ananias gave up the ghost after being exposed by the
Holy Ghost, but his wife fell dead at the feet of the Apostle
Peter after he specifically spoke a divine sentence on her.

PROVERBS 16: 10
"A divine sentence is in the lips of the king: his mouth
transgresseth not in judgment." (KJV)

Before this episode, all the miracles in the early church were
miracles of mercy. But here, we encounter the first miracle of

judgment in the New Testament Church. It is important to see that the miracle of judgment brought the fear of the Lord to the saints and to all who heard about it. The time is now for apostles of the contemporary church to rise with a word of authority and power. Many sins run rampant in the church because the apostles are not manifesting the apostolic word of authority. Some feel they need to ride the middle road of patience, whether from fear of being stigmatized and judged as bringing curses upon the people, or by pure ignorance. Nevertheless, the devils enjoy it and wreak havoc in the local churches. It is common to see saints without any respect for their spiritual authority. We see apostles receiving no respect from their people and sometimes even being the laughing stock and subject of criticism over dinner after church. Why? Because of no authority and no demonstration of the divine sentence of God. People can see miracle after miracle of mercy, but until they see the miracle of judgment, many will never have the reverence they are called to have for the man of God. Pharaoh saw many miracles, but when his son became a sign, he let the people of God go. A miracle of judgment can sometimes be a key to bring genuine fear of God and of the man of God. And I am deliberate in saying, "of God and of the man of God". Church is not called to put the man of God at the same level of God but is still called to respect, reverence and believe in the servant of God. The miracle of judgment activated by the word of the man of God not only brought the fear of the Lord, but also the fear of the servant whom the Lord put in authority over His people. It took the divine sentence spoken by Peter to bring about the death of Sapphira and to release the divine fear of God, which brought a mighty apostolic breakthrough.

The authority and power through Peter's decree brought the fear of the Lord (verse 11), many signs and wonders (verse 12), respect, reverence, and honor to the men of God (verse 13) and a tremendous harvest of souls (verses 14). But where are the apostles of this generation who will step up and flow in that divine level of authority and power through their decrees? It is no wonder certain churches do not experience mighty signs and wonders: no fear of the Lord. And the fear of the Lord cannot be initiated because the apostle is lacking the boldness to speak the divine sentence that will bring it to pass.

In this skeptical, doubtful, arrogant, non-submissive and disrespectful generation, it will take a sign to bring the fear and respect of the man of God, of the Word of God and of our precious Lord. And this sign will not be a sign of life brought about by healing or deliverance, but a sign of death demonstrating the judgment of God.

Exodus 14: 30-31 insists by saying,

> *"Thus the Lord saved Israel that day out of the hand of the Egyptians; and Israel saw the Egyptians dead upon the seashore. And Israel saw that great work which the Lord did upon the Egyptians: and the people feared the Lord, and believed the Lord, and his servant Moses."*
> *(KJV)*

Here, once again, the miracle of judgment by death brought the fear of the Lord into the heart of God's people. When the Israelites saw the Egyptians dead upon the seashore, they feared the Lord and believed the servant of God. Is this declaration too strong?

Apostolic Word of Correction

PROVERBS 15: 10

"Whoever abandons the right path will be severely punished; whoever hates corrections will die." (ESV)

ECCLESIASTES 7: 5

"It is better to hear the rebuke of the wise, than for a man to hear the song of the fools."

The Word indicates here that human nature will bring saints to abandon the right path at some time or another. Now rebuke is meant to come from the wise. The apostolic office is equipped with a great grace of wisdom to handle corrections. I believe that authority and power in the word of the apostle needs to be exercised to administer correction. Apostles are given the rod of correction for this purpose.

1 Corinthians 4: 21 declares,

"What will ye? Shall I come unto you with a rod, or in love and in the spirit of meekness?"

2 Corinthians 10: 6 says,

"And having in the readiness to revenge all disobedience."

The apostle, being the ministry gift with spiritual authority in the church, has been equipped by the Lord with the grace, wisdom and authority to bring correction to the saints of the church and the Body of Christ. Much disobedience is left untouched in the churches, due to the lack of authorities of God who have the boldness to overrule sin and disobedience.

Belial, Jezebel and their demonic maneuverings intimidate many ministers. The apostle is gifted by God to rise from anonymity to confront and throw down the reign of these principalities in the church. The devil, being fully aware of that, will capitalize thoroughly when that authority is not exercised, whether it's from lack of knowledge or from any other foolish reason. Henceforth, many churches are paralyzed and some even end up closing, because of a lack of apostolic authority that is able to come with the rod of correction to reckon with the forces that wage war against her destiny.

The Lord will inform apostolic leadership of the miscues and mishaps of the saints, the deacons, as well as the elders in the church. Some of these flaws or wrongs will need correction to be straightened out. In the normal life of the church, there are certain situations that can be taken care of with a word of counsel or even a word of wisdom. But there are certain other situations that will never change unless given a strong word of correction. Patience, meekness, love will not do it. Rebuke and a corrective warning are the only solution. In these cases, if the apostle of the house wants to play the middle road, the situation will only disintegrate and bring chaos to the saint involved. This can also spread like a cancer and affect other saints and pollute the assembly. Apostles of God, the Lord has imparted to you this divine capacity to bring correction. When the time comes, the Spirit of God will dictate it to you. Do not fight the unction of the Lord and do not draw back. Use it and see the salvation of the Lord!

The apostle Peter spoke the word of rebuke and judgment upon Sapphira and saved the assembly from falling prey to deceiving and lying spirits, as well as having its finances and material blessings cursed.

Signs and Wonders

2 CORINTHIANS 12: 12
"Truly the signs of a TRUE apostle were PERFORMED through SIGNS, WONDERS AND MIGHTY WORKS." (ESV)

Where are the signs and wonders wrought by the apostles of our day? We do not need anymore flaky and spooky ministers with a couple of rhythms or a shout and a dance, but we need ministers who have a profound word that comes with authority and power. One of the signatures of the apostolic ministry is signs, wonders and mighty works. Notice that these signs were not talked about but performed. Sufficient testimonies of those signs were performed in the life of such and such minister from abroad, or from a powerful minister of the previous era, or of what the Lord did in Bible days. I believe the Word when it says, "Jesus Christ, the same yesterday and today and forever" (Hebrew 13:8). Are you an apostle? Where are the signs and wonders that follow you? We are not talking here about a headache disappearing but strongholds coming down, principalities bound, regional demons expelled, massive healing and deliverance. The church and the world are yearning for an apostolic ministry that shows forth divinity, for we are partakers of divine nature. No true apostle can escape the miraculous, signs and wonders aspect of apostolic ministry.

I've seen a lot of so-called apostles talking at length about the theoretical aspect of the demonstrative power in apostolic ministry, yet I seldom see it manifested in them. But the apostle Paul said to the people of Corinth in 2 Corinthians 10: 10-11,

"For his letters, say they, are weighty and powerful; but his bodily presence is weak, and his speech contemptible. Let such an one think this, that, such as we are in word by letters when we are absent, such will we be also in DEED when we are present."

Where are these apostles that will shut the devil's mouth with the exercising power of signs, wonders, miracles, and mighty deeds? There is nothing that can shut the mouth of religious lecturers and detractors of the Gospel more than the manifestation of the finger of God in a given situation. There is a level of respect and recognition of Christ that will not be given, but taken by the manifestation of signs and wonders of God. After the healing of the lame man at the gate called Beautiful, the religious leaders of Jerusalem wanted to oppress the Christians through their condescension and threats, but the miraculous hand of God zipped their mouths.

ACTS 4: 13-14
"Now when they saw the boldness of Peter and John, and perceived that they were unlearned and ignorant men, they marveled; and they took knowledge of them, that they had been with Jesus. And beholding the man which was healed standing with them, they could SAY NOTHING against it."

I can remember in one of our local church Bible studies, we were teaching about false religions. Some Muslims heard of our session on Islam and came to oppose us. These religious devotees manifested much debating and much arrogance, but at the end of the service, a deliverance case broke loose.

And we said, "Today we will see if it's the name of Jesus that casts out demons, or if it's the name of Mohammed." You see, there is a time to talk, but then there is a time to demonstrate the power of God. Mount Carmel caliber confrontation needs to happen in certain circumstances to let all see that our Jesus is in a class of His own. As the demons were manifesting, when adjured to come out in the name of Mohammed, they started laughing. When asked why they were mockingly laughing, in front of the Muslims, they said, "Mohammed is dead." Now we told them that there is One who is not dead, yet lives forevermore. It should come as no surprise to you that the demons' mocking laughter of Mohammed changed to terrorized lamentations at the power in the name of Jesus. In no time, the name above all names, the name of Jesus, was enough to expel those demons and that young lady was set free from the devil's hold.

After this demonstration of the sheer power of God, the Muslims had no choice but to stop their debating and acknowledge the supremacy and lordship of the greatest prophet of all time. Jesus Christ is truly the King of kings and Lord of lords. Nothing can confirm it better than the manifestation of His lordship over lives, the earth, the weather or any circumstance or situation. Miracles, signs, wonders and mighty deeds are not optional in the ministry of the apostle, but compulsory.

THE FUNCTION OF THE APOSTLES

We have understood from the characteristic of the apostolic office their great authority and power. We need to ask ourselves now, what do apostles do? What is the ministry they are called to fulfill? Well, an irrevocable fact is that apostles establish strong apostolic churches. How tragic to have ministers calling themselves apostles starting the ministry with a handful of saints and after many years in ministry still having only a handful of saints. In such a case one should question himself on his apostleship.

Apostle Paul says in 1 Corinthians 9: 2,

"If I am not an apostle to others, yet doubtless I am to you. For you are the seal of my apostleship in the Lord."

An apostle may start a ministry with a handful of people but they will grow in number and maturity, in the revelation of Jesus Christ and in fruit. You see an apostolic church is one that through apostolic anointing, every saint is equipped to reach his prophetic destiny in Christ. There is no one-man show in an apostolic house. The apostle is not a superstar that is alone to minister, preach, teach, lay hands and cast out devils. As in a pastoral house, everyone is used to gravitate around the pastor and his family to the fulfillment of their call, the apostolic house on the other hand, under the apostolic grace, raises an apostolic people that are identified, trained, mandated and sent out to fulfill their destiny for the advancement of the kingdom of God. An apostle is called to establish strong apostolic churches, able to make a statement in transforming their community and region for Christ.

Fathering Anointing

1 CORINTHIANS 4: 15
"For though you might have ten thousand instructors in Christ, yet you do not have many fathers; for in Christ Jesus I have begotten you through the gospel. Therefore I urge you, imitate me."

In this portion of the Word of God, Apostle Paul exhorts the Church of Corinth, which he had established some time before. He told them that they could have ten thousand masters in Christ, but they could not have many fathers for he begot them in Christ Jesus. In other words, it is possible for a local church to have many different ministers who are used by God to bless the assembly spiritually; however, it may only have one father. This statement by Apostle Paul opens our understanding regarding the fathering capacity of the apostolic office towards the Church.

EPHESIANS 4: 11-12

"And He himself gave some to be apostles, some prophets,
some evangelists, some pastors and some teachers, for
the equipping of the saints for the work of the ministry,
for the edifying of the Body of Christ."

The Lord Jesus Christ has given five gifts to the church for its perfecting and edification. However, when we take a spiritual look at these five ministry gifts, we can see the pre-eminence of the apostolic office. The apostle is named first in Ephesians 4: 11 and in 1 Corinthians 12: 28. As we study the ministry of the apostle, we discover the great spiritual responsibility and spiritual authority that this office has in the Body of Christ. Many profound men of God have been used insightfully by God to expound on the ministry of this ascension gift for the edification of the Church. Among these men is Apostle John Eckhardt, a spiritual general of the 21st century in the Body of Christ who has written many valuable books on the apostolic ministry. God endows the apostle with a tremendous spiritual capacity to establish churches. One of his many graces is the capacity he received from God to "beget".

When reading 1 Corinthians 4: 14-16, we see the apostle Paul (without pretension) addressing the church at Corinth as his beloved children saying that he is the father who begat them in Christ. The apostolic office has received the capacity from God to spiritually father the saints of the Kingdom of God in the local church.

You see in the Corinthian culture, the upper echelon of that society had servants and guardians who would accompany the young sons to school and take care of them. So apostle Paul uses this cultural reality of that time to tell the saints of Corinth that they may have had many spiritual guardians (such as Apollos) who were taking care of them, and keeping them in the faith. However, they did not have many fathers, for it was he who had begotten them in Christ Jesus. Many learned theologians limit the apostle Paul's claim of being the Corinthian saints' father only to the extent that he led them to the Lord and founded the church of Corinth. With all due respect to these scholars, I believe that the capacity to beget in a biblical sense transcends the fact of simply bringing someone to the knowledge of Jesus Christ. Otherwise, any Christian who brings another person to the Lord in a legitimate way would automatically become that new born in Christ's spiritual father.

What are we to say of evangelists who bring multitudes of people to Christ, do they father them for this simple fact? The responsibility of spiritual fatherhood transcends that of the new birth and of putting the first stepping-stones in the life of the new believer in the local church. When we meticulously and spiritually analyze the ministry of apostle Paul to the Corinthians, we will see that this master builder had deposited in that local church some solid foundations and was able to propel the people into their destiny. To beget, in its full and biblical revelation, literally means to give birth and deposit the necessary foundations enabling the nurturing and blossoming of the spiritual child or children for the fulfilling of their spiritual destiny. The responsibility is certainly greater than simply bringing someone to the Lord or merely giving some basic faith and fundamental principles. The Apostle Paul will speak of his ministry to the Corinthians by saying in 1 Corinthians 1: 4-7,

> "I thank my God always concerning you for the grace of God which was given to you by Christ Jesus, that you were enriched in everything by Him in all utterance and all knowledge, even as the testimony of Christ was confirmed in you, so that you come short in no gift, eagerly waiting for the revelation of our Lord Jesus Christ."

The Apostle Paul, in the span of a year and a half deposited such revelatory depth in the saints of the church of Corinth, that they had all the riches concerning the word and knowledge, the testimony of Christ Jesus being solidly established in them. He had done more than simply preach a few evangelical messages in order to bring them to salvation and accomplish a few miracles so that the people would recognize the power that resides in the kingdom of God. The gifts of the Spirit were not uncommon to them; they possessed them all. Apostle Paul had clearly done in-depth work in the establishment of the Corinthian Church. He was rightfully allowed to speak of the people of Corinth as being his children in the faith. He was truly their spiritual father.

In the same way that the husband is placed in authority in a God-fearing household, the apostle is placed in authority in the spiritual home according to 1 Corinthians 12: 28. And one of the major reasons for this position of authority is his divine capacity to beget, to give birth to and to work at the maturing of God's people for the fulfillment of their destiny in Christ Jesus. Apostle Paul declares in 1 Corinthians 9: 1-2,

> *"Are you not my work in the Lord... for you are the seal of my apostleship in the Lord..."*

What validated his spiritual fatherhood of the people of God at Corinth was not simply the fact that he had given birth to them spiritually, or the fact that he had given them revelation on a certain principle in the Word. It was rather that through his teachings, he had given them the necessary tools to be solidly anchored in their faith in Jesus Christ and be positioned for the fulfillment of their spiritual destiny. Therefore the question for you is: Who has been instrumental in giving you not simply some messages but a solid foundation and the biblical truths which have been or are paramount to the fulfillment of your maturity? Furthermore, who has nurtured you to the realization of who you are in Christ to allow you to reach your destiny in Christ Jesus?

Discovering of Spiritual Identity

1 TIMOTHY 1: 18
"This charge I commit to you, son Timothy, according to the prophecies previously made concerning you."

2 TIMOTHY 1: 5-6
"When I call in remembrance the genuine faith that is in you, which dwelt first in your grandmother Lois and

your mother Eunice, and I am persuaded is in you also.
Therefore I remind you to stir up the gift of God which
is in your through the laying on of my hands."

We see here in these verses the apostle Paul speaking of Timothy's spiritual identity, his legitimate son in the faith. He recalled to Timothy that his identity was recognized through the prophetic word and the laying on of hands that he received from him. In the example of Apostle Paul, a spiritual father has the capacity and grace from God to help their spiritual sons discover who they are in the Lord. Unfortunately, many Christians spend years under the covering of a man of God without ever discovering their spiritual identity in Christ Jesus. Whereas when you get under the anointing of the apostle who walks you through your ministerial process, he will be able to help you find your spiritual identity. You will not be released in his identity but in yours. He will not impose upon you who he is or even the part of the plan of God on his life that he failed in or that he did not have the courage to fully accomplish, but you will be enlightened on your spiritual identity. I have witnessed entering particular congregations where everybody speaks like the pastor, walks like the pastor, dresses in the same style as the pastor. Those who bring the Word to the congregation, preach like the pastor. We would surely think that we're in a soft drink plant manufacturing a single product with a single brand and a single flavor. But such is not the will of God. This is why the apostolic office has been established as first in the Body of Christ. The apostle has the capacity to release originals and not copies in the church of God. An apostle's mature sons can be seen by the singularity of their spiritual identity. The apostolic office is able to release apostles as well as the other gifts in the Body of Christ. The depth of the grace of this minister is able to groom ascension gifts in the same office having their particularities, with different graces and different mandates.

Let me give you this example. An apostle may have many sons who are called to the prophetic office, but he will be able to identify them in their respective gifts and graces. One may therefore be a governmental prophet, another a shamar prophet, powerful in intercession and spiritual warfare, another a social prophet and another an administrative prophetess. All are prophets but identified in their gifts, graces and respective mandates. He helps his sons clarify their horizons. His spiritual children will not have to step on one another's toes in the ministry. They will not have to overlap on the ministry of another, but they will be identified and joyfully and blissfully maximize who they are and what they're called to do in the Lord. There is no need to be jealous or competing against each other, since all in the Body of Christ have their position and their importance in the fulfillment of the plan of God. The Lord has prepared a good work for us to accomplish. He uses the apostle for our spiritual identification in order that we might accomplish the good works that have been prepared for us by the Lord.

Educates and Trains Spiritually

2 TIMOTHY 1: 13
"Hold fast the pattern of sound words which you have heard from me in faith and love which you have heard from me, in faith and love which are in Christ Jesus."

The apostle not only has the capacity to identify his spiritual children but he is also able to educate and train them spiritually.

Apostle Paul told his spiritual son Timothy to hold fast the pattern of sound words that he received from him. Timothy had therefore been educated and trained by his spiritual father, Apostle Paul, in the ministry. As much as a natural child needs to be educated and trained by his parents, a child who enters the spiritual family of God needs also to be educated and trained spiritually. This spiritual upbringing may even incorporate the care he had not received from his natural parents. The spiritual education and training that the apostle gives to his spiritual children are instrumental to the fulfillment of their destiny. They can therefore not be underestimated and neglected. How many premature ministers we see in the Body of Christ? How many servants of God do we see with flaws in their gifting or in their character, or both? Why, because of the absence of a spiritual father or because of a premature rupture of the educational and ministerial training process. Truly, for many the calling and potential were there but the complete spiritual training was lacking.

The son who is wise will accept to be spiritually educated and trained in order to be properly prepared for ministry in the process of fulfilling his destiny. And for this he will need certain traits. The son who wants to fully complete his training will need a lot of humility.

Proverbs 16: 18 says,

> "*Pride goes before destruction and a haughty spirit before a fall.*"

Chapter 18: 12 continues by saying,

> "*Before destruction the heart of a man is haughty, and before honor is humility.*"

Then 1 Corinthians 8: 2 adds,

"And if anyone thinks that he knows anything, he knows nothing yet as he ought to know."

Understand that a prideful son will have difficulty benefiting fully from the education and training of his spiritual father, because the prideful man has difficulty recognizing his true level. He oftentimes believes he masters what he has not mastered at all. Therefore he brings confusion and spiritual stagnation to his life, since if anyone thinks that he knows anything, he knows nothing yet as he ought to know and cannot therefore think he can grow. We need to understand that the first step to progress is to recognize one's ignorance. Since the prideful has a biased understanding of his ignorance, it is difficult for him to receive the education and training necessary for his progress, from his spiritual father. To remedy this condition, the son who has wisdom will seek to grow in humility to maximize the education and training he is called to receive from his spiritual father. He will have to be conscious of his vulnerability and weaknesses. The truth of God needs to illuminate us on our vulnerability, on our weaknesses and on our ignorance before it can allow us to progress. When we recognize these shortcomings, we can then benefit from another fruit of the word: spiritual progress.

There are several stages in the life of the son who is in spiritual training: infancy, adolescence and spiritual adulthood. In each of these stages the needs of the son differ. Every stage has its newness of apprenticeship and of revelation. Each season has the need for adjustments, corrections and reproofs for their success. The apostle has no difficulty bringing the necessary adjustments and corrections for the success of the training of his son.

PROVERBS 15: 10

"Harsh discipline is for him who forsake the way, and he who hates correction will die."

ECCLESIASTES 7: 5

"It is better to hear the rebuke of the wise than for a man to hear the song of fools,"

Correction and reproof are part of the ministry of the apostle. The Lord has given him the grace to encourage and celebrate you at the opportune time, as well as to correct and rebuke you when it's necessary. A son who dodges correction, and fights correction, will attract death in the area of his life where the Holy Spirit wants to correct him in his spiritual process. There will be harmful repercussions in the life of the son who refuses correction. The shortcomings, which the Holy Spirit wants to address, will surface and haunt him in his spiritual walk one day or another.

Proverbs 22: 15 says,

"Foolishness is bound up in the heart of a child; the rod of correction will drive it far from him."

Whereas Proverbs 23: 13-14 declares,

"Do not withhold correction from a child, for if you beat him with a rod, he will not die. You shall beat him with a rod, and deliver his soul from hell."

Here the Bible gives us wisdom in the way to raise our children. Whether in the case of a natural or a spiritual child, correction should be part of a normal educational process.

However today's psychologists say that one should not physically correct a child and governments which are ignorant of the wisdom of God in the educational dynamic of children's upbringing have legislated in agreement with them. The Word of God on the contrary tells us not to spare the child from the rod. Notice the Bible does not tell us to physically abuse a child with a rod but to correct him with a rod when the follies of the child demand it. The Bible is clear that the rod of correction will spare the child from follies. The ones who are anticorrection with the rod will say that this particular verse only connects rod with the hardship of correction. However, verses 13 and 14 of Proverbs 23 give precision on the subject. The Word clearly states that if we beat a child wisely and opportunely with a rod, he will not die. Rather, the correction with the rod will save his soul from decadence. When man wants to take his own foolish path and rebel against the Word of God, the consequences always follow without any doubt. Since certain societies have forbidden parents to physically punish their children, they have also clearly experienced and witnessed escalating negative social issues with the youth. Disrespect, rebellion, disobedience and kids who want to follow their own whims are only a sample of the social issues that these societies have been encountering. The social professionals have found no rest with the issues of the youth and are only able to diagnose the problems without successfully finding any viable and effective prognoses. What is therefore the reason? It is disobedience to the Word of God.

Natural parents as well as spiritual parents are called to correct their children. The apostle with the role of spiritual father needs therefore to take a stand and correct his spiritual sons, although he needs to do it according to the spirit and not the flesh. He will correct his spiritual child with the spiritual rod, which is the Word of God. Sometimes he will be obliged to give a correction or a rebuke to his spiritual son, which will surely cause some carnal discomfort. Nevertheless, offered with spiritual comfort, it tends toward the saving of his soul. The flesh is the only part of a spiritual child that can be affected when his spiritual father divinely corrects him; the spirit can only be edified. Proverbs 15: 10 states, "A harsh discipline is for him who forsakes the way." You therefore, who is a son, though you can receive multiple compliments and be constantly encouraged, know that the authentic spiritual father without a doubt will one day have to correct or rebuke you. You can neither intercede nor fast to prevent that from happening. It is a normal occurrence in the apostle-apostolic saint relationship that is healthy and favorable to the spiritual child for growth and maturity.

Therefore spiritual education and training demonstrate that the apostle is not only a man of words but of action. The authentic apostolic fatherhood will not only help you recognize your spiritual identity, but it has the necessary capacity to train you through divine revelation. In this way you would not be a frustrated child, but mature to be a servant walking in the path of the Most High to manifest the good works that God has prepared in advance for you.

Releases Spiritual Blessings

The Bible tells us in Genesis 27: 27-30, 33,

> "And he came near and kissed him; and he smelled the smell of his clothing and blessed him and said: 'Surely, the smell of my son is like the smell of a field, which the

> Lord has blessed. Therefore may God give you of the dew of heaven, of the fatness of the earth, and plenty of grain and wine. Let peoples serve you and nations bow down to you. Be master over your brethren, and let your mother's sons bow down to you. Cursed be everyone who curses you, and blessed be those who bless you!' Now it happened, as soon as Isaac had finished blessing Jacob, and Jacob had scarcely gone out from the presence of Isaac his father, that Esau his brother came in from his hunting... Then Isaac trembled exceedingly, and said, 'Who? Where is the one who hunted game and brought it to me? I ate all of it before you came, and I have blessed him and indeed he shall be blessed."

We can see in these verses the power of the declaration of an apostolic type father on a son. After the Jacob's trickery, his father released a blessing on him that was irrevocable even if the intention of Jacob was to bless his firstborn son Esau. In spite of Esau's distress and his desire to receive the blessing that was the portion of the firstborn, his father had released that blessing upon Jacob and could not go back on his word. Therefore the blessing that Isaac pronounced on Jacob followed him all through the course of his life. In reading the rest of Chapter 27, you will discover that Jacob by his father's prophetic decrees, received superiority over Esau and his other brothers and became their master. His blessings therefore superseded theirs. We can further see in Chapter 49 the prophetic blessings that Jacob declared on his sons and their posterity who became the twelve tribes of Israel. These spiritual blessings were their portion without missing a jot.

These two examples were from apostolic type fathers who recognized their spiritual authority and released the blessings on their children. But we also see the example of Moses who released the spiritual blessings on Joshua who was not his natural son but his spiritual son. This will permit us to fully grasp the spiritual character of the capacity of a father to release the blessing on his children.

1 Chronicles 23: 15 lists the biological sons of Moses: "The sons of Moses were Gershon and Eliezer."

The Bible also declares in Deuteronomy 34: 9,

> "Now Joshua the son of Nun was full of the spirit of wisdom, for Moses had laid his hands on him; so the children of Israel heeded him, and did as the Lord had commanded Moses."

Notice, Moses had biological sons, however Joshua distinguished himself as a spiritual son by the quality of his service to Moses. He received the blessing of the mantle of authority that Moses had to lead the people of God. The Lord used him to continue the ministry of Moses. Moses was the liberator used to take the people of Israel out of bondage from the Egyptians, but Joshua was the conqueror used by God to lead His people into the Promised Land. His ministry was initiated by the laying on of hands that he received from Moses, who released the spiritual blessings to him. Our verse of predilection says that Joshua was filled with the spirit of wisdom because Moses had laid his hands on him. This spirit of wisdom was in full fledge operation only after Moses released the blessings on Joshua. The words of Jacob followed his sons as much as the prophetic words of Moses, another apostle type of the Old Testament, also accomplished their course. Growing under the teachings and perfecting of a spiritual authority cannot be negligible. It has the capacity to release the blessings on the spiritual children of the spiritual authority.

I would like to elaborate on two particular ways of being anointed for service. It is true and biblical that some by divine election may develop a particular anointing without having one minister that can clearly be recognized for having fully trained them. This type of anointing is the portion of some apostles who are patriarchal since they are called to start a specific move of God or groom a certain generation in a specific revelation of God. Jesus had a patriarchal anointing, Abraham had a patriarchal anointing and apostle Paul also had a patriarchal anointing, since he started a ministerial lineage without clearly having a spiritual authority that trained him in the ministry. This situation is quite different from the twelve who were trained by Jesus in his earthly ministry. Jesus had a direct influence on their perfecting for the work of the ministry. The patriarchal anointing starts a lineage and initiates a movement of the spirit that affects a generation. You should however know that this type of anointing is very particular. It is not for "Mister Everybody" who decides to leave a local house to be directly trained by God without the covering and training of a spiritual father and the elders of the local church. After analysis and observation of the workings in the Body of Christ, you will notice that more often than not, those who say that they have a special call of God and are not called to grow under a specific ministry are simply not called by God. It appears as if they are called to make special pilgrimages in different ministries before launching their own ministry. These are the arrogant, full-of-oneself saints under the hold of Leviathan (the demonic principality that infests men with pride), who refuse to submit themselves to anyone in the church that the Lord has placed them in to receive adequate training for the fulfillment of their destiny. And this is primarily due to the fact that they cannot accept the necessary corrections for their growth. Instead, they want liberty to do and say what they want, without being accountable to follow the principles of God to grow upright.

Nevertheless, God raises up ministers with a ministerial process in which they cannot pinpoint and fully define a minister as being their spiritual father. They rather had different men of God mature and experienced fathers in the faith who gave them a certain level of training and perfecting. Those mature fathers are used by God to inculcate in them the necessary notions to the completion of their destiny. This does not mean that they will not grow in a local church and under authority. But there is a genuine and particular anointing that is not fathered by a man of God but truly given by God. It is nurtured through a personal relationship with God, for a certain and specific mandate given by God, when He Himself chooses and traces this path for one. In the majority of cases, the path chosen by God for the transferring of the anointing and the grace for the ministry is through the father-son relationship. Elisha received his spiritual heritage from his spiritual father to start his ministry, after he received the mantle of Elijah that represented the succession of anointing and of prophetic authority; the Bible explains the fashion in which Elisha started his ministry.

2 KINGS 2: 9, 11, 13

"And so it was, when they had crossed over, that Elijah said to Elisha, "Ask! What may I do for you, before I am taken away from you?" Elisha said, "Please let a double portion of your spirit be upon me. Then it happened, as they continued on and talked that suddenly a chariot

of fire appeared with horses of fire, and separated the two of them; and Elijah went up by a whirlwind into heaven. He also took up the mantle of Elijah that had fallen from him, and went back and stood by the bank of the Jordan. Then he took the mantle of Elijah that had fallen from him and struck the water, and said, "Where is the Lord God of Elijah?" And when he also had struck the water, it was divided this way and that; and Elisha crossed over."

Elisha started his ministry with the anointing that was on his spiritual father, Elijah, represented by the mantle of the trainer-prophet Elijah. The anointing of God is transferable. One of the representations of the presence of God in the Scriptures is oil. You see, a person who is soaked with oil is able to transfer some of this oil by rubbing himself onto another. Another good example is perfume. A person who keeps contact with one who is perfumed will also smell of the same perfume. A saint who serves in a ministry, a son who "rubs shoulders with" his spiritual father through the teaching and the ministry that his father brings him will see the grace of his father manifested in his life. I still remember after having interpreted for a man of God for a year and a half, I started ministering with the same type of anointing as this man of God. In fact, after he would finish preaching, he would make an altar call and have two prayer lines: one for him and the other for me. The extraordinary thing is that: the same manifestations of healing, deliverance and miracles that he had in his line, I saw them also in mine. I received an impartation of the anointing on the life of this man of God by simply being submissive and obedient in serving him and receiving his teachings. I was able to grow in the ministry of deliverance and healing in that fashion. The mistake that some people make though is to prematurely start their ministry because they see the manifestation of the power of God while they are serving a man of God. They ignore growing in maturity and waiting for God's timing. The anointing that we may manifest while we are serving a man of God or as we are submitting ourselves in the local ministry is foundational to start us up in ministry. However we need to grow in the teachings received from our spiritual father and the ministry of the local assembly. Then we can reach our full potential in having our own identity in the Lord. In my personal case, although in my first ministerial steps I was ministering like the man of God for whom I was translating (to the point that the way I was praying and the tone of my voice resembled his), as I grew in maturity some years later after my pastoral ordination, I had an entirely different way of ministering healing and deliverance. Like Elisha, I started with the anointing that was transferred to me through my service and proximity to the man of God. That anointing then grew into an anointing pertaining to the call and mandate of God on my life through my spiritual growth in the Lord. It is therefore imperative to understand that it is our duty to wisely receive the impartation from our spiritual father to make our first steps in ministry. We should not be prideful and arrogant, and wanting to establish a particular anointing and "unique ministry", when we have not received that direction or grace from God.

Elisha did not fall in the trap of individualism that is common in this era. After witnessing the departure of his spiritual father in chariots of fire, he recognized that he received the anointing of Elijah. Notice he asked, "Where is the Lord God of Elijah?" when he struck the water that divided. Many who are ignorant of the revelation of the principle of spiritual father and of spiritual authority would have thought that statement to be heretic, demonic or even idolatrous. These false notions are common since our modern society has so many people who want to be independent, self-trained, self-perfected and be directly led by God without submitting themselves to any spiritual authority. But Elisha had grasped the abundant blessing in his relationship with his spiritual father. Furthermore this first miracle was instrumental, for it brought him the respect of his peers.

The Bible tells us in verse 15,

> "Now when the sons of the prophets who were from Jericho saw him, they said, "The spirit of Elijah rests on Elisha." And they came to meet him, and bowed to the ground before him."

The Lord is the one who established the principle of authority and He will surely put His stamp of approval on it. A spiritual authority has been granted by God a special grace because of his role and responsibility pertaining to the care of the people of God.

The Bible says in Numbers 12: 4-9, after Aaron and Miriam spoke against Moses the servant of the Lord,

> "Suddenly the Lord said to Moses, Aaron, and Miriam: Come out, you three, to the tabernacle of meeting. So the three came out. Then the Lord came down in the pillar of cloud and stood in the door of the tabernacle and called Aaron and Miriam. And they both went forward. Then He said, Hear now my words: if there is a prophet among

you, I, the Lord, make Myself known to him in a vision; I speak to him in a dream. Not so with My servant Moses; He is faithful in all My house. I speak with him face to face, even plainly, and not in dark sayings; and he sees the form of the Lord. Why then were you not afraid to speak against My servant Moses? So the anger of the Lord was aroused against them, and he departed."

In this Scripture, the Lord is greatly displeased with Aaron and Miriam who dared compare their position and spiritual authority with Moses', His Sent One. The Lord was very clear about the sharp difference that existed between their authority and the authority of his servant Moses. He reminded them that He had communicated with them through visions, but He had spoken to his servant Moses face to face. This statement illustrates how directly and with great clarity, He spoke to the set apostle who is over the whole congregation. Aaron and Miriam were delegated authorities under Moses. It is true that the Lord God loves all his children. Nevertheless, this does not change the fact that the apostolic office, by reason of its responsibility and accountability, has a greater grace to be able to accomplish its mandate.

Spiritual Covering

The capacity to be used by God to bring spiritual security and covering to the apostolic house is another portion of the apostolic grace. There is a special anointing granted to the apostle for the spiritual security of the apostolic saints. There is havoc that the devil cannot wreak on a saint who stays under authority of his apostolic covering.

Exodus 32: 30-33

"Now it came to pass on the next day that Moses said to the people, "You have committed a great sin. So now I will go up to the Lord; perhaps I can make atonement for your sin." Then Moses returned to the Lord and said, "Oh, these people have committed a great sin, and have made for themselves a god of gold! Yet now, if You will forgive their sin but if not, I pray, blot me out of Your book which You have written." And the Lord said to Moses, Whoever has sinned against Me, I will blot him out of My book."

Numbers 14: 11-17, 19-20

"Then the Lord said to Moses: How long will these people reject Me?... I will strike them with the pestilence and disinherit them. And Moses said to the Lord: Then the Egyptians will hear it, for by Your might You brought these people up from among them, and they will tell it to the inhabitants of this land. They have heard that You, Lord, are among these people; that You, Lord, are seen face to face and Your cloud stands above them, and You go before them in a pillar of cloud by day and in a pillar of fire by night. Now if You kill these people as one man, then the nations which have heard of Your fame will speak, saying, Because the Lord was not able to bring this people to the land which He swore to give them, therefore He killed them in the wilderness. Pardon the iniquity of this people, I pray, according to the greatness of Your mercy, just as You have forgiven this people, from Egypt even until now. Then the Lord said: I have pardoned, according to your word."

Scripture shows us here, Moses as the "the apostle of God," interceding for the people of Israel who had sinned against God. Because of his God-given mandate as spiritual authority over the people of God and accordingly to his privileged relationship as spiritual guardian of the people of God, the Lord honored his petition and forgave the sin of the people of Israel. The apostle in his position of authority has the capacity to intercede to the Father and have a special attention from God with respect to the people he is called to nurture and protect.

In fact, the devil cannot do what he wants with a people who are under the spiritual covering of an apostle sent by God to lead them. When the apostle lifts his voice to God on behalf of his congregation, heaven gives special attention. There is a level of attack of the kingdom of darkness that cannot touch a people under apostolic authority and covering. That was the case for the people of Israel during the spiritual watch of the prophet Samuel. The word says this in 1 Samuel 7: 13,

> "So the Philistines were subdued, and they did not come anymore into the territory of Israel. And the hand of the Lord was against the Philistines all the days of Samuel."

Because the prophet Samuel provided spiritual covering to the people of Israel, the Philistines were unable to affect the people of God. There is a level of attack that you will not get when you are under spiritual authority. It is imperative to be spiritually planted in a local ministry and have an authority cover you. How tragic it is to have itinerant saints just visiting assemblies or being here and there, erroneously thinking that they are connected to God. There are some situations you will go through in the process of accomplishing your destiny that will require a spiritual authority and elders to seek God on your behalf. The Philistines were subdued and could not affect Israel all the days of Samuel.

Establishes Biblical Foundations

EPHESIANS 2: 20
"Having been built on the foundation of the apostles and prophets, Jesus Christ Himself being the chief cornerstone."

Establishing biblical foundations in the Body of Christ is another part of the function of an apostle. A local house can have many apostles and all are called to fulfill the mandate of equipping the Body of Christ for the work of ministry and the edification of the Body of Christ. How can this be done? Will they minister the Word alternately and when they are not ministering do they sit in the local house and wait for their next turn? No, not at all. Although it is biblical for ascension gifts to sit and receive in the local house, much remains to be done for the expansion of the kingdom on earth. Therefore, some apostles in a local house are also called to be sent out to set foundations in churches abroad or churches that they had previously built. A church may be lacking in the ministry of deliverance, which is a pillar for a strong apostolic house. An apostle with an apostolic team can go to that church to establish the foundation of deliverance in that local house. After completing his assignment, he returns to his local house. Although Apostle Paul had many fruitful apostolic trips he would always return to his local congregation, the church at Antioch.

Acts 14: 26-28 talking about the return of apostle Paul and Barnabas to their apostolic house says,

> "From there they sailed to Antioch, where they had been commended to the grace of God for the work, which they had completed. Now when they had come and gathered the church together, they reported all that God had done with them, and that He had opened the door of faith to the Gentiles. So they stayed there a long time with the disciples."

Therefore there is ministry for every apostle commissioned in the local house. And yes, more than one apostle can be in the same local house. The church of Jerusalem had twelve whom we know of and they were able to function and minister together for the advancement of the kingdom of God in Jerusalem. In fact not all apostles are called to lead an apostolic center, although they are called for equipping and edification. Apostles in the same local house will all have a specific mandate from God for advancing the kingdom. Some will be called to church planting, others to establishing foundation in different churches, in different regions of the world, with strength in different principles: ministry of deliverance, spiritual warfare, apostolic structure, spiritual authority, prosperity, etc., within the perspective of apostolically expanding the kingdom of God in the regions of the world.

Missionary Works

The word "missionary" has widely been misused and abused in evangelical circles. The main purpose of a missionary in the first century church was to be sent out in a specific region to establish the kingdom of God. The gist of the work was spiritual; making disciples of all nations and not primarily bringing running water to a region and feeding the poor. Nevertheless missionary work is part of the apostolic ministry. In 2 Corinthians chapters 8 and 9, Apostle Paul is soliciting offerings from the saints of the church at Corinth to alleviate the needs of the poor in Jerusalem. The overall well being of man is incorporated in the gospel of the kingdom. Therefore, a missionary works to fulfill the different physiological and material needs of a certain region is also the mandate of the apostolic office.

APOSTLES' PITFALLS

Pride

With great authority and leadership, one should always be wary of pride. The apostle in the maturity of his office will have great revelation, power and breakthrough. For this specific reason he must beware of the trap of pride. He needs to be very sensitive to pride sneaking up in his life. Those who are beguiled by pride are the last ones to know. Others will see the manifestation of pride while the affected one thinks he only has strong conviction from the Lord, not recognizing that the lord in question is Leviathan and not the Lord Jesus. At times the plurality in the eldership and accountability with other apostles in the Body of Christ provides a safety net for an apostle. God never called any ministry to be self-sufficient, whether it is for the fulfillment of one's calling or for the edifying of one's call. Every minister needs the ministry of another minister, the apostle included. No matter how powerful and learned you are of the mysteries of Christ, you need to receive from somebody sometime in your ministry. Ministers who had not understood that truth stumbled and destroyed the mandate of God on their lives; some died before their time because they would not listen and accept ministry from a peer. The Lord knowing the weaknesses of man speaks of the church as a human body having many parts interlinked with one another. It is anti-biblical to be so prideful as to be self-sufficient and not recognize the need to receive from others. The need to receive from fellow apostles and ministers in the Body is instrumental in dismantling the works of pride. This is one reason why it is vital not only to connect with ministers under our authority but to also have horizontal accountability. The need to have apostles who are peers and are not afraid to biblically challenge our doctrine and spiritual paths for soundness is crucial.

Control and Intimidation

The strong character of an apostle subject to the Spirit of God can manifest control and intimidation. It is important for an apostle to have his accountability in these areas, because the line between control and intimidation with leadership and spiritual guidance can be quite thin.

The word tells us in Romans 14: 23,

> "Whatever is not the fruit of conviction is sin."
> (Louis Segond's French Version)

Although the apostolic office has great leadership capacity, the leadership needs not to be forceful with the people of God. The saints need to grow in learning to have conviction from

God and the Word of God. As apostles of God, we are not called to bring the people to believe in us but in the veracity of the Word we preach and teach. We are called to direct them toward the Almighty God whom we serve and His divine purpose and not toward us.

John 16: 8 speaking of the Holy Spirit says,

> *"And when He has come, He will convict the world of sin, and of righteousness, and judgment."*

The Holy Spirit leads in all truth, the Holy Spirit convicts of sin, righteousness and judgment and not control and intimidation.

Deficiency in the Measure of Rule

1 Samuel 13: 8-11

"Then he waited seven days, according to the time set by Samuel. But Samuel did not come to Gilgal; and the people were scattered from him. So Saul said, "Bring a burnt offering and peace offerings here to me." And he offered the burnt offering. Now it happened, as soon as he had finished presenting the burnt offering that Samuel came; and Saul went out to meet him that he might greet him. And Samuel said, "What have you done?"

What had Saul, with the royal anointing, who is an Old Testament figure of the apostolic anointing in the New Testament, done? He had derogated to the principle of the measure of rule. He had not recognized where his authority as king started and ended. This is a deficiency that an apostle needs to hearken. Because of his many graces and his level of authority, he can fall in the trap of enlarging his sphere of authority and measure of rule beyond what has been given to him by God. The apostle Paul had understood the importance of this principle. He understood his sphere of authority and measure of rule and made the effort to stay in them.

2 CORINTHIANS 10: 12-15A

"For we dare not class ourselves or compare ourselves with those who commend themselves. But they, measuring themselves by themselves, and comparing themselves among themselves, are not wise. We however, will not boast beyond measure, but within the limits of the sphere which God appointed us a sphere, which especially includes you. For we are not overextending ourselves (as though our authority did not extend to you), for it was to you that we came with the gospel of Christ; not boasting of things beyond measure, that is, in other men's labors."

In this portion of Scripture, Apostle Paul confirms this fact by telling the church of Corinth that being the one that beget them in the Lord, he was in his measure of rule and sphere of authority when it concerned them. God mandated Apostle Paul to reach the Gentiles and Apostle Peter was mandated to reach the Jews with the Gospel. It is very important for an apostle to clearly know the mandate God has given him, because the authority he has will be divinely appointed and operational only in the measure of rule that the Lord's gives him. There is not such a thing as a universal Apostle who has authority and rule everywhere in the world. Jesus is the only "Universal Apostle".

PROPHETS

MINISTRY OF THE PROPHETS

Many leaders refuse to accept the establishing of the prophetic office and the gift of prophecy in the local churches. There is a visible lack of prophets in the churches. We seldom see ordained prophets in the leadership of local houses. Prophets teamed up with apostles in establishing biblical foundations in the Body of Christ are virtually nonexistent. In the apostolic restoration movement taking place in the Body of Christ, we cannot undermine the importance of the office and ministry of the prophets, since the apostolic and prophetic team is clearly a biblical key to the establishment of strong apostolic houses in the plan of God to expand His kingdom on earth. To clearly understand the role and ministry of the prophets and of prophetic ministry in the local house and the Body of Christ, one should not base himself on the position of denominational creeds or the sayings of religious leaders, but as the people of Berea, we should search the Scriptures to base our belief and conviction on the function and ministry of the prophets. Therefore: What does the Word of God teach us concerning the prophetic ministry in the New Testament? For all people, unanimously accept the establishment of prophets and the prophetic ministry in the Old Testament.

Well clearly as mentioned in 1 Corinthians 12: 28 and Ephesians 4: 11, the prophet is a governmental gift established in the apostolic structure of the local house of the New Testament churches. He is an elder called and established in the government of the local houses. He carries great authority and utterances. The kind of ministry he executes is one that requires a lot of boldness and character. He is sometimes distant but only to receive a fresh 'Thus said the Lord' for the people of God. The prophet Elijah took time to set himself apart on the mountain. The modern day prophets might not have a mountain to set themselves apart, but they must spend time on their own with God to be effective in their governmental call and ministry. This is absolutely not a basis for not being submitted and under authority nor being participant in the normal life of the local house.

Definition of prophet: (from the Greek, *prophetês, prohemi*) **Pro:** before, *phemi:* say, declare. Hebrew, *Nabhi:* him who announces.

From the etymology of the Greek and Hebrew translation of the word we can understand the definition of this governmental gift. A prophet is one whom God speaks through by prophetic teachings. Prophets preach to edify, console, strengthen, exhort, correct, warn and reprimand a saint, the local church, the Body of Christ, city, state, country or nation.

ACTS 15: 32
"And Judas and Silas, being prophets also themselves, exhorted the brethren with many words, and confirmed them."

1 CORINTHIANS 14: 3, 4, 24
"But he that prophesieth speaketh unto men to edification and exhortation, and comfort. But he that prophesieth edifieth the church. But if all prophesy, and there come in one that believeth not, or one unlearned, he is convinced of all, he is judged of all." (KJV)

JEREMIAH 38: 1, 2
"Then Shephatiah the son of Mattan, and Gedaliah, the son of Pashur, and Jucal, the son of Shelemiah, and

Pashur, the son of Malchiah, heard the words that
Jeremiah had spoken unto all the people saying, thus
saith the LORD."

The Bible also calls the prophet a seer (1 Samuel 9: 9). The
term "seer" has been polluted by the world from its spiritual
integrity. In the secular world a seer is a person who speaks
on one's life in exchange for money. He does this through the
demonic influences of the spirit of divination. On the other
hand, the seer, expression used in the Old Testament, was a
man of God anointed by the Holy Spirit and used mightily to
speak to His people.

2 SAMUEL 24: 11
"For when David was up in the morning, the word of the
Lord came unto the prophet Gad, David's seer."

The seer obtained God's will or directives for public affairs
as much as for private one's or even for the spiritual direction.
Imagine the importance and impact that this ascension gift
could have in the contemporary governmental affairs. When
we see the carnal and demonic influences upon governmental
decisions, the Body of Christ should take as example the
prophet Daniel. Instead of refuting and denigrating these
ministry gifts, we should cry out to God that He might solidly
establish these prophets in the local church so that the fruit
God intends to produce in the Body of Christ as well as in the
nations would be seen.

DANIEL 6: 1-3
"It pleased Darius to set over the kingdom an hundred
and twenty princes, which should be over the kingdom;

and over these three presidents of whom Daniel was first: that the princes might give accounts unto them, and the king should have no damage. Then this Daniel was preferred above the presidents and princes because an excellent spirit was in him; and the king thought to set him over the whole realm."

Prophets flow in the revelational gifts: word of knowledge, word of wisdom and discernment of spirits and the inspirational gifts of prophecy, diversity of tongues and interpretation of tongues, all found in 1 Corinthians 12: 1-11. These ascension gifts have a very strong prophetic gift. They prophesy, although not all who prophesy are prophets. Some saints may prophesy through the gift of prophecy without necessary hold the office of the prophet. The prophetic anointing and prophetic realm of a prophet is much greater than the saint or leader with the gift of prophecy. The office holds authority to bishop over the saints in the college of elder lead apostolically. They can be used to discern what affects and is needed in a particular region. Prophet Isaiah, Prophet Jeremiah and Prophet Ezekiel were used by God to give spiritual guidance to kings and entire nations. Personal prophecy is great- encouragement and exhortations are needed, but in this season we need prophets to arise with the word of the Lord with clear directions for the fulfillment of the divine purpose and destiny for the regions. Prophets having the *"nabhi"* grace are anointed to create and bring to life things that were lost or dead of the blessings of God on a nation, a city, a church or a saint's life. Strong and mature prophets are able to bring direction and clear solutions for the apostolic house.

A fundamental key to understanding the different aspects of the prophetic ministry is the fact that all prophets prophesy but not all those that prophesy are necessarily prophets. There is quite a difference between the saint who has the gift of prophesy and the saint who is called, trained and established in the office of the prophet. The prophetic anointing is much greater in the ministry of the prophet than the saint who has the gift of prophecy. The gift of prophecy will edify, console and strengthen. A saint can prophesy to another saint for his edification, but he does not have the mandate of God and authority to correct nor rebuke prophetically a saint. The elders over this saint are the ones mandated for warning, correcting, rebuking and reprimanding. Now a saint's prophetic sphere and grace will exceed edification and exhortation to evolve and mature to include a level also of correction, warning and reproof when he is called into the office of the prophet. The prophet is an ascension gift for the local church and for the Body of Christ. His very person, even among the saints, is a blessing, a gift to the Church.

> EPHESIANS 4: 11
> *"(...) some, apostles; and some, prophets (...).*
> *The words some imply persons, individuals,*
> *saints in the Body of Christ."*

> 1 CORINTHIANS 12: 7-11
> *"But the manifestation of the Spirit is given to every man*
> *to profit withal. For to one is given by the Spirit the word*
> *of wisdom (...) to another prophecy (...). But all these*
> *worketh that one and the selfsame Spirit, dividing to*
> *every man severally as he will."*

Prophecy is a spiritual gift (1 Corinthians 12: 10). This gift is an instrument distributed by the Holy Spirit to whom He pleases, among the saints of the local church, for the common use of the church. Prophecy therefore is a gift used by a saint under the direction of the Holy Spirit, while the prophet is a saint who is himself a gift. The prophet has received from the Holy Spirit the gift of prophecy. In comparison, a prophet in a mature state of his ministry has a greater maturity in the gift of prophecy than a saint who has the gift of prophecy. The depth and prophetic sphere of a prophet are much greater than the saint who exercises the gift of prophecy.

The Church has a great need to be healed of the wounds inflicted by the wrong administration of spiritual gifts. These wounds affect the church's acceptance of the prophetic office. However, these mistakes toward the Word of God should not produce the removal of the Word of God. Our local churches have a great need in regards to the discerning of spirits and prophetic direction. God is reforming His church, shaking the ecclesiastical human structures established in the local churches. Time has come for the restoration of the integrity of the prophetic office.

THE FUNCTION OF THE PROPHETS IN THE APOSTOLIC CHURCH

One of our great challenges after we embrace the prophetic ministry in the apostolic restoration is to sort out how this tremendous ministry can be functional, effective and efficient for the purpose and mandate of the Body of Christ. This has truly been challenging. I have seen partial use and understanding of this aspect. I have also seen total abuse of the function of the prophets and the prophetic ministry in the local houses and Body of Christ to the point that some churches, although they understand the need of the prophetic anointing, completely shy away from it for fear of negative repercussion of this type of ministry on their vision and ministry.

ACTS 13: 1
"Now there where in the church that was at Antioch certain prophets and teachers."

1 CORINTHIANS 14: 29
"Let two or three prophets speak, and let the others judge."

The Antioch church had prophets in its leadership. The apostolically structured church encourages a plurality of prophets in the local house. In 1 Corinthians 14: 29 Apostle Paul encouraged the church of Corinth to let more than one prophet minister in their local house. Now if two or three are encouraged to minister and that the other prophets are called to judge, it is therefore understood that there is more than one prophet established in the local church. The sensitivity to the Spirit of God of the prophetic office makes it a strong addition to many departments and ministries in the local church. From this stems the importance of having a plurality in the assembly, for they are called to fulfill many functions in the mature apostolically structured house. What are the different functions of the prophetic office in the apostolic church?

Establishes Biblical Foundations with the Apostles

1 CORINTHIANS 12: 28
"And God has appointed these in the church: first apostles, second prophet third teachers."

EPHESIANS 2: 20
"Having been built on the foundation of the apostles and prophets..."

In the first century church, the prophets had a preponderant role in ministering alongside the apostles in the establishing of biblical foundations in the local churches. The apostles traveled with prophets in order to maximize the efficiency of edifying local churches in the regions. The prophetic office was used to establish biblical foundations through prophetic teaching and preaching to affect lives, churches and nations.

In 1 Corinthians 12: 28, the positioning of prophets between apostles and teachers is truly strategic. The prophets bring balance in an apostolic team of apostles and teachers. The apostles carry the vision, carry the blueprint, bring structure and give leadership. The teachers' strong doctrine, relate Scriptures to biblically strengthen the churches and the prophets bring balance in connecting vision and dogma with direction of the Spirit and the Word of the Lord. The prophet is able to download imprints from heaven, connecting the Spirit to the vision of the apostles and the instructions of the teachers to establish the local churches with biblical foundations.

In both verses, notice that the prophets were not the leading ascension gifts in the apostolic team, the apostolic office had the leadership. The apostolic office has the first rank authority to cover the apostolic team and apostolic houses. This by no means implies that a prophet cannot lead an apostolic and prophetic team to missions. This simply acknowledges the fact that prophetic ministry needs to be under apostolic authority. The apostolic office has the authority and grace to cover spiritually the prophetic office and to help them develop and fulfill their divine destiny.

Preaches and Teaches Prophetically

ACTS 15: 22, 30, 32

"Then it pleased the apostles and elders with the whole church, to send chosen men of their own company to Antioch with Paul and Barnabas; NAMELY, Judas, surnamed Barsabas and Silas, chief men among the brethren. So when they were dismissed, they came to Antioch: and when they had gathered the multitude together, they delivered the epistle. And Judas and Silas, being prophets also themselves, exhorted the brethren with many words, and confirmed them." (KJV)

In this portion of the Word, the apostles of Jerusalem sent out prophets Judas and Silas to the church of Antioch. God used them powerfully with confirmed prophetic preaching to establish the faith of the saints of Antioch. Some prophets have a great gift for preaching and teaching the Word of God through prophetic utterances and exhortations to strengthen the Church of Jesus Christ. In such a case they are more on the forefront of the local assembly for they labor in the Word and doctrine.

Spiritual Watchmen

EZEKIEL 3: 16-17

"Now it came to pass at the end of seven days that the word of the Lord came to me, saying, Son of man, I have made you a watchman for the house of Israel; therefore

hear a word from My mouth and give them warning from Me."

While some prophets may have tremendous gifts for preaching and teaching the Word of God and be on the forefront of the assembly, others may never be called upon for preaching and teaching but are called as spiritual watchmen for the local apostolic house and the Body of Christ. These particular prophets have very keen spiritual eyesight to discern what enters the church and warn the people of God. They are seers in the apostolic house. When a witch comes in the church or witchcraft rears its ugly head in the lives of saints in the house, the spiritual watchmen become important for they are able to pick these things up before they affect the life of the church. They can see poverty, danger or death before it strikes; they can discern these things. These prophets might not be preaching nor be teaching but they can see and warn and implement the power of God to bring peace in the church of the Lord. They faithfully and humbly report the word and discernment given to them by God to the presiding apostle of the house and the leadership team. Notice that the Lord in the Book of Ezekiel, gives revelation on the work of the watchmen. These prophets are able to hear from God and speak to the saints of the Lord, warning them of impending danger or breakthrough and blessings that are spiritually discerned. They might not be in the spotlight of pulpit ministry but they are satisfied in doing a work undercover, and it is subtle but greatly needed and important for the spiritual growth and the fulfillment of the vision of the local apostolic house in its region.

They are able to give prophetic counsel and guidance to the leadership of the church by assisting the apostolic office.

Amos 3:7 enlightens us to this truth by saying,

*"Surely the Lord does nothing, unless He reveals His
secret to His servants the prophets."*

The Almighty reveals His secrets to them so they can speak
with accuracy, not after things happen but before. Have you
ever seen the so-called prophets who are only able to give
what they receive after the situation has happened? The
prophet speaks before — the secrets that the Lord gives are
for us to prosper. The spiritual watchmen therefore need to
be respected and the church needs to take heed to the words
they receive from the Lord. The watchmen prophets will also
discern the strongholds that are affecting the church or the
region. These seers will expose and come against the works of
darkness in the church by the power of the Holy Spirit. They
will depict the spiritual needs of the church and the region and
are able to prophetically put in motion the solutions needed
to bring change by their powerful and spiritually resounding
utterances.

The real watchmen will be specific and clear. I still
remember before leaving for an apostolic trip one of my
watchmen prophets gave me clear insight on a situation the
apostolic team would be facing in the upcoming trip. Led by
the Spirit of God, she said that at the end of my meetings, one
person would come to bring me a gift in a box well packaged.
That person would say that this gift is to thank me for the
tremendous revelation she received in the conference. I was
directed by the Holy Spirit not to take that gift and not even
allow it to enter my hotel room. Well this situation played out
exactly as the watchmen had received from the Lord. As I was
signing some books at the end of the conference, one lady came

and offered a well packaged gift box, in acknowledgement to the revelation received in the conference. Right away, the Lord reminded me of the word he had given me through that seer prophetess and without any notice, I handed the gift to my assistant on that trip who was also present when the prophetic warning was given. He understood right away and before entering our hotel room we disposed of the so-called gift that was simply a set up by the devil.

In order to do effective and efficient apostolic ministry, true anointed and mature watchmen prophets are needed, because the enemy only sends his agents in ministries that are truly exposing his kingdom and sabotaging his works by enforcing the kingdom of God in their region. Why would the enemy seek to affect a church that has absolutely no relevance or spiritual and natural impact in a region that he is already dominating?

Intercession-Spiritual Warfare

EZEKIEL 22: 30

"So I sought for a man among them who would make a wall, and stand in the gap before Me on behalf of the land, that I should not destroy it; but I found no one."

HABAKKUK 2: 1-2

"I will stand my watch and set myself on the rampant, and watch to see what He will say to me... Then the Lord answered me and said..."

The prophets have a tremendous spiritual capacity to move things in the spirit realm. In Ezekiel 22, the Lord was concerned that He was unable to find prophets to intercede for

His nation. Spiritual degradation was rampant among those in exile in Babylon greatly because the prophets who had the anointing, authority and power to shift things in the Spirit were not consecrated and in position. The prophets who have the grace for intercession and spiritual warfare, are called to persevere and be like the prophet Habakkuk in their watch, to see what the Lord will say and fight for the breakthrough and the fullness of God's blessings for His people.

Daniel had consecrated himself and fasted 21 days, when the angel of the Lord delivered the answer to his prayer.

DANIEL 10: 12-13, 20

"Then he said to me, do not fear, Daniel, for from the first day that you set your heart to understand, and to humble yourself before your God, your words were heard; and I have come because of your words. But the prince of the kingdom of Persia withstood me twenty-one days; and behold, Michael, one of the chief princes, came to help me, for I had been left alone there with the kings of Persia. And now I must return to fight with the prince of Persia; and when I have gone forth, indeed the prince of Greece will come."

The angel of the Lord gives us important revelation on intercession and spiritual warfare in his comments to Daniel. Notice he said that the prince of Persia fought him on his way down to give the answer to Daniel's prayer and on his way back he will be fighting the prince of Persia and then have to face the prince of Greece. Understand that the angel was not going to face a human prince of Persia or Greece. The princes here are calibrated principalities, chief angels of Satan that are in charge of a certain region to inflict havoc and reinforce the devil's grip on a particular region or nation on earth. In order for the angel of God to bring the answer to Daniel, spiritual warfare was needed. Likewise, in our generation different regions are affected by different demonic princes that need to be dealt with in order for the church to breakthrough in a particular area. Spiritual warfare prophets are the governmental gifts equipped to face and dethrone these princes. Prophetic intercessory prayer and spiritual warfare are therefore one of the prominent roles of the function of the prophets. Because of the weakness in this area, the people suffered, in the time of the prophet Ezekiel. We will not be able to have any significant breakthrough in a particular region without this function of the prophet being fulfilled. These mighty man and woman of God step up in the realm of the spirit and put themselves in the gap between the church and demonic princes, confronting them and defeating them to the glory of God for the advancement of the kingdom of God. They are the shamar prophets (prophets at the gap) who rise not only to pray for deliverance at the level of the saint in the church, but deliverance in the realm of the spirit for the whole Church, a region, a country and a nation.

It is important to understand that the prophet intercessor is not one to only pray religiously in tongues for a long period of time. In fact he is a mature prophet versed in the Word of God and learned in the things of the spirit, that is why he is able not only to discern which kind of demonic prince affects a region but he also receives insight from God to know the proper steps for dethroning such a prince. I have seen many prophets come short of their calling because of ignorance in the prerequisite knowledge and maturity needed for their prophetic intercessory grace. Some die before their time, others serve God wholeheartedly but are afflicted in their relationships, finances or even in their health, but please know that this is not the will of God. Intercessory-warfare prophets are called to be fully blessed as they accomplish their mandate in the governmental leadership of the church. Let it be known that in this season, revelation, knowledge and wisdom of that call is being released in the Body of Christ and we will see a whole new dimension of intercessory warfare prophets in position for dominion in the advancing of the kingdom.

Prophetic Praise And Worship

1 Chronicles 25: 1-6

"Moreover, David and the captains of the army separated for the service some of the sons of Asaph of Heman and of Jeduthun, who should prophesy with harps, stringed instruments, and cymbals. And the number of the skilled men performing their service was: Of the sons of Asaph..., the sons of Asaph were under the direction of Asaph, who prophesied according to the order of the King. Of Jeduthun, the sons of Jeduthun... under the direction of their father Jeduthun, who prophesied with a harp to give thanks and to praise the Lord. Of Heman, the sons of Heman... All these were the sons of Heman, the King's seer in the words of God... Asaph, Jeduthun and Heman were under the authority of the King."

A sector in church ministry that has been suffering for the longest time is the ministry of praise and worship. It is so common to see talented musicians and psalmists raised in the church ending up singing impure songs, releasing an impure sound living a proverbial life to the shame and detriment of the Body of Christ. Why? Because very often, the church has prostituted the gifting of the praise and worship ministers. They have been seen for too long as those preparing the way for the anointed preachers. Their ministry very often has been reduced to entertainment. How different from the role of praise and worship ministers in the Bible days. Contrary to what we see in too many churches, praise and worship ministers in the Bible were anointed ministers consecrated to the important service of taking the people of God to the throne of God, the presence of the Almighty. The praise and worship ministers were not entertainers but powerful ministers of the Lord. King David understood that praise and worship was a weapon needed for victory, an instrument to access the presence of God for deliverance, healing and direction. Therefore, we see in 1 Chronicles that the praise and worship ministers were truly prophets in a strategic position of ministry. This is a function of the prophetic office that has been misunderstood and ignored for the longest time. Many musicians, chorists and worship leaders are truly prophets of God who have not been trained to fully attain their spiritual potential. In fact all musicians, ministers and psalmists are prophetic. They might not all be prophets, but if they do really have the gift of music at whichever level it is, they are all prophetic. The prophetic anointing gives the capacity to create music, songs, prophetic dancing, painting and different graces in arts and entertainment. But unfortunately, they have been relegated to a second level ministry that supports supposedly the real thing... preaching.

1 Chronicles 25: 1-6 instruct to the fact that Asaph, Jeduthun and Heman were all prophets of the Lord leading their prophetic families to the ministry of praise and worship in the reign of King David.

They were able to sing forth the new song of the Lord.

PSALMS 40: 3
"He has put a new song in my mouth- Praise to our God; many will see it and fear, and will trust in the Lord."

PSALMS 149: 1-4
"Praise the Lord! Sing to the Lord a new song, and His praise in the assembly of saints. Let Israel rejoice in their Maker; Let the children of Zion be joyful in their King. Let them praise His name with dance; Let them sing praises to Him with the timbrel and harp. For the Lord takes pleasure in His people; He will beautify the humble with salvation."

2 KINGS 3: 15
"But now bring me a musician." Then it happened, when the musician played, that the hand of the Lord came upon Him."

1 SAMUEL 16: 23
"And so it was, whenever the spirit from God was upon Saul, that David would take a harp and play it with his hand. Then Saul would become refreshed and well and the distressing spirit would depart from him."

In these verses we can see the prophetic aspect of praise and worship. King David who was a prophet of praise and worship in Psalms 40 declares that the Lord had put a new song in his mouth. He understood the importance of having a new song for every new season in his life. He understood that his Lord was an ever-glorious God renewing His graces every day, always having a fresh word and blessing for him, which was released through his songs. How tragic that many churches have been singing songs, hymns of old to get a sense of the anointing of old when the Lord is more than willing to give a fresh anointing through a new song for a present and current need. In these religious settings praise and worship has been reduced to singing hymns from a book and spending a religious half hour to an hour in a boxed spiritual ambiance that is sometimes filled with emotions but lacking the true presence of God. The time has come for reformation and restoration of the prophetic in praise and worship so that as in the days of King David through prophetic praise and worship coming forth with new songs of the Lord, the people could experience God's presence and fear Him once again. No wonder we do not see miracles, signs and wonders but only people who sing and clap; the new songs are not released for the presence of God to manifest and show forth Almighty God's authority and power in action.

The praise and worship team is called to minister and prophesy. Praise and worship is not supposed to be a boring, lifeless, religious segment of a service but should be full of life, singing new songs, praising God with instruments and dances, because the Lord takes pleasure in His people adoring and magnifying Him. Notice that Psalms 149: 4 even speaks of the beautifying effect of prophetic worship. How powerful!

In these verses we clearly see the importance of musical instruments in the praise ministry. Musical instruments are not only there to produce sounds but prophetic sounds fostering the presence of God creating the spiritual atmosphere so that the Lord could speak to his people. In the episode of 2 Kings 3: 15, we see how an anointed musician's ministry brought a conducive spiritual atmosphere for the prophetic ministry of

Prophet Elisha. David who was a prophet of God had so much anointing that he was able to bring deliverance to King Saul in 1 Samuel 16: 23, without uttering a word: simply by playing his harp, demons were being cast out of the afflicted King. Notice, if the hands of David were able to release, without him singing, the anointing of God for deliverance, instrumental new age music and demonically inspired musicians can also release evil spirits without pronouncing a word. So do not fool yourself in thinking that all instrumental music is harmless, the spirit of the musician can easily be released for evil or for good depending on his spirit and allegiance. How saddening when Christian musicians and ministers seek the work of ungodly and worldly artists for guidance and inspiration, forgetting that they are serving a jealous God who requires our complete consecration, adoration, worship and dependence on Him.

2 CHRONICLES 20: 21-22, 25-26
"And when he had consulted with the people, he appointed those who should sing to the Lord, and who should praise the beauty of holiness, as they went out before the army and were saying: Praise the Lord, for His mercy endures forever." Now when they began to sing and to praise, the Lord set ambushes against the people of Ammon, Moab and Mount Seir, who had come against Judah. When Jehoshaphat and his people came to take away their spoil, they found among them an abundance of valuables on the dead bodies, and precious jewelry, which they stripped off for themselves, more than they could carry away. And on the fourth day they assembled in the Valley of Berachah."

Prophets should be trained and set in prophetic praise and worship position so that the army of the Lord can take full victory. King Jehoshaphat understood the power that resided in praise and worship for he put the musicians in front of his army and his people in the quest of combat. Through prophetic praise and worship, the enemies of Judah were ambushed and the people of God were blessed in the valley of Berachah (the valley of blessing) with abundance of riches above what they could carry away. Oh! How much abundance of blessing the Church of Jesus Christ is forfeiting because of the lack of prophetic praise and worship. Prophets of praise and worship certainly are not to be disregarded in the implementation of a strong apostolic house.

Teaching, training and activation of the prophetic ministry is key to the success of the prophetic pillar in the apostolic Church. It just cannot be neglected. Many churches and church leaders want to have a strong prophetic ministry, understanding its importance in the apostolic ministry, but fall short in taking the adequate steps for their prophetic ministers to be trained. In the praise and worship ministry, it is no different. Prophetic praise and worship ministers are critical to the raising of a mature prophetic praise team therefore training cannot be undermined. In fact in our ministry, my wife is in charge of the prophetic praise team. Before any new minister is released to participate in the praise ministry, he is channeled to training and teaching of the prophetic ministry. The mistake some churches make is to become enamoured by the musical talent of some saints and undermine the importance of making them go through proper teaching, training and impartation. A lot of gospel singers and musicians have absolutely no power and anointing. They can be technically sharp with great sound effects but without power and anointing. Why? Because they truly do not know God and what it means to be in His presence. They do not know or understand their function in the Body of Christ; they are not trained or equipped for the spiritual ministry they are called by God to do. Therefore many finish singing in some gig or if they are more talented they end up singing professionally for the secular music scene. Now those in the church that hang by a thread they are attacked by all kinds of impurities. Truly this is not the will of God. Certainly they can bring a level of ministry with the gift, but in order for them to reach their full ministerial potential and fulfill their destiny, they will need to sit under anointed teaching and training and receive prophetic activation to be fully propelled in their destiny. There are various prophetic areas of ministry that need to be trained: Arts — people that are in television, graphic designers, painters, fashion designers, movie professionals that create the sound of programs and movies. It is a prophetic grace, to have the capacity to connect the proper sound to a certain movie. One needs to be prophetic to be able to connect the people with the image. You may not be called to be a prophet preaching in the house of the Lord but have the prophetic gift to radically affect the movie industry with that ingenious talent of sound creation. Comedians are prophetic. The capacity to make people laugh by stand up comedy is a branch of prophetic grace. But the religious church would never accept to raise a prophetic comedian in the house. How ridiculous! Church should have comedians with clean humor to release the joy of the Lord and even send some out in the world to use comedy to sow seeds of righteousness, forgiveness, patience, kindness, long-suffering and the multitude of other principles that are in the Word of God, that can bring salvation and transformation to the world. We need prophetic writers who are able to write stories instead of renowned writers like J.K. Rowling (Harry Potter trilogy) infesting society with demonic stories. We need prophetic ministers with the capacity to write stories to release the principles of God to transform society to the knowledge and greatness of God. Advancing the kingdom by having apostolic saints' books being used to make blockbuster movies. The Lord wants to raise praise and worship ministers but also apostolic saints penetrating the secular music world. For who can sing better on love, joy, peace, change, transformation and every other need of society than the anointed apostolic person sent by God who has the answer from the omniscient God of Abraham, Isaac and Jacob? Imagine a son of God winning the American Music Awards. Imagine a saint of God winning an Academy Award and going up the stage releasing the fear of God through sheer prophetic decree to the movie industry with millions in the world watching. Truly the prophetic gift needs to be activated in the apostolic house. This brings us to another area of ministry of the prophetic office.

Identification And Activation

1 Timothy 4: 14
"Neglect not the gift that is in thee, which was given thee by prophecy, with the laying on of the hands of the presbytery." (KJV)

Another function of the prophet in the apostolic house is identification and activation of the gifts in the church. Some prophets are very strong in this area of ministry. They should be therefore part of the presbytery that does the laying on of the hands to release the saints in their gifts and callings.

PROPHETS' PITFALLS

Biblical and Ministerial Deviations Through Ignorance of the Word

I feel it important for us to touch some of the pitfalls of the prophetic ministry and in so doing bringing balance in the teaching of the prophetic office.

> EZEKIEL 3: 3-4
> "And He said to me, "Son of man, feed your belly and fill your stomach with this scroll that I give you." So I ate, and it was in my mouth like honey in sweetness. Then He said to me, "Son of man, go to the house of Israel and speak with My words to them."

It is so unfortunate to see the number of great prophets who started their ministry really well and end up deviating biblically. Very often, these deviations are the result of lack of depth in the Word of God. Prophets are called to be adept in the Word of God and in doctrine, being careful not to count only on their capacity to receive spiritual things. The devil also speaks through the spirit and ministers can also speak from their flesh. It is for this purpose that Ezekiel was commanded by God to eat the scroll in the above passages in the book of Ezekiel.

Why was Ezekiel able to speak? He had the Word. Some prophets come to the assemblies of the saints with their eyes shut during the preaching of the Word being so called under a strong anointing communing and touching God, forgetting that God is also speaking to them through the preaching of the Word. They are therefore not exempted to take notes as everybody else. God is speaking and they are waiting for the anointing. When we speak about prophets we are not speaking about spooky people. Prophets need to know that the Word of God is prophetic. Every prophetic utterance of God comes from the Word of God. Too many potentially great prophets never fully reach their destiny because of the lack they have in the Word of God. They would tell you they see in the spirit, they are seers. They have such an exponential intimacy with God that they can communicate what God is saying, therefore they don't need to indulge in the Word like everybody else. What great ignorance!! That attitude is just the beginning of the meltdown and the downfall of some, cutting short some potentially great prophetic ministries because of biblical deviation. You see very often the enemy will not push you in the ditch at once: he does it by steps. Before you fully realize it you have deviated and even have started some religious, heretic cult. Most of the time the devil uses deviated prophets to start the most demonic cults. Because they see in the spirit, Jesus talks to them... That is why sound biblical foundation and continual growth in the Word of God is key to a stable and long-suffering prophetic ministry. Ezekiel ate the scrolls and was able to give the "Thus said the Lord" Not "Thus said Ezekiel" nor "Thus said the devil". The more a prophet has depth in the Word of God and has been sitting under sound teaching the more depth he will have in his prophetic ministry. The prayer and fasting of a prophet, his setting himself apart and his consecration are great but without showing himself approved and rightly dividing the Word of Truth, he still has the potential to be an instrument of the devil for destruction.

Spiritual Pride

Some prophets unfortunately fall into spiritual pride because of their prophetic grace, thinking they are the only one who can receive prophetic revelation. Although Prophet Samuel was tremendously gifted in the prophetic and had a tremendous communion with God, he nevertheless did not initially know who God was going to release as the next king after the fall of king Saul. In 1 Samuel 16:5, the prophet Samuel was convinced that Eliab was the next king, yet God had chosen David. The prophet did not know everything. There are certain truths that God will not tell you to keep you humble. God does not have to tell us everything. We need to beware of spiritual pride. God does not have to pass through a prophet to confirm every prophetic word he gives the body. Prophet of God you are not indispensable and are not the final judge of the *rhema*, that is the Word of God, therefore when the thought pops in your head that everything you receive comes from the Throne and that you should have the last confirmation on every word given to the Body, shake Leviathan and the spirit of pride before it destroys you. The Lord gives us in part so that we can learn to humble ourselves and function in a Body. Notice that in 1 Corinthians 14:29, two or three prophets were encouraged to speak and the other prophets were to judge. Not one "Mr. Prophet, King Prophet, Queen Prophetess of the Lord", but two or three. In the church of Corinth, there was no Super Prophet who was the only one with the Word of the Lord, but two or three spoke and still others were present not speaking but judging the accuracy of the prophetic word. This is the reason why in a mature apostolic house there is more than one prophet, to help him not fall in the trap of the spirit of pride and think he is the 'Sent Prophet of God' with the only final and accurate word possible from God. Prophet and Prophetess of God no matter how accurate and mature you are in the prophetic ministry, know that you can miss it and that you don't have the full council of God. There are 7000 other prophets who have not bowed to Baal. As Lord told Prophet Elijah when he thought he was the only one ministering the Word of the Lord in Israel (1 Kings 19: 18).

Isolation

Isolation is another pitfall of the prophetic office. When a prophet feels that he always needs to be by himself and starts dodging church fellowship something is wrong. For one is not called only to minister prophetically but to be part of the apostolic house. We are a body. Sometimes the prophetic anointing will call the prophet aside to receive certain downloads from heaven but this can only be periodically and not the majority of the time. Prophet Elijah got into that trap of isolation in thinking that he was the only prophet left serving God and coming against the work of the enemy, but God quickly brought him back to reality (1 Kings 19: 3). When a prophet gets in his dry spell of not feeling understood or even feeling left behind, not respected at his proper place, he can fall into that place of isolation. The only problem is that the enemy very often tries to make sure that he can finish the work of crushing the prophet in his state of emotional vulnerability. Every saint, being human, will experience challenges, justified or not, in such case, isolation is the worst thing. When one is imprisoned, he needs someone on the outside with a key to open the prison door to let him out. The Lord uses other ministers to help us out and the prophet is not exempt from such situations. Isolation can be lethal for a prophet.

TEACHERS

MINISTRY OF THE TEACHERS

1 CORINTHIANS 12: 28
"And in the church God has appointed, third teachers"

The teacher is the third governmental gift cited in 1 Corinthians 12: 28. Very often overlooked in some ministerial cases as a Sunday school teacher, a theologian who completed a Ph.D. or given a honorary degree, the teacher has been disregarded as a governmental gift in the apostolic house and Body of Christ.

Definition of a teacher: (from the Greek: *didaskalos*) a term, which signifies a teacher, master, or instructor.

The teacher is not one who only has obtained a doctorate degree in theology, nor one who seeks prideful gratification in elaborating Greek and Hebrew words to the apostolic house, but he is an elder mandated and particularly anointed to teach God's Word. This teaching is not simply brought in an intellectual way, but with the Spirit of God, authority, power, conviction and confirmation. Our Lord Jesus is our perfect example in the teaching office.

JOHN 7: 15
"And the Jews marvelled, saying: how does this man know letters, having never studied?"

MARK 1: 21-27
"And they went into Capernaum; and straightway on the sabbath day he entered into the synagogue, and taught. And they were astonished at his doctrine: for he taught them as one that had authority, and not as the

scribes. And there was in their synagogue a man with an unclean spirit; and he cried out, saying, let us alone; what have we to do with thee, thou Jesus of Nazareth? Art thou come to destroy us? I know thee who thou art, the Holy One of God. And Jesus rebuked him, saying, Hold your peace, and come out of him. And when the unclean spirit had torn him, and cried with a loud voice, he came out of him. And they were all amazed, insomuch that they questioned among themselves, saying: what thing is this? What new doctrine is this? for with authority commandeth he even the unclean spirits, and they do obey him." (KJV)

There are certain particularities of a teacher that come forth in this portion of the Holy Scriptures cited above. The teaching of the Lord Jesus Christ was very distinct. He did not teach like the scribes, who were the theologians of His time. Different from the scribal teaching of theologians, the teacher anointed by the Holy Spirit teaches with authority and power. The teacher deposits in the spirit of the listeners conviction and opens them up to spiritual enlightenment. The power of the teacher's teaching resides in the understanding and conviction of the Word of God brought to the spirits of the listeners by the Holy Ghost. The Jews were bewildered by the Lord's doctrine not because of the letter but because of the power of the Spirit, which accompanied it. Are the teachers who minister with revelation, authority and power by the Holy Spirit all gone? Are the teachers who instruct with revelation and with the simplicity of the Lord Jesus Christ without using complicated and equivocal language, are they all lost?

When we look at some Sunday school instructors we see a reduced format of this authority of God in the teaching of the Word. Here, we say reduced, since these instructors are sometimes ascension gifts who have not been fully released in their calling, having therefore their authority watered down. Unfortunately, they are not recognized in their rightful office and value for the tasks that they do. The church does not recognize them as spiritual authorities, nor as elders. On the other hand, please remember that not all those who teach in Sunday school, in services or in home cell meetings are necessarily ascension gifts of Christ with a teacher's calling. These may simply be saints who are ministering with the teaching anointing.

What are the differences between the teacher and the Sunday school instructor? The teacher is a bishop the Lord has established, by the laying on of hands of the elders, as an authority of God in teaching. The degree of knowledge, revelation of the Word of God and the teaching anointing are clearly much greater for the teacher than for the Sunday school instructor who teaches.

PSALMS 119: 130
"The revelation of your word enlightens, it gives intelligence to the simple hearted."

The teacher possesses a special grace from God in regards to the knowledge, understanding and profound wisdom of the Holy Scriptures. He has a tremendous capacity to retain biblical verses. He has a divine aptitude to make the link and to find the relationship between verses of the Word of God. The other gifts should not have less depth of the Word of God, but the teacher is rather the specialist in this aspect of the ministry. What differentiates the teacher from the other ascension gifts is his supernatural ability to bring the saints of God revelation of biblical principles. Notice that the Word tells us that it's the revelation and not information that enlightens. The spiritual doctor of the Word does not simply diagnose the problem; he is also the spiritual pharmacist who gives the right biblical prescription to bring remedy. The revelatory teaching of a teacher enlightens a biblical principle that is unclear for a saint in spite of multiple edifying sermons on the subject.

We must understand that preaching and teaching are instruments in the ministry of God's Word, which are clearly different one from another. The Lord preached and taught the Word of God.

Matthew 9: 35 tell us,

> *"And Jesus went about all the cities and villages, teaching in their synagogues, and preaching the gospel of the kingdom"*

Preaching brings a biblical truth to the saints for their edification, exhortation, fortification, while teaching brings the saints to the enlightenment of biblical principles. Preaching on the power residing in the Word of God for divine healing brings healing by faith to a saint, whereas teaching on divine healing brings the saint to the revelatory understanding of the biblical principle of divine healing.

IS THE PASTOR AUTOMATICALLY A TEACHER?

Many pastors who are church leaders attribute the teacher's office to themselves because of the conjunction of coordination that joins the words "teacher" to "pastor" in

Ephesians 4: 11. But, in this verse, we must simply understand the presence of five different gifts of Christ that God has established in His Church, for the purpose of bringing perfecting and edification to the Church of Jesus Christ. Is it not possible that the only objective of this coordination conjunction was to simply conclude the enumeration of the different ascension gifts and not to obligatorily attribute to the pastor the teaching office?

The teacher's ministry was again mentioned and specified in Acts 13: 1 which declares,

> *"Now there were in the church that was at Antioch certain prophets and teachers as they ministered to the Lord."*

It must be understood that in the Church of Antioch there were pastors who were mandated to the care and needs of the saints. However, in the text in question the emphasis is placed on the governmental gifts. We see the teacher clearly established in the government of the church of Antioch without being joined to the pastor. Although a pastor can minister under the teaching anointing, that does not obligatorily makes him a teacher. It is the teacher's fruit that qualifies him for the office and not the title of that position.

MATTHEW 7: 17, 20
"Even so every good tree bringeth forth good fruit. Wherefore by their fruits ye shall know them." (KJV)

Acts 13: 1 distinctively presents us the office of the prophet and of the teacher in operation in the local church. This passage explicitly mentions teachers and not pastor/

teacher. The relationship made between the prophet and the teacher allows us to believe the service and the special authority that these two offices hold in regards to teaching in the Body of Christ. The teacher is one who is more systematic while the prophet teaches with prophetic exhortations.

TEACHER'S PITFALLS

Biblical and Doctrinal Pride

1 CORINTHIANS 9: 13
"For we know in part, and we prophesy in part."

Because of the outstanding depth in the teaching of the Word that he is called to have, the teacher must beware of biblical and doctrinal pride. Notice that the Scriptures remind the saints that their knowledge is finite not infinite; we only know in part. The teacher receives insight from the Spirit of God who leads in all the truth, but he does not possess the totality of the truth. No matter how profound and impressive a teacher you are, you will always have some aspect of the Word of God that someone else in the Body of Christ will teach you. Therefore let arrogance and pride of biblical knowledge be put in check so you may receive from others' preaching and teaching. You can be a great teacher but you don't know it all and you will never know it all. Humility will help you stay open to receive all that God has for you through the rest of the eldership in the house or whoever else the Lord wants to use to bless you with more knowledge.

Doctrinal Deviations and Heresies

1 Corinthians 8: 1-2

"Now as touching things offered unto idols, we know that we all have knowledge. Knowledge puffeth up, but charity edifieth. And if any man think that he knoweth any thing, he knoweth nothing yet as he ought to know." (KJV)

Biblical and doctrinal pride can lead the teacher into another terrible trap-doctrinal deviations and heresies. Although this may seem a paradox for one who is gifted to dissect the truth of the Word of God, pride leads to destruction. Pride can convince a teacher that his doctrinal understanding, of a certain principle or Scripture is correct though it may be completely heretical. If he does not accept to be corrected by other ministers, this can be very detrimental. As we examine 1 Corinthians 8: 1-2, we can extract the root of that pitfall. Whenever one believes he knows, he is learned, he is profound in the things of God, he is already close to the fall. Therefore he should not take lightly the danger of doctrinal deviations in the course of his ministry through the carnal result of pride. You see the prideful thinks he knows everything. Therefore if he deviates, he will be stubbornly and heretically sure that he is on the right track in his biblical truth although he is totally and completely off the chart of sound doctrine. So know that as a doctor of the Word, you still need to beware of doctrinal deviations and heresies that loom over your ministry. Pride is a door that can permit doctrinal deviations to enter you ministry. No matter how educated you are in the Word and how decorated you are as a biblical scholar always remember that you know in part.

Quenching the Spirit of God

1 THESSALONIANS 5: 19

"Quench not the Spirit."

A teacher having the strength in methodology, order, structure and doctrine can be so structured that he takes the Spirit of God out of his program. A doctor can desire so much to impart the Word that he does not let the power of God move to solidify the ministry he is bringing. Therefore the teacher needs to strive to have balance as much as the teaching of the Word is important it cannot be done without the input of the Holy Spirit who leads in all truth. Intellectual teaching touches the mind but teaching by the power of the Holy Spirit touches the spirit and brings transformation. Jesus never ministered without demonstrating the power of the word and the Spirit. He never put his biblical teaching over the direction the Holy Spirit wanted to take. The teacher needs to remember that it's not by might nor by power but by the Spirit of the Lord. The Spirit of God and His power need to be present confirming the word being taught.

LUKE 5: 17

"And it came to pass on a certain day, as he as teaching, that there were Pharisees and doctors of the law sitting by, which were come out of every town of Galilee, and Judaea, and Jerusalem: and the power of the Lord was present to heal them."

The Lord Jesus did not quench the Spirit. While he was teaching the power of God was constantly present to demonstrate as He willed. As a teacher never become so dogmatic and structured that the Spirit of God has no place to maneuver through your teaching to confirm the Word.

PASTORS

MINISTRY OF THE PASTORS

We have elaborated on the office and function of the governmental gifts in the apostolic house and have understood their major responsibility, but this does not take away the relevancy and importance or undermine the ministry of the pastor and the evangelist. To be able to understand the revelation of the apostolic structure, one has to truly renew the understanding he had of the pastoral office. Pastor comes from the Greek word, *"poimenos"* which means shepherd: one who takes care. The pastor is the ascension gift that has a tremendous grace to take care of the spiritual, emotional, physical and material needs of the saints in the apostolic house. A mistake I have seen churches make in bringing light in the revelation of the ascension gift of pastor is mixing the term of the spiritual authority: the shepherd of the house or the angel of the house with pastors or shepherds that are part of the ministry gifts for the perfecting and edifying of the saints in the local house. The office of pastor is the ascension gift in the eldership that works with the other four ascension gifts under the authority of the visionary of the local house; which in an ideal apostolic setting is an apostle, to perfect the saints for the work of ministry.

Acts 20: 28
*"Take heed therefore unto yourselves, and to all the flock,
over the which the Holy Ghost hath made you overseers,
to feed the church of God, which he hath purchased with
his own blood."*

JAMES 5: 14

"Is any sick among you? let him call for the elders of the church; and let them pray over him, anointing him with oil in the name of the Lord."

1 TIMOTHY 3: 2

"A bishop then must be blameless, the husband of one wife, vigilant, sober, of good behaviour, given to hospitality, apt to teach."

Pastors are the bishops who oversee the important need of the well being of the saints in the house. They are the elders who will do the important task of visiting the sick, taking care of the poor, participating and representing the eldership in an important family event of a saint of the house. One can appreciate the ministry of a pastor in his capacity to remember the name of the saints and greet them with such warmth of Jesus. The other elders will also minister to the needs of the saints at a certain level that cannot be topped with the excellence and thrust of the pastor in that respect. In fact, the larger the church is, the more pastors are needed to take care of the flock. Knowing the role and function of the pastors, understand that it is impossible for the saints in a house of 1,000 members to have only a few pastors. Every need of ministry of every saint in the apostolic house is called by God to be taken care of. Unfortunately many mega-churches only have audiences and not an edified church that is taken care of, or the number of ordained pastors would probably be 10 to 20 time more, but often time the pastor and those ordained are only the presbytery with the wrong title and office.

Pastors usually flow in the gift of counsel, word of knowledge and wisdom as well as the gift of prophecy that are needed in their multiple counseling sessions and pastoral visits.

The pastoral office was not prominent in the early church, in fact it is named only once in the New Testament in Ephesians 4: 11. That brings me to a question. How can one refuse to accept the ministry of the other four ascension gifts of Ephesians 4: 11 when they are listed with the pastor which is only mentioned in that particular verse? If one acknowledges the ministry of the pastor, he has no other choice but to acknowledge the ministry of the other ascension gifts for the perfecting and edification of the church.

The primary function of a pastor in the early church was to minister directly to the saints in a little group setting. They were not teaching, preaching and leading in a global setting. Acts 13: 1 mentions the governmental leaders of the church of Antioch. They were prophets and teachers, although certainly pastors were present to take care of the flock. Throughout the first century church, the prominent gift ministries who were dealing with the leadership and direction, teaching and preaching to the saints were apostles, prophets and teachers; pastors took care of the saints and evangelists brought in the souls and helped the church stay focused on the needs of the world for Jesus Christ.

PASTORS' PITFALLS

Ministerial Emotionalism

Because of their proximity and great desire to see the needs of the saints met, pastors need to beware of the pitfall that I call ministerial emotionalism. Ministerial emotionalism is when a minister gets emotional with a certain need or the situation of a certain saint. This is problematic since we are called to walk by the Spirit and not by the flesh. We certainly cannot take care of the spiritual needs of the saints whether they are physical or material without the Spirit of God. Ministerial emotionalism will draw the pastor in all types of traps from bad judgments to relational and sexual sins.

Conservativeness and Neutrality

Another pitfall of the pastoral office is conservativeness and neutrality. The desire to be the glove that fits all can affect the pastor's ability to draw the line in a particular case or be direct and succinct in his judgment, position and counsel in specific cases. We need to remember that love speaks the truth, chastises, rebukes and corrects. It does not only encourage and comfort. Therefore, the pastor will be called to rebuke and correct the saint who takes the crooked path and this will sometimes come with severity (Proverbs 15: 10).

EVANGELISTS

MINISTRY OF THE EVANGELISTS

Of all the ascension gifts the evangelists are one of the most spoken of in the Body of Christ. However, such recognition is often based on ignorance. Many saints and leaders see the evangelistic ministry as simply a stepping-stone to the pastoral office. For the leadership of many churches, the evangelistic ministry is just a preparation stage. He is but an apprentice minister that has the gifting to one day become a pastor, but is not yet mature and lacks enough wisdom and spiritual depth for it. For many local houses and denominations the evangelist has an extraordinary preaching grace with impressive boldness but he is still lacking maturity, therefore he is in a training period to one day be promoted to the "real leadership office... the pastoral office." Unfortunately there are some ordained pastors who are simply dizzy and lost evangelists in an ecclesiastical system, which is handicapped and cancerous. This system, which demonstrates no biblical foundation, yet is well in place by many denominations, who lead these evangelists directly toward the pastoral office. Because according to them, the only true and viable option for a saint with so much potential in preaching is to become a minister of the Word epitomized in the position of a pastor. For this reason many evangelists are clustered in an incongruous ecclesiastical and evangelical environment.

In fact, the pastor, being the supreme authority in the majority of ministerial circles where the evangelist ministers, perceives the evangelist as a threat to his position. Also since there is such a lack of teaching on this subject, the saints do not give the evangelist the respect that he deserves as an elder. The evangelist is often perceived as a brother who preaches well and who serves as an excellent support to the pastor.

By letting the Holy Spirit shed light in the function and position of this ascension gift in the apostolic house, we discover an elder who is endowed with an extremely bold character. The evangelist is God's number one instrument to set ablaze the gospel in the world. The evangelist is the charger among the elders. We can see certain traits of the evangelistic character when we consider the Apostle Peter. It was he who jumped out of the boat and started walking on water to go and join the Lord Jesus while the rest of the disciples trembled in fear in the boat, waiting to know if it was really the Lord. Despite the fact that he began to sink halfway, we cannot overlook his boldness and courage in that episode (Matthew 14: 22-33).

What about the legendary declarations of the apostle Peter, in Luke 22:33, "Lord, I am ready to go with thee, both into prison and to death." When the Lord had announced to His disciples that he would be captured and killed before resurrecting, Peter finished by denying the Lord Jesus three times before the rooster crowed in that episode. However, the desire to protect the cause of Christ was revealed in Peter's attitude. Peter was the flamboyant, impulsive and dynamic evangelistic apostle who was first in the assault whenever the occasion sprang up. His evangelistic charisma allowed him to bring three thousand souls to conversion in his first evangelistic sermon after Pentecost.

Definition of evangelist: (from the Greek *euaggelistès*) he who declares in advance good news.

EPHESIANS 4: 11
"*And he gave some apostles and some, evangelists; and some, pastors.*"

2 TIMOTHY 4: 5
"*But watch thou in all things, endure afflictions, do the work of an evangelist, make full proof of thy ministry.*"

ACTS 8: 26-31, 35
"*And the angel of the Lord spake unto Philip, saying, Arise, and go toward the south unto the way that goeth down from Jerusalem unto Gaza, which is desert... a man of Ethiopia, an eunuch of great authority under Candace*

queen of the Ethiopians, who had the charge of all her treasure, and had come to Jerusalem for to worship, was returning, and sitting in his chariot read Esaias the prophet. And Philip ran thither to him, and heard him read the prophet Esaias, and said, Understandest thou what thou readest? And he said, How can I, except some man should guide me? Then Philip opened his mouth, and began at the same Scripture, and preached unto him Jesus." (KJV)

Evangelists are ascension gifts who are elders in the Church of Jesus Christ just as much as pastors. They are neither assistants nor the "boys of the pastors." The office of evangelist is absolutely not to be considered an intern for someone who aspires to the pastoral office.

By the grace that they have received from the Lord Jesus Christ, evangelists have a tremendous anointing and passion for lost souls. They are the ministry gifts that connect the unsaved to the local house and the saints of God. Unfortunately, some have called themselves evangelists and ministered from church to church, bringing the salvation message sometimes to people who are already saved. If one has a strong evangelistic anointing his fruit should be lost souls found. Although the strong exhortation and preaching anointing of the evangelist can be used to bless the local house and churches, this gift should be primarily used to expand the kingdom of God with new souls for Christ. Churches suffer in growth because of the lacking in that office. Every saint is called to bring people to Christ but the evangelist has a greater grace and is anointed to stir up the evangelistic anointing and bring revelation to the apostolic house for greater impact in evangelism.

ACTS 8: 6-7

"When the crowds heard Philip and saw the miraculous signs he did, they all paid close attention to what he said. With shrieks, evil spirits came out of many, and many paralytics and cripples were healed." (NIV)

To show forth the fruit of their ministry, the Lord has equipped the evangelists with a strong anointing for healing and deliverance. Facing the unbelief and doubt of the world, the power of God manifested in his ministry is used to authenticate and bring conviction in the gospel of Jesus Christ. The demonstration of the Word of God breaks the yoke of unbelief.

Notice that in the above verses the people of Samaria had no choice but to pay close attention to the words of Philip, since they saw it was not all talk. The word of God was confirmed and demonstrated with many healings and deliverances. How unfortunate that in our era there are too many talk show preachers having all the nice rhythms and cute slogan sayings, but no power and demonstration of the power in the gospel of Jesus Christ. The crowds of today, like those of the past, are not impressed with simply the expression of nice words. No wonder some find no difference between an evangelical preacher and another 21st century preacher of another religion. In our era polluted by the influence of false prophets, as Raël, and his sexually emancipated troop that preaches the liberty of sexual expression, we need true evangelists. There is the crowd of Joseph Smith, the Mormons who preach on the three kingdoms. There are the followers of Charles Taze Russel, the Jehovah Witnesses, who have preached many dates that have come and passed of the coming of the Lord, and there are many more. For the gospel of grace to be able to break through all these layers of lies proliferated by these multiple religions and religious sects, it must be preached in its fullness with a demonstration without showing the least bit of ambiguity. The crowds of Samaria did not just receive words, but they saw the explosive demonstration of the Word of God. Where are these evangelists who do not simply stimulate the human intellect but also demonstrate the power of the Word of God that will lead to conversion?

The peop le of Samaria saw the manifestation of the power of God and just could not dodge the King of kings behind the power. The evangelist in the apostolic house is raised to preach with depth and clarity the revelation of salvation with signs and wonders that follow bringing forth salvation for kingdom expansion.

EVANGELISTS' PITFALLS

Itinerancy

ACTS 14: 26-28

"From Attala they sailed back to Antioch, where they had been committed to the grace of God for the work they had now completed. On arriving there, they gathered the church together and reported all that God had done through them and how he had opened the door of faith to the Gentiles. And they stayed there a long time with the disciples." (NIV)

In spite of the itinerant aspect that may be reflected in the evangelistic ministry, the Lord Jesus Christ never called the evangelists to be itinerants. But it is unfortunate that many international evangelists advocate an itinerant ministry; not having a local church. They believe themselves as indispensable to the Body of Christ and to the perishing world means their timetable is saturated with engagements. Consequently, they do not have time to sit down and receive the word in their local church, contrary to the apostle Paul who returned to his local assembly in Antioch after his mission trips (Acts 14:26-28).

Despite his magnificent evangelistic ministry out of Jerusalem, Phillip the Evangelist had understood the principle of belonging to a local church. Today, many evangelists have adopted a system of "Evangelistic Ministry Inc.", equipped with a head office and administrative council similar to secular businesses. Other five-fold ministers who are also itinerants or are close to retirement, serve as members of their council. They serve as ministerial counselors and as the Body of Christ to whom these great ones of the evangelical ministry must give an account. Very often a conflict of interest arises, since the one who is accountable to the council is also the one who pays the salaries of the ministerial council. However, the Lord Jesus Christ rather speaks to us of the Body of Christ, the local church, elders who take care of the needs of the flock and not of an independent administrative council or ministerial councils. These evangelists who have their own post-biblical systems dismantle the concept of a college of elders.

This type of non-scriptural itinerancy in regards to the evangelistic ministry sometimes gives birth to evangelists who exempt themselves of all accountability to a local church and to a college of elders. In that case, unity with the other elders of the local church is slanted. The ministers who function in that way, in certain cases, are difficult to educate and correct. The weaknesses that could be addressed in the framework of a college of elders and an apostolic house are easily brushed off among subjective counselors in the core of an administrative council and, all too often, the results are not very convincing.

The itinerancy of a lone ranger evangelist can be the fruit of disobedience and ignorance about the importance of his accountability to a local house and eldership. Also, in many cases, due to his lack of training in the normal life of the local house, proper protocol, respect for authority and other principles inherent to a proper ministry are undermined.

Lack of Biblical Depth

Another area of attention that an evangelist needs to focus on if he wants to fulfill his call is biblical depth. Often evangelists will lack biblical depth because of their heavy preaching engagements. It is very hard to deepen his revelation if he is constantly on the road preaching the same message in different places without taking time periodically to sit under the anointing of the other elder's ministry of the word in the local house and spend time at the feet of the Lord.

A FULLY FUNCTIONAL ASCENSION GIFTED APOSTOLIC HOUSE

Therefore in the mature apostolic house every ascension gift, whether the apostles, prophets, teachers as well as the pastors and evangelists are identified, trained and established in their divine position and calling of God. The apostles edify the church, the prophets bring the prophetic word of the Lord, the evangelists bring the souls to Christ whom the teacher teaches and whom the pastors take good care of. In the light of the elaboration of the function of the ascension gifts, we can see how a plurality of each ascension gift can be fully functional in the same apostolic house. In that aspect, each ascension gift can focus in a specific area of ministry in the frame of the gifts of their ministry. Now remember that God in his sovereignty and diversity has different combinations of gifts that can take place amidst the ascension gifts, offices and ministries. Although, we need to remember that only Jesus was able to function in the fullness of the grace of the five ascension gifts; we need to be careful when a minister says he is an apostle, prophet, evangelists, pastor and teacher. The apostle, because of his prominent mandate, can flow in the grace of all the other four ascension gifts when he is sent by God to establish a church in a region but that does not make him one who possesses the five gifts of Ephesians 4: 11. He can minister in them for a set period, for a specific season and purpose but he is not partaker of the gifts and anointing of the five offices.

Now it is imperative to understand that all the saints in an apostolic structured house are not all ascension gifts. The word in Ephesians 4: 11 says that *some* are... not *all*, therefore what are the other ministries in the apostolic structured house?

DEACONS

PHILIPPIANS 1: 1
"Paul and Timotheus, the servants of Jesus Christ, to all the saints in Christ Jesus which are at Philippi, with the bishops and: deacons."

As we continue to analyze this verse, we notice that the apostle Paul sent his salutations to the deacons. The deacons are part of one of the three categories of saints found in the local church.

Definition of deacon: (from the Greek *diakonos*), one who serves, who helps, who brings a service toward his master. Deacons are therefore ministers who are helpers who bring a service to the elders in the apostolic house. It is in this fashion that Tychicus helped the apostle Paul in Colossians 4: 7. Deacons also bring a service to the saints. It is in this light that some tasks in the apostolic house are given to the deacons by the elders to maximize functioning of the normal life of the local church. There is a special honor given to the saints who are promoted and who properly fulfill the ministry as deacons.

When speaking of deacons, 1 Timothy 3: 13, declares the following,

> *"For they that have used the office of a deacon well purchase to themselves a good degree."*

And Romans 13: 7 says,

> *"Render therefore to all their dues: honor to whom honor."*

The deaconship, the office of deacons and the eldership, the office of the elders are two distinct ministries in the apostolic structured church. The deacons cannot therefore, by this simple fact, be established as an elder in the college of elders. Although deaconship may be, in certain cases, a preliminary to a five-fold minister's establishment in his office, Phillip functioned in the deaconship before entering into the office of an evangelist. He was counted among the deacons who were elected in Acts 6: 5, but later, he is mentioned as being an evangelist in Acts 21: 8.

INSTITUTION OF THE FIRST DEACONS

ACTS 6: 2-6

*"Then the twelve called the multitude of the disciples
unto them, and said, it is not reasonable that we should
leave the word of God, and serve tables. Wherefore,
brethren, look ye out among you seven men of honest
report, full of the Holy Ghost and wisdom, which we may
appoint over this business. But we will give ourselves
continually to prayer and to the ministry of the word.
And the saying pleased the whole multitude: and they
chose Stephen, a man full of faith and of the Holy Ghost,
and Philip, and Prochorus, and Nicanor, and Timon,
and Parmenas, and Nicholas, a proselyte of Antioch:
whom they set before the apostles: and when they had
prayed, they laid their hands on them."*

We see for the first time in the New Testament church, the
institution of deacons in this portion of the Holy Scriptures.
The establishment of the ministry of deaconship came to
lighten the load and the service of the elders, which had become
too heavy due to the multitude of believers who were saved in
the church of Jerusalem. The deacons therefore took care of the
distribution to the saints, permitting the elders to continue to
apply themselves in their primary tasks, that of prayer and the
ministry of the word.

ACTS 6: 1-2

*"Now in those days, when the number of the disciples
was multiplying, there arose a complaint against the
Hebrews by the Hellenists, because their widows were
neglected in the daily distribution. Then the twelve called*

the multitude of the disciples unto them, and said, it is not reasonable that we should leave the word of God, and serve tables."

As we notice in the church of Jerusalem, the apostles understood that it was not desirable as elders in an apostolic house to leave the word of God and serve tables. They were appointed by God to primarily perfect the saints for the work of ministry and not to perform administrative work and daily distributions. Many church leaders are entangled and stalled in ministry from lacking to establish an effective deaconship able to take care of administrative task in the local house, thereby enabling them to focus on the perfecting of the saints.

ACTS 6: 3-4

"Brothers, choose seven men from among you who are known to be full of the Spirit and wisdom. We will turn this responsibility over to them and will give our attention to prayer and the ministry of the word." (NIV)

A lot of elders are lacking time to pray because they are doing so much of the administrative work of ministry. Elders need to get their time to fellowship with God in their prayer time to receive fresh revelation of the word, insight and direction for healthy growth of the people of God.

THE RELATIONSHIP BETWEEN THE DEACONS AND THE ELDERS

When we scrutinize with an eye of revelation Acts 6: 2-6, we notice that the institution of deacons was not official but after the approval of the elders. After having prayed to receive confirmation of the Lord, the elders laid their hands on the deacons demonstrating that they were consenting to the choices made.

1 TIMOTHY 5: 22
"Lay hands suddenly on no man, neither be partaker of other men's sins."

It would have been uncalled for to have the elders lay their hands on the saints chosen for the deaconship if they had doubt about their choices or clearly received otherwise from the Lord. The laying on of hands that the chosen saints for deaconship received from the elders is also a conferring of authority by the elders to them. By this, we see the spiritual authority that the elders have upon the deacons. The elder is therefore a spiritual authority on the deacons and on the saints in the local church, whereas deacons, by their given position in the local ministry, have a delegated authority on which ever position they are given by the eldership. The spiritual and biblical structure of the local church, in the order of spiritual authority, is established in the following way: the elders, the deacons and the saints.

Romans 13: 1 specifies,

"Let every soul be subject unto the higher powers."

The saint must not seek to submit only to the five-fold ministers, but to all superior authority, which includes deacons. The elder is chosen by God and is consecrated by the laying on of hands of the college of elders. The deacon is chosen by the saints and approved by the elders. The elders can replace the deacon, whereas the anointing that is on an elder is irrevocable.

PSALMS 105: 15

*"...Do not touch My anointed ones, and do My prophets
no harm." (KJV)*

We cannot revoke the anointing on an elder. On the other
hand, God may replace him.

Job 34:24 tells us, when speaking of God,

*"He shall break in pieces mighty men without number,
and set others in their stead."*

Ephesians 4:12 emphasizes the fact that an elder is called to
equip and to edify the saints. In the same way, some deacons
can also be used in the ministry of the Word to edify the saints.
Stephen, the deacon, in Acts 6: 8-15; 7: 1-60, was used by the
Lord to propagate the Word of God with great wisdom and
with the Spirit of God. Phillip, the deacon, preached with a
strong evangelistic anointing in Acts 8: 5-10.

ROMANS 16: 1

*"I commend to you our sister Phoebe, a servant of the
church in Cenchrea." (NIV)*

Deaconess Phoebe was so anointed that she was
commended for her service. Apostle Paul acknowledged and
recommended her personally, due to her extraordinary support
and service in ministry.

ACTS 6: 8-10

*"Now Stephen, a man full of God's grace and power,
did great wonders and miraculous signs among the
people. Opposition arose, however, from members of*

the Synagogue of the Freedmen (as it was called) Jews of Cyrene and Alexandria as well as the provinces of Cilicia and Asia. These men began to argue with Stephen, but they could not stand up against his wisdom or the Spirit by whom he spoke." (NIV)

Stephen is another outstanding example of the grace that is called to follow deacons. He had so much wisdom and knowledge of the word accompanied by anointed utterances demonstrated with power that the sects of his time could not withstand him. You see it is not enough for the contemporary deacons to serve communion on the first Sunday of the month. Deacons are called to service to alleviate the ministerial weight off the elders. It is not enough for them to come on members meeting and sporadically on Sundays. Let the real deacon boards arise to service!!!

THE FUNCTIONS OF THE DEACONS

From a biblical point of view, the term "deacon" denotes a help and a service brought to. Deacons serve as help to the elders for the maintenance of the tasks in the apostolic house. They may be supervisors of different ministries, the elders being the authorities of the local house to which they are called to be accountable in proper apostolic structure. They can be in the administrative structure of the house as a treasurer or secretary. They can be head musician, head usher, head logistics and so on.

We cannot underestimate the qualification of the deacons in the apostolic house. It is not enough to come faithfully to church and be a smiling "Yes man" to the leader to be positioned as a deacon.

ACTS 6: 3

*"Wherefore, brethren, look ye out among you, seven men
of honest report, full of the Holy Ghost and wisdom."*

1 TIMOTHY 3: 8-13

*"Likewise must the deacons be grave, not double tongued,
not given to much wine, not greedy of filthy lucre; holding
the mystery of the faith in a pure conscience. And let
these also first be proved; then let them use the office of a
deacon, being found blameless. Even so must their wives
be grave, not slanderers, sober, faithful in all things. Let
the deacons be the husbands of one wife, ruling their
children and their own houses well. For they that have
used the office of a deacon well purchase to themselves a
good degree, and great boldness in the faith which is in
Christ Jesus."*

The one who aspires to the charge of a deacon can be a man
or a woman; Phoebe was a deaconess in the church of Cenchrea
(Romans 16: 1). The deacon must have a good testimony among
the saints, and among the unsaved. This good testimony has
all its importance, since the establishment of a deacon is done
according to the choice of the saints. His election is influenced
by his devotion toward the work of God. This exemplary
devotion toward the work of God gains him the respect of the
saints. Such a respect gives him a position over the saints on
which he now has a delegated authority. He must therefore be
tested before being promoted to the ministry of deaconship.

Deacons must be filled with the Holy Spirit in order to be
able to make good decisions. John 16: 13 tells us this, "Howbeit
when he, the Spirit of truth, is come, he will guide you into all
truth." Being regularly in a decisional position, honesty and

wisdom must be absolutely part of their qualifications. They must also be done away with duplicity.

The excesses of wine destroy the credibility and the confidence that deacons build, thanks to their good testimony. These servants must therefore run away from this like the plague! The department of finance in the local church is one of many areas of ministry in the core of the Body of Christ that deacons can minister. They must therefore be done away with dishonest gain and greed. Many have fallen in these traps and attract curses upon themselves by taking funds mischievously from the church. Others have stopped the flow of financial blessing in a ministry by being in an unclean spiritual state in the area of their personal finance and the application of the principles of kingdom of wealth. They must also conserve the mystery of the faith in a pure conscience allowing them, at all times, to bring a ministry with full conviction and with full assurance.

Proverbs 28:1 declares,

"The righteous are bold as a lion".

Impure conscience in this ministry can take away the boldness of the deacon in the assertiveness of his function and of his sayings.

By unveiling the qualifications of deacons, the Lord Jesus Christ puts a special emphasis on their families. Deacons must be faithful to their wives and hold their children in submission. Their homes must be exemplary. Being a leader for the many homes that compose the local church, it would be difficult for a deacon to give some household advice, if his family lives in disorder. Matthew 7: 5 tells us how could they remove mote in another's eye, when they themselves have a beam in theirs?

By making a revelational investigation on the qualifications and establishment of deacons, we can see a transparency and impartiality in the choices made. They were not in any way unwise or commonplace choices. They were not puppets led by the carnal hands of manipulative elders. They were not under the hold of the elders, but under the direction of the Holy Spirit. They were not men without conviction, but men filled with the conviction of the Holy Spirit. They did not seek to please men, but to please God. They did not speak with arrogance but with wisdom. Can we testify this of our contemporary deacons? Can you say the same regarding your deacons in a local church?

SAINTS

What are the saints called to do in the apostolic house's structure? Are they called to sit and clap, criticize the missing links for the local house to be excellent according to their haughty opinion? According to the spiritual and biblical structure of the local church unveiled in Philippians 1:1, we do not find there mentioned only elders and deacons; there are also saints who make up the members of an apostolic house. For too long the saints of God have been confined in the walls of passivity in what concerns ministry in the church. Too many saints are content with simply being a spectator to the services brought by the ministry of praise and worship and to the elder or preacher who preached the word of God. A saint of God has much more value than this, and his participation in the local church has much more importance than we may think, for the accomplishment of the work of God. The saints are not called to be the audience clapping and cheerleading the process to the success of a preacher and his family.

EPHESIANS 4: 11-12

"It was he who gave some to be apostles, some to be prophets, some to be evangelists, and some to be pastors and teachers, to prepare God's people for works of service, so that the body of Christ may be built up." (NIV)

The saints are called to minister. The elders are called to equip and perfect the saints. But the saints are called to do the work of the ministry. They are called to **work**. It is not normal for a local house to have a small percentage of saints ministering. In fact the apostolic church's success is linked to its capacity to raise the saints to their divine call, God-given position and purpose. The saints are not called to be Sunday morning benchwarmers, but effective ministers of Jesus Christ. For a long time the saint who had a calling on his life was called to be a pastor. Know that every saint in a church is called for a God-given purpose. In the apostolic house you are there to be identified, equipped and perfected, mandated and sent out in your God-given position and destiny. The church is a filling station. You cannot come to a gas station to stay and live. You come to fill your tank and go. Jesus said, "Go ye in all nations and make disciples". Unfortunately, many religious saints stay instead of going. They stay in the four walls of a building, receive preachings and teachings until they die and go to heaven or until the fulfillment of all things. It was never the plan of God for a preacher and worship team to be the only highlights of his army. The saints are called for ministry. They are called to go and penetrate every societal system and transform and impact it for the kingdom's expansion. They must return on Sundays, not only with themselves but also with souls touched by the power of God that moved through them in their area of influence.

We are not called to go and start our new church, if God did not appoint us for that, but we are called to bring salvation to the world and enhance the kingdom of God. We have made churches a healing center but it really is supposed to be a Perfecting Center. See, Jesus poured into the 12 disciples perfection and revelation. If Jesus had said to his followers "I want to pray for you for your sicknesses and for a job only", we would have never gotten the gospel. He, on the contrary, trained his disciples who became "sent ones", apostolic to be fishers of men. Know that each saint has a call on his life and as you become perfected, you are destined to infiltrate, influence and transform the different sectors of society.

ACTS 11: 26
"and it came to pass, that a whole year they assembled themselves with the church, and taught much people. And the disciples were called Christians first in Antioch."

In Acts 11, the believers were called Christians for the first time in Antioch, and this qualified their actions. They were imitators of Jesus Christ. Doing the works of the Lord was a normal part of life for these Christians. Souls were saved, the sick were healed, and the captives were set free, lives passed from spiritual death to abundance of life in Jesus Christ.

Acts 11: 21, tells us,

"And the hand of the Lord was with them: and a great number believed, and turned unto the Lord."

God's hand, being upon Christians, allows them to demonstrate the power of God. This power is always manifested by souls who come to the knowledge of Jesus Christ. There was not only a few conversions, the Bible also tells us that a great number of people believed in Him and were converted unto the Lord. An apostolic house is a fullfledged functional army where everybody is effective in its destiny as a Jesus Christ demonstrator in his environment. Nobody should be cheerleading, but everybody should be positioned to be a light in the region of darkness where he lives and functions. The grace of God must always be seen through the lives of Christians and through their works. Barnabas had seen the grace of God in the lives of the believers of Antioch (Acts 11: 23).

The raising of apostolic churches is not a movement but the will of God for every church. Every church was called to be apostolic, equipping and releasing sent ones in the world to advance the Kingdom of God on earth.

When people look at you in the world, they have to look at you and yearn to resemble you. They need to know, what it is that you have that keeps you going the way you're going. You don't even have to release Jesus "loves you". They need to see it. You see, the problem with churches today is that we have been going around with our "Jesus" tie, and our "Jesus scarves". People are tired of seeing your tie and your scarf, they want to see you as a witness, they want to see you breakthrough in the field you are at. There is a level of result that you are able to bring forth in your sector of society that people will want to ask: "What do you have that I don't have?" You won't even have to talk about Jesus; your stepping out and being a testimony will push them to know where you go. Less talking needs to be done and more showing of the transforming power in the gospel of Jesus Christ.

GENESIS 1: 26

"And God said, Let us make man in our image, after our likeness: and let them have dominion over the fish of the sea, and over the fowl of the air, and over the cattle, and over all the earth, and over every creeping thing that creepeth upon the earth."

Notice the Lord said; "Let us make men in our image according to our likeness, let them have dominion." Man lost dominion because of sin. But through the redemptive act of our Lord Jesus, man has regained dominion.

Romans 5: 17 says,

"For if by one man's offence death reigned by one; much more they which receive abundance of grace and of the gift of righteousness shall reign in life by one, Jesus Christ."

We the heirs of the kingdom of God are called to reign. Notice that it says; in life. You are not only called to be blessed in heaven, God wants to bless you right here on earth. Understand that our greatest blessing is eternal life in Christ Jesus. It is a tremendous blessing to have received Jesus and be heirs of heaven. Heaven is definitely a tremendous blessing, but God said he wants us to rule and dominate in this life. If you don't dominate and if you don't reign in this life, there's a problem. Let us stop saying, "Maranatha! Jesus is coming back" and start concentrating on the task at hand: reigning in this life!! Some Christians are so concentrated on walking on gold in heaven that they have forgotten that they are called to reign on the earth.

Now, one major problem is that too often we are ruling in the church. But the Lord did not say to rule and reign in church. He said on the earth. So it is not just in church that you need to be powerful, the time has come for you to be positioned to be powerful in the world. If you can sing, if you can dance and if you can shout for Christ, that's great. I sing, I dance, I shout in the presence of God, but we cannot stop it there - we need to rule in life, we need to rule in the world. For too long we have been dominant in the four walls of the church, for too long we have been dominant and powerful in church. But it's time to be powerful in the world. That's why the kingdom has not advanced in the level of impact that God has called it to have, because we have not been powerful enough in the world. In fact we would be shocked to know that 90 % of Christians have two lives, they have the life in church and a life in the world. They just put up the jacket and step into the church and say glory hallelujah! Hallelujah Jesus! Brother, Sister how are you...? And all the evangelical terminologies and then step out in the world and have their second life: their life in the accounting firm, their life in the government, their life in the school, their life in the office and their life in the hospital. If that is your situation, you are in the 90% of Christians having two distinctive lifestyles. Oh! Sure you make your effort to be as godly as you can in your workplace, but unfortunately it has its language, style and way of life. You have not been able to implement the principles you acquire in church, out of the church setting... you are a two lives Christian! And it's ok because I believe as we recognize that we are not truly reigning in life, we are ready for a turnaround. Unfortunately one can be successful in its sphere of influence and yet have no impact for the kingdom of God. This is due to not being able to transmit the kingdom revelation received in the assembly of the saints, in the world to advance the kingdom of God. The mandate of God for this book is to give strategic revelation in how to be positioned in your sphere of influence as a Christian and clearly have impact to advance the kingdom of God on earth.

Many Christians have this common dilemma. I understand the gospel and what God is saying but how do I translate the principles of the kingdom that I have learned in church into clear kingdom impact in my sphere, as a director, as an engineer, as a teacher, without just spreading out my Jesus flyer. People are solicited so much by different religions that they are starting to get tired of fanatics just throwing their religion at them. A strategy needs to be unfolded to the saints for kingdom impact in the world. They know how to have an impact in church but the time has come for the Body to learn strategically how to have an impact in the world.

3

Fulfilling the Reform
Mandate

PSALMS 24: 1
*"The earth is the Lord's, and the fullness thereof; the
world, and they that dwell therein."*

Understand that every person in this planet is a creature
of God. But not only the people, the world is also God's.
Literally, the kingdoms of this world are God's, the systems
that encompass our society belong to God.

In Genesis 1: 26, God speaks and says,

> *"And God said, let us make man in our image,*
> *after our likeness and let them have dominion...*
> *over all the earth."*

Man was created by God to rule the earth, to have dominion
on the kingdoms of the earth. The will of God was for Man to
have dominion on earth. The sin of man not only took away

man's communion with God but man also at the same time gave the devil dominion of the kingdoms of the world.

"Then the devil, taking Him up on a high mountain, showed Him all the kingdoms of the world in a moment of time, and he said to Him; All this authority I will give You, and their glory; for this has been delivered to me..."

The word "authority" used in this verse is the Greek word "exousia" that literally means the legal right to exercise. The devil was saying that because of the original sin of man. Man gave him the legal right to exercise authority over the kingdoms of this world. The devil had legitimately received the legal right from man to exercise authority over the kingdoms of this earth, but he had forgotten that the Lord God had a plan B. The Holy Trinity after deliberating on the eschatology of human destiny had already planned the solution for the redemption of man. The Son was chosen to come on earth, die and resurrect to fulfill the mandate for the redemption of man from the deadly hold of sin.

PHILIPPIANS 2: 6-10

"Who, being in the form of God, did not consider it robbery to be equal with God, but made Himself of no reputation, taking the form of a bondservant, and coming in the likeness of men. And being found in appearance as a man, He humbled Himself and became obedient to the point of death, even the death of the cross. Therefore God also has highly exalted Him and given Him the name which is above every name, that at the name of Jesus every knee should bow, of those in heaven, and of those on earth, and of those under the earth."

Jesus made himself of no reputation and humbled Himself to the point of the death of the cross for the salvation of man.

Hence Romans 5: 17 says,

"For if by the one man's offense death reigned through the one, much more those who receive abundance of grace and of the gift of righteousness will reign in life through the One, Jesus Christ."

This is such a powerful truth. It states, that although the offense of Adam brought death upon humanity, all those who receive Jesus Christ as Lord and Savior also receive the abundance of His grace and the gift of righteousness from God. This righteous stand before God gives us the right to reign in life through Jesus Christ.

Matthew 28:18-19 confirms this when it says,

"And Jesus came and spoke to them, saying, All authority has been given to Me in heaven and on earth. Go therefore and make disciples of all the nations..."

Because of Jesus' innocent blood shed on Calvary for the sin of man, the devil had no choice but to give Him back the authority over the world and its kingdoms that he had manipulatively taken from man. Notice that the devil did not give back some authority but all authority was given back to Jesus. Being coheirs with Christ in God we have therefore received authority to implement His authority on earth and on the kingdom of the earth. Jesus has literally given us the power to rule on earth again! What the devil had stolen from us, our Lord Jesus took it and gave it back to us!

As a newborn believer in Christ Jesus you have the capacity to reign on earth. You cannot simply wait for heaven, but God is calling you to reign in life. You are called to reign on earth. You cannot be the tail you must be the head, you cannot be beneath, you must be on top. You cannot be last you must be first. We have the legal right to reign in life. We have the legal right to rule on the earth. But it is imperative for you to know that there is a power struggle on earth. The devil will not release the luxury he had, the right, which he had for thousands of years without a fight.

James 4: 6 says,

> *"Submit unto God, resist the devil and he will flee from you!"*

There's a power struggle for the dominion on earth. Jesus took the keys of Hades and of Death and He gave power to the Church to advance His kingdom on earth, but the devil previously had control. He will not relinquish his hold on the earthly systems and man so easily. Understand that it is not just because you are a believer that the devil will submit unto you. He will begin to submit willfully when he sees that you have spiritual knowledge of who you are and when you begin to apply your kingdom rights adequately with the legal rights that you have received from Christ. If the Word of God asks us to resist the devil, it means that there is a counter-resistance from him. He does not want to let go of the rule of the earth, he is resisting. The devil had infiltrated and was dominating the systems of the world. He will fight to stay in control. But I want you to realize that you have the authority to rule, for we have received power from God to reign in life. No matter what life seems to throw at you, no matter what situation that seems impossible to you and the circumstances that would want to tell you otherwise. God gave you the power to reign in life. The quicker you understand that, the faster you will be on your way to fulfill your mandate of societal reform and social transformation.

THE PURPOSE OF APOSTOLIC REFORMATION AND RESTORATION

The apostolic reformation was inspired and directed by God to bring order in a disordered Body of Christ. It has permitted insight to the church to strategically restructure the local house in order for it to be effective. Because it would have been unreasonable to think that we could change a world if the church was incapable of caring for the incoming souls saved from the different societal systems of the world. It is one thing to have a church that is able to take care of a people who are down and out or in the lower echelon of a community. It is another thing to have a church that is equipped to take care of people coming from the different echelons of society. It is also one thing to have a church that has an audience cheering on the gifting of an individual with his family and his sidekicks. It is another thing to have a church established with the capacity to identify, train every saint in order for them to receive their mandate from God and to be sent out and affect the societal systems of the world to advance the kingdom of God. For this purpose, God has been speaking of apostolic reform throughout His Body all over the world. Nevertheless, we would fall short of God's purpose to think that His purpose was only to have a solid apostolic church that has elders, deacons and saints properly positioned if we are unable to advance His Kingdom in the world, or affect the systems in our society. Adam was called to have dominion on earth. Jesus redeemed us to also have dominion in our world. Therefore the fundamental purpose of apostolic reformation and restoration was to position the church for the fulfillment of its original mandate: having communion with God and having dominion on earth, which will enable it to bring salvation to man and to our world. We will not be able to do it to the fullest because our Lord Jesus Christ at an appointed time of God will take care of the fullness of things. That truth should not stop us though from fulfilling our destiny of reigning in life. Apostolic reformation and restoration is not and should not be an end but a mean to an end. In many reformation eras the church has built a monument out of a move of God, a reformation brought by God in His church. We are running into the same problem in this season of apostolic reformation in the Body of Christ. We are running into the temptation of making the apostolic reformation a monument, making it become a doctrinal statement fundamental to a denomination. How tragic to see churches that have received apostolic revelation, turn it into a weekly basis for worship, preaching, teaching, praying and prophesying. The purpose of apostolic reformation and restoration was to set us up for societal reform. The Church of Jesus Christ is properly edified to have the necessary tools to change the world and to be able to take care of the world that will be saved. If we don't get societal reformation to advance the kingdom of God in the world, we will have come short of the fullness of our mandate.

WHAT IS SOCIETAL REFORMATION?

This term comes from two words: societal and reformation. Here are some definitions of these words:

Societal

Noting or pertaining to large social groups, or to their activities, customs. etc. (dictionary.com)

Of or relating to society (Merriam-Webster.com)

I particularly like the definition of the French dictionary (*le-dictionnaire.com*) that translates as: Relating to a society, its values and its institutions

Reformation

The act or process of improving something or someone by removing or correcting faults, problems, etc. (Merriam-webster.com)

Taking an analytical approach to the word reformation it literally means: Improvement in the existing form or condition of institutions or practices with the intent to make a striking change for the better in social or political or religious affairs.

In light of these different definitions societal reform is strategic changes applied in the systems of our society to improve it. We could take education as an example. Societal reform in education would be bringing changes in that particular system in our society to improve its functioning and results.

You see the church has worked very hard to change individuals and their lifestyles but came short of the system reformation. We have used the power of God for healing and deliverance and personal breakthroughs, but we have not maximized the usage of the power of God to change systems. When I speak of a societal system, I am speaking of the different societal structures that encompass the functionality of a society. The time has come for us to use the power of God strategically to change societal systems. Understand that it is a wonderful and marvelous thing to see an individual's life changed by the power of God. But in this season God wants to direct our attention in receiving wisdom to change systems. We can't continue to bring people to Christ and sit them in the waiting room for heaven. Too many people receive Jesus Christ and just wait to go to heaven, forgetting that salvation is simply the door that permits us to enter the kingdom of God. We should rather enter the kingdom of God and benefit from all its riches, advance the kingdom of God on earth and go to heaven after we've accomplished our mandate on earth in the manner of King David who lived full of days, riches and honor (1 Chronicles 29: 26) and Apostle Paul who said this in 2 Timothy 4: 7-8, "I have fought a good fight, I have finished my course, I have kept the faith."

It is imperative for the church to know that we were never called to have church or just be the church but advance the kingdom of God in the world. Peter, James and John did not have a building called "The Holy Ghost Temple", but they transformed their world. In fact when the Lord prophesied the coming of the Church, He was not talking about a physical building but living stones in a spiritual building (1 Peter 1: 5). Now please understand that there is nothing wrong with having a building called church but sometimes we can be so addicted to the building that we forget our mandate for our city and nation. We can be so connected to our "members" and building that we forget that the devil is taking our community and systems to hell. I believe God for a new generation of ministers who will praise God with their best but will also put their best in humanity, because Christ did not die only for our "members" and some denomination but for the world. For too long we have been saving people, hiding them and cuddling them inside the building to the point that some saints are afraid to be with non-believers. There are some saints who are so religious that they cannot even have a normal conversation with a non-believer, since every second word they say, they have to stick a "Hallelujah!" But look what the Lord says here in John 17: 15, "I do not pray that you should take them out of the world, but that you should keep them from the evil one." His prayer here is what we commonly name the sacerdotal prayer and specifically states that His disciples are edified for the world not the synagogue. The people of God are not raised for the church building, but for the world. Our training should not be purposed for us only to be good ushers, praise and worship singers, part of the dance team or multimedia ministry, but we are purposed to change the world. We are edified to be sent out to shift things in the systems of our society for the kingdom of God. The world should be our workplace. We need to affect our communities, cities and nations. Coming to church to praise and worship God, testify His goodness and listen to a good message for our personal enhancement is all good but the assembly of saints should also be ready to receive revelation in order to grow in wisdom and come out of the church building and affect our spheres of influence with the principles of the kingdom.

We need to go and change the world. Let's go and make disciples of nations. When the results and changes stemming from societal reform mature we reach the state of social transformation. There is no use speaking of any kind of social transformation if we don't have societal reform.

SOCIAL IMPACT VS SOCIETAL REFORM

Social Impact

In our quest for societal reform, it is relevant to know the difference between societal reform and social impact. These two terms are not necessarily the same or inter-changeable. The church in our generation has had social impact. It has been feeding the poor; it has clothed people and taken care of the needy. We have had a level of impact in the systems of the world. But having impact in a societal system does not stop the devil from continuing to control that specific system. Let me give you an example. We can give food to the hungry. We can send bags of rice and do social work of purifying the water in certain nations to permit the hungry and the thirsty to have a meal and drink water where they had not been able to have a regular meal and have drinkable water. This is social impact. Now understand that this is all good but still can be a mirage from taking care of the deeper issue. As this social impact is being done, the devil has already set his agents within the system's hierarchy and the decisional positions to control the food industry and how it is regulated. So ministries are giving bags of rice and sending nurses to take care of a few infirmities in a region. In the meantime, the international governing boards of the food industry and the major pharmaceutical corporations that are able to give food and medication, without even making a dent in their revenues, would rather destroy the goods or regulate them to maintain their global control of the market, instead of focusing on alleviating or eradicating a social global need. Therefore the church is having a certain level of social impact but the devil is controlling systems and having societal impact. This pattern can unfortunately be seen in all the major systems that control a particular nation, and that is in too many nations.

Societal reform is a whole other dimension of strategic apostolic ministry in our mandate of advancing the kingdom of God on earth. In order to have societal reform, we need to penetrate the systems of our nations and seek to have kingdom ministers positioned in places of authority and be decision makers, to affect the decisions, the operation and the fulfillment of that system. Only then, are we able to bring kingdom influence by using the principles of God to bring godly changes in that specific system. In so doing, we will not only have social impact but bring societal reform affecting and totally transform the system.

Let us take the example of education. Even if we have good teachers who are doing a good work of implementing kingdom principles and kingdom values in certain schools, that endeavor is good, they are great teachers and making great social impact but unfortunately that will not change the decisions taken and values implemented by the executives in the educational system. The educational system can still release ungodly values and principles globally to the schools and affect the greater majority of students and drastically affect the knowledge and beliefs of a nation and a society. The devil, by putting his agents in the upper echelon and decisional positions of the educational system, can push his demonic agenda. No wonder in schools today, essays and studies are being made to laud the goodness of witchcraft. At a very tender age, kids are learning that homosexuality is genetic, that a person is born a homosexual and there is absolutely nothing wrong with that. Students are being taught that spirituality and the notion of God are relative and can be found in different ways. It is important to understand that people in the hierarchy of the educational system have their values and it is but normal for them to push those values in the system they work in. The devil being strategic assures himself to put his agents in the positions of power in that system while the Christians continue to have social impact by having a good teacher making the best he could by changing the education of some students. Social impact is very often a good but superficial and external work that does not reach nor is able to change the core function, the lack or corrupted fundamental values that hold a system. Unfortunately, in a general scale ministries and churches have only invested time and energy in having social impact, which doesn't intimidate the devil nor affect in a broader scale, his agenda of destruction of man and society. This is why it is so imperative for us to strive for societal reform. Positive, pious social impact is good, but societal reform is another level and the Body of Christ needs to emphasize more on that. We need to reach the level of "sandwiching" the devil by defusing our efforts and results in social and societal reformation. Bringing forth social impact and societal impact in a global sense influences and affects a system for the advancement of the kingdom of God.

SOCIETAL REFORM

Societal reform speaks of transforming a societal system by bringing changes in its philosophy, re-organizing its structure and systematic functions. You see social impact is applying external efforts to affect the internal working of a system. Going back to our example of the educational system, social impact is the pious teacher having an external impact to the education system by being a great teacher to his students and bringing changes on a small scale. Societal reform on the other hand is striving for transformation by bringing internal changes in the educational system by seeking to set kingdom agents in the decisional positions of the system. It is affecting the core of the system by changing its philosophy and re-organizing its systematic functions. This will henceforth affect the system globally and bring changes in a larger scale. Societal reform strives to enter the upper decisional echelon of a system to bring global change to that system and therefore bring social transformation. It's an inward-outward transformation, where social impact is an outward-inward transformation. The devil is not afraid of external changes in a system. The devil is not afraid of a teacher trying to change a little group of students. But what scares him is the infiltration of Christians in the administrative boards of schools, executive councils in the educational system with decisional power and beginning to bring transformational changes to the core of the system. This strategic work will result in a greater external impact of social transformation. In this generation, we therefore need to imitate Joseph's strategy. He was able to penetrate the decisional position of a governmental system. Through the wisdom brought forth by the Spirit of the Lord, he was able to prosper the nation of Egypt and bring recognition, prosperity and respect to the people of God. Through that manner, respect was given to the God of Joseph.

RELIGIOUS FACTORS BLOCKING SOCIETAL REFORM

There are religious factors that are severely affecting our capacity to be instruments for societal reform. We will have to deal with these factors to be able to launch out and bring effective societal reform for social transformation in our communities and nations.

The Escapist Mentality

For too long preachers preached the gospel of salvation, preparing the believers for heaven. The problem is that the Lord never called us to preach the gospel of salvation but the gospel of the kingdom giving revelation to the Body of Christ for dominion on earth. You see salvation is only the door to enter the kingdom but the gospel of the kingdom permits us to have dominion. The "Escapist Mentality" preached by religious preachers has separated the church from the reality of society and its responsibility to change it. It has hindered us from having dominion on earth.

In 2011, Harold Camping falsely prophesied the rapture of the church and the end of the world for the 21st of May 2011 at 6:00 p.m. This lunacy made a mockery out of Christianity. I can still remember in a sports network the report of a baseball play caller saying on the air, "Oops its 6:01pm the prophet missed it, we are still here!" The media capitalized on that nonsense to discredit the validity of Christianity. Because we have concentrated so much on the rapture, we have forgotten that we are called to dominate on earth. We have concentrated so much on the rapture that we have forgotten our fundamental mandate by God to dominate on earth. The gospel of the kingdom is called to release the Church in the epicenter of every culture and societal systems of its communities and nations.

Being in the systems gives us the ability to change and transform the world we are living in. For a long time, we have been great in the four walls of a church building and have no impact or minimal impact outside of the doors and the walls of the church. It is therefore normal that we have little impact in society because we have segregated the church. We cannot be hiding within the four walls of a church building waiting for heaven. Unfortunately, too many religious churches are still singing and concentrating the majority of their energy on the time when they will be walking on streets of gold in heaven meanwhile the devil is dominating and polluting the systems of the world and taking millions at a time to hell. This "Escapist Mentality" has therefore diverted the church's attention from the task at hand of advancing the kingdom of God on earth by bringing wholeness to systems and having rule on earth, not understanding that it can only have the resulting effect of touching and affecting more people with the gospel of the kingdom and increasing the amount of salvation. Truly the wage of sin is death but the free gift of God is eternal life. It is a divine truth and a tremendous blessing for the believers. We should be blessed as Christians that heaven is waiting for us, but we should also be focused to change the systems that are affecting our societies in order to advance the plan of God on earth.

Preachers Raising Believers Not Christians

The preachers have been raising believers and not Christians in the Body of Christ. What is the difference between a believer and a Christian? The believer received Christ as his Lord and Savior, he is a believer. In Acts 11: 26, the believers are called for the first time Christians because the non-believers were frustrated in seeing them do the same works the Lord Jesus Christ was performing when He was on the earth. (So today we have believers that are called Christians, although they are not worthy of this name since they have not manifested the work of Jesus Christ. As Christians, we should be able to do the work of God without our pastors, because our pastors are biblically called with the elders to equip the saints, so that the saints are able to do the work of ministry in the sphere of influence in their society. If you have received the Lord for years and have not been able to bring someone to Christ, cast out a devil in an afflicted person, there's a problem. You are a believer but come short to rightfully be called a Christian. Jesus built a disciple-based movement. They were able to do what the Master was doing. But we've been preaching and raising good believers. We will not change a nation with believers but we need Christians, we need disciples, kingdom enforcers. We need *kingdomizers* able to advance the kingdom of our King Jesus in their sector of influence on earth.

Preachers Have Been Raising the Body of Christ for Church Gatherings Not the World

Preachers have been raising the Body of Christ for the church gathering and not for the world. We have raised Christians and disciples to be ushers, to be deacons, to do praise and worship, to take care of multimedia, to take care of the youth and of the women. So we have raised the Body of Christ to be good in the church, but when the believers step out of the church, they are lost; they don't know what to do, because we raised them to be good churchgoers. In the church, they are comfortable but in the world they are uncomfortable. But Jesus did not raise his disciples for the synagogue, He raised them for the world. So, this needs to change! We need to start getting messages and teachings that make the Body of Christ become not only great in church but also even greater in the world. Until you are able to be great in your work place, you are still a spiritual child. I see people who can prophesy, they can pray in tongues and lay on of hands when they are in church, but they are unfortunately ineffective in their sphere of influence, in making known the principles of the kingdom. They are unable to advance the kingdom of God in their society.

You see church is like a gas station. When we come, we come to be filled up, but we never stay in a gas station. You come, you take gas and you leave. Every time we gather, we gather to be filled up, to receive revelation, to receive depth so that we can step out. The elders' ministry starts when you come, your ministry starts when they finish.

Ephesians 4: 11-12 says,

> *"God gave some to be apostles, some prophets, some evangelists, and some pastors and teachers, for the equipping of the saints for the work of Ministry..."*

Your work of ministry is not in the praise and worship, it is not to just come and usher. This is part time ministry, but you are called full time as a kingdom enforcer to affect your societal system in the world. This is your work. But unfortunately, church showed us how to be good Believers. Therefore, we can now do the basics as a churchgoer. We know how to say,

"Hallelujah!" We know how to jump, we know how to shout, we know how to fall under the power, and we know how to act spiritual. Some people think being spiritual is talking and walking slowly. Don't be fooled. Humility is not the way you speak and the way you walk, it is first a heart thing. We are called to be Christians 24/7.

Daniel 1: 8 says,

> *"But Daniel purposed in his heart that he would not defile himself with the portion of the king's delicacies... therefore he requested..."*

It is important as kingdom enforcers that we are 24/7. If you are going to change the nation, you need to position yourself to be a Christian 24/7. The world will present you its portion, it will present you its language, its style, but we need to be able to stand our ground and be a witness of our King Jesus seven days a week and 24 hours a day!

Using the Spirit Forgetting the Brain

The secular world is reaping the consequences of the religious church's error of focusing solely on spirituality and leaving the field of knowledge in the hands of the unbelievers. The spiritual quest that takes so much place, coupled with waiting for heaven, from the narrow-minded, unwise teaching of the eminent return of Jesus Christ, has caused a lack of intellectuals in the church. A large number of religious believers are solely focused on increasing their biblical knowledge to be ready for heaven and ignorantly forsaking the acquisition of academic knowledge necessary to be strategically positioned in the upper echelon of the systems of the world. Some religious churches have directly and indirectly discouraged higher education, ostracizing higher studies, rendering them a futile quest because "the return of Jesus is eminent". For example, many religious preachers and believers think it is ungodly or non-Christian to be in politics or to be a lawyer. All politicians are supposed to be crooks and lawyers are liars. It is almost inconceivable for the religious believer, for a true Christian to be in arts and entertainment, because they say, all entertainers are dominated by lust and impurity. The devil is capitalizing on the fact that the church is not emphasizing the importance of education among its disciples. This has created a lack of sound Christians raised up as enlightened minds, philosophers, thinkers, and decision-makers to head and be in decisional positions in the upper echelons of the systems of the world. So as we are constantly fasting and praying, the witches and the secret societies are sending their adepts and children to school with the objective of not just penetrating the systems of the world but to also continue strategically leading them to advance their demonic agenda.

Singing and dancing in the presence of God is good, but God has given us a brain and we need to use our intelligence. It is great to have elders to raise the people of God in the principles of the kingdom and in the things of God. However, the people of God need to be raised up academically if we want to change systems, we need educated and professionally trained saints in the different societal systems. If the saints leave school prematurely and do not maximize their academic potential, they lower their possibility of reforming and changing the different sectors of society.

For this purpose, this new generation in Christ needs to be filled of the Holy Ghost, deep in the things of God but also educated and positioned like Daniel. He was a pious and spiritual Christian who took his spirituality very seriously but he was also trained at the university of Babylon. He graduated as an elite among his peers, which was instrumental in placing him in the king's inner circle. Too much potential has been wasted in the church. People are jamming the pulpit thinking that it is the only place possible to accomplish one's Christian destiny. How tragic! We cannot all be preachers. It is time for us to understand that there are other pulpits that we are called to master. Who will penetrate the sectors of government, science, education and the various other societal systems that are affecting our world? We need to continue to raise saints with higher education, with bachelors, masters and doctorate degrees for them to be positioned in the upper echelons of the systems in our society.

We don't need to raise simply intellectuals, but ministers full of the Holy Spirit, able to connect their knowledge and academic education with the revelation of God. The church needs to raise educated ministers instead of being intellectuals. You see intellectuals have knowledge but when one is educated, he possesses applied knowledge. He puts in application the knowledge that he has. When we look at the meaning of the word educated, application of knowledge generally comes out of it, whereas the word intellectual speaks of possessing knowledge. Knowledge by itself is not enough to change a society until it is applied. Having a bunch of intellectuals in a certain field is therefore not enough to bring transformation in that field. We have Christians who are intellectuals, but they are unable to bring reform. It takes applied knowledge connected with the wisdom that the Holy Spirit gives in order to penetrate and change systems.

"Drive-Less" Christians

Another negative effect of religiousness in a believer's life is the loss of drive that it causes. Many who were active and determined to succeed lose that drive while they are waiting for heaven. Many who were on top of their game in the secular have become losers in the kingdom of God. Saints who were feisty, tough and hard to be discouraged lost their fighting spirit. Their once bold attitude without God has become cowardliness in Christ. No more creative ideas, no more drive, no more desire to breakthrough. It is as if the saints live under the influence of spiritual sedatives hindering them from using their full capacity, cognitive wisdom and knowledge. The devil is a liar; that is a religious demon. You are called to be the head and not the tail, on top and never beneath; first not struggling as last. It is truly demonic, because salvation is not meant to dry out your drive but enhance and channel it by the help of the abiding Holy Spirit. Our zeal in Christ should increase. Our desire and determination to succeed should greatly increase as the relationship with our Creator has been restored. Who can better direct us than He who has prepared good works for us to accomplish from before the foundation of the world? There is simply too much potential in the Body of Christ to have the saints just satisfied sitting in the pews listening to feel good messages, too much potential to be only waiting for heaven. This religious spirit that sedates believers after they have received the Lord needs to be broken over their lives in order for them to maximize their potential.

You see the church is full of potential hiding under the dust of speaking in tongues and waiting for heaven. The saints are full of potential but they are so into the atmosphere of the spirit that they don't take time to grow that potential. I'm not saying we should not pray and not understand the things of the spirit but we need to build the potential in our people. Some saints have the potential to change arts and entertainment, some have the potential to change business, some have the potential to change education but they are stuck in just doing spiritual exercises and participating in church services. Some saints could have had their master's degree already, but fell in the trap of believing that it would take too long. The only problem with that is the fact that the statement was said five to 10 years ago. They said that it would be too long but unfortunately those years were wasted without any true professional advancement. Was that really from God? Some churches in parts of the world have 21-day revivals and 50 days of praying and fasting. If the saints have to come for 21 days and 50 days straight in church, when will they work, when will they go to school and have time to study? When will they have time to develop their potential? We need to develop the Christian potential. If we are only praying, masonic politicians will continue to take over government and Mormon teachers will continue to affect education by teaching our kids. It's time to increase the Christian potential. We are in a generation where we are called to raise multifaceted disciples. It is not enough to be educated and learned in one field, we need to have knowledge in different fields. Use your gift. Use your Christian potential. You are too great to not bring forth fruit. You are called to be a teacher, you are called to be a lawyer, you are called to take control of the banking system. Let the will of God be done. It is not enough to just pray in tongues, it is not enough to just cast out devils; we need to raise the potential of the Christians. There will be no reform if we do not raise the potential of God's people. It is not so much the gift you have, but it is to develop it. All the different gifts and potential in the believers are needed to influence the different systems. Not everybody is called to be an Apostle Paul, we need some to be Apostle Peter. Paul was called for the Gentiles and intellectuals but Peter was called to the Jews. We can have different gifts and touch different areas. We cannot all be preachers. Who will be the professional athlete, who will enter arts and entertainment, who will transform the media, who will be in science and find the cures for diseases? We cannot all be in the same kingdom and do the same thing. We cannot all be pastors. We cannot all be apostles. The word in Ephesians 4: 11 said, "...some are apostles...", not all. There are different members in the Body. We cannot all be eyes or else the Body would be monstrous. But we need to be eyes, ears, noses, hands - that's a Body! These days everybody wants to be at the pulpit, but your pulpit might be in education and for another government, arts and entertainment, another mechanics and as you penetrate that system as a disciple, power will be released to shift that sector for Christ.

We need to invest in the potential of the Christians. We need to raise up Christian professionals. The church has professionals. We have professionals in the political arena, in the media, in arts and entertainment and so forth. We have professionals in the societal systems of the world. We have professionals who are believers. They speak, act and function like the secular professionals, but they are believers. Good saints but they have absolutely no impact in their spheres. No societal reform, because they have not been able to translate the principles of the kingdom in their position and societal system. So they have two lives. They have the life in the church and the life in the workplace. They put on their "professional jacket" and have another life in the workplace. They are professional but they have no impact because they are professionals who are believers. Understand that what we need is not professionals who are believers but Christian professionals. So you can be a tremendous lawyer and be a devout saint, but when you go in your office you enter the cultural setting of your profession without having any kingdom impact in it. You can be a great philosopher or a great teacher but nobody on the school board has been impacted by you because you are simply in the system. Therefore a lot of professionals are believers, but we do not have enough Christian professionals. You participate in the vain office conversations, you speak intellectually and you talk as a great knowledgeable person but you have unfortunately brought no systematic change. You are a physicist, you are an accountant who is a Christian, but you are not a minister who is a physicist, you are not a minister who is a teacher. So a lot of believers have absolutely no impact in their workplace. You have two lives; what you do in church and what you do at work. But God in this season is bringing forth revelation to raise up Christian professionals who are versed in the principles of the kingdom with an agenda to devote their life in bringing transformation in their sphere of influence for the advancement of the kingdom of God.

Normalities Are Abnormalities

As I took the time to analyze various evangelical circles, I have come to the conclusion that unfortunately, certain things that are supposed to be common sense and normal in the secular world are abnormal and an issue in the Body of Christ. Many saints have been so overwhelmed by the spiritual that they forgot that they are living in the natural. I have witnessed how hard it is for Christians to be on time, when it is only normal for them to be on time at work. They can respect Mammon the god of money, but disrespect the God of their salvation, edification and blessing. The same people who saw nothing wrong with financing political campaigns with billions of dollars, who themselves participated, very often are the same ones criticizing financing the kingdom of God. Some others who have spent thousands of dollars on drugs, alcohol, and frivolous and destructive lifestyles are now saved and have become stingy and frugal in their financial support for the work of the kingdom of God. Some even dare speak against paying for a conference when they spend three or four times more for a secular conference. It is truly time to step out of the religious bubble. Religiousness is killing the common sense of the believers. In order for us to be put in the proper path for societal reform, we need to deal with the religious factors in the Body of Christ.

KINGDOMS OF INFLUENCE IN THE WORLD

In our quest to be positioned to advance the kingdom of God in the world, it is imperative for us to have clarity concerning the kingdoms of influence in the world.

LUKE 4: 5

"And the devil, taking him up into an high mountain, shewed unto him all the kingdoms of the world in a moment of time."

In this Scripture, as the Lord was taking a time of consecration and fasting before entering full-time ministry, the devil comes and tempts him. In the period of temptation, probably in the spirit realm, he takes Jesus up onto a high mountain and shows him all the kingdoms of the world in a moment of time. The devil was showing the kingdoms of influence of the nation. There is an American movie, "The Devil's advocate", with Al Pacino and Keanu Reeves, that poignantly depicts this biblical episode. In that movie, Al Pacino, representing the devil, takes Keanu Reeves, depicted as a great lawyer, on top of a high building and shows him the downtown view of a capitalistic city with many corporate and industrial buildings and said: "If you serve me you'll get all of these." He was showing him the kingdoms of the world. Different kingdoms that affect a society influence a nation. In fact there are seven kingdoms that influence any given nation at any given time.

KINGDOM OF RELIGION & SPIRITUALITY

The first kingdom that needs to be addressed is the kingdom of religion and spirituality. Religion and spirituality is the kingdom that influences the spirituality and the principles of life in a nation. In many nations religion is instrumental in the values, the morals, the way of life and the culture of the people. The Islamic nations are a perfect example of this fact. Islam has transcended the religious effect on these nations to reach a level of having a cultural bearing on the Islamic nations. Islam is more than a religion, it is a way of life. It affects the beliefs and the way these societies function. Notice that during the time of Ramadan, that period of fasting in the Islamic calendar, many non-practicing Muslims will fast from six to six. They might not open the Quran for the whole year and not even step inside the mosque once a year but they would still practice

Ramadan. It has clearly become cultural more than spiritual because religion and spirituality will affect your culture. The spirituality of Ramadan has therefore been reduced to a religious practice with no spiritual emphasis. In fact, some of them say, "Man, when will six o'clock come so I can eat my hamburger". Because it's cultural they just do it. In Christianity we have similar situations. Some saints are so cultural that they come in church just for special events. They come during Christmas, Easter or baby christenings. Some come to service and by late afternoon do not even remember the message of the preacher. Being part of a Christian circle and a religious cycle and practice, has affected the culture of these religious saints to a certain extent. The principles received in one's religion will have a bearing on their morality and how this person conducts himself. The spiritual information is often applied or affects a person and how he interacts with his society and environment. Hence, a devout evangelical will stand for marriage of a man and a woman. He will be pro-life and have an issue with abortion. The Hindus will deify certain animals and show lenience to these animals in the cultural and societal dynamics of their countries. Because of cultural traditions and morals set by religious teachings, to this date a known homosexual will be vehemently persecuted or even killed in some nations. In some nations women are being persecuted, abused and have very few rights because of cultural beliefs based unfortunately on religion and spirituality.

FAMILY

Family is another kingdom that influences a nation. A nation is constructed with the common denominator called the family. A nation consists of a multitude of families. From that perspective, the interaction, the operation and the interrelationship of the members of families influence the nation in its uniqueness. Society is filled with families. The composition of families and the healthiness of the families will clearly influence a nation. A society is impaired when the families are broken, dysfunctional or unhealthy. Some sociologists are predicting that in 10 to 20 years a significant number of families will be comprise of two men and a woman or a man with two women or similar types of trends. These types of family nuclei will definitely have a psychological and conceptual effect on our society. These family structures are without a doubt a dubious plan of the devil to humiliate the biblical foundation of family. The people of God therefore need to rise up and take their position in influencing societal systems of families. As in the example of North America, specifically the United States and Canada which are sister nations, the day the Word of God was taken out of schools, they started having problems. But the family has the power to set what we call family education. Because of family education, there are things a person cannot ethically imagine himself doing. There are certain things you will not do because your parents showed you otherwise. Even though school has a level of influence on students, because you have received certain teachings at home, there is a behavior you could never have. In fact, some family teachings can affect a person for the rest of his life. In my family education, I was taught to have reverence and a certain level of respect for elders. Through the years, this teaching has influenced the way I carried myself. Although I am the spiritual authority of an apostolic ministry and local house and receive a particular respect and reverence from the local congregation, I still address an elderly person in a specific reverent way because of my family education. I still have great difficulty to call an elderly son or daughter by their first name since my family education has taught us to use "Sir" or "Mam" with an older person. Family values henceforth have an impact in the society we live in. Education received within the family setting will have its share of influence on a person and thus the society he lives in. It is for this reason that parents cannot underestimate the importance of the teachings they give their kids at home. As a parent you cannot say, "Well, let the school system or children's ministry in church teach my kids." Parents have the responsibility to inculcate family values and teachings to their children, independent of the teachings received in school and in church.

That's why the Word of God says in Proverbs 22: 6,

> *"Train up the child in the way he should go: and when he*
> *is old, he will not depart from it."*

The family therefore has the power to affect society through the values, teachings given to its members and their relationships.

EDUCATION & SCIENCES

The kingdom of Education and sciences influences the knowledge and the orthodoxy of a society. It affects what is taught in that nation. Education is a key factor for the edification of a nation. An educated nation has a lesser propensity of being affected by certain social turmoil. As we take a look at the social statuses of the nations of the world, we observe that oppressions and afflictions are suffered more often than not by uneducated societies. Knowledge and education give people a greater capacity to establish more balanced social systems. The political structure, the social rights and the level of education of a population will affect standards, the livelihood and the lifestyle of a nation. Education affects the systems, structures and functionalities of a nation. Therefore a low level of education will have a clearly negative impact on a nation. The lack of education in a third world country radically influences its progress. The effect of the lack of education can be also seen in the difficulty an uneducated person coming from a third world country to adapt to a more educated country with more complex societal systems. Such persons will have difficulty adapting to the way of life in a more industrialized and technological country. A simple procedure such as taking an escalator, using the Internet or a banking machine is a daunting task.

It is important to know that education is conducive to the growth of the different entities of a society. Education will shape the thinking process of a nation, helping it to evolve systematically. Any level of upgrade in a society becomes difficult where the leadership lacks education in the different systems of that society. The higher the level of education the leadership has in the different systems in a society, the higher its tendency to emancipate and have success.

ARTS & ENTERTAINMENT

Arts and entertainment is another kingdom of influence in a society. Arts and entertainment influences the trends in a society. It will affect what is in and what is in style in a society. You see, the way we dress, the way we talk, the way our hair is styled is very often influenced by what we see in arts and entertainment. Let me prove it to you. In Europe, football is a national phenomenon and greatly influences the style of people. Young children's attire and style is very much impacted by football players. If a certain boy's favorite player styles his hair in a certain way, the boy will be prone to style his hair in that same way. Why do Americans wear Air Jordan and not a "no name" brand of sportswear? It's simply because there was a basketball player named Michael Jordan who dominated his sport and was an icon for his fans. His promotional value skyrocketed. Some business partners teamed up with him and capitalized on his popularity by introducing basketball shoes bearing his name. This business venture subsequently broke out to sporting wear to finally end up a giant in the merchandising industry worldwide. Michael Jackson, named the king of pop music, had a similar impact on his fans. There was a time that a large number of black men were styling curly hair with a leather jacket from the impact of his music videos that completely took over the market. Michael Jackson had such a profound impact on pop culture that some people to this day, since he has passed away, are still dancing, singing and dressing like him. In fact, he is grossing record revenues still after his death, making more money than the large majority of entertainers that are still yet alive. To what can we attribute this phenomenon? It is attributed simply to the fact that arts and entertainment have the power to influence the lifestyle of a society. Why do we see people dressed a certain way? It is because they are very often influenced by their entertainment icons. A new trend has hit western society; body piercing and tattoos popularized by artists, entertainers and athletes. Arts and entertainment has the power to affect the way people dress, talk and style their hair. They will influence what is in, what is trendy and what is in style. Whoever your superstar will have the capacity to affect your style and behavior. Why do women read hair magazines? It is not because they are bored on their way to work on the bus or in the subway, but to learn how to style their hair. You do not open your Bible and say, "Lord give me a revelation on how I should style my hair"... you look at a hair magazine or how your favorite star styles theirs. You are looking at their hairstyles to see what is trendy, what is happening, and then you turn to page 25 and say, "I want it like this!" Well, the person that is on page 25 is part of the arts & entertainment. And because of the influencing capacity of that kingdom, you decide to imitate that look. Entertainers have the capacity to affect the trends of a nation. If in a particular movie, an actor drives a Mercedes, you look at the movie and you silently say to yourself or mumble without disturbing the person next to you; "I want to have that car". Arts and entertainment has the capacity to influence people's trends and lifestyles.

MEDIA & COMMUNICATION

Media and communication influences the information that touches and affects the faith of our society. A couple of years ago, the media announced the spread of a virus called H1N1. Television, radio and newspapers started reporting on people dying from swine flu. They started publicizing and raising the awareness of people to the devastating effects of that virus. They cautioned the population to be careful and that kids in daycares were very susceptible to catching that disease. As the news of this epidemic start growing, even saints in churches started getting paranoid and nervous about the virus affecting them and their families. The media then started vocalizing the importance of taking the swine flu shot, then believers started to contemplate choosing the vaccine that clearly had inconclusive medical testing to it. Many saints even gave the vaccine to their kids and took it themselves. When the media continued vehemently professing that the kids and elders were in greater danger of catching the disease, babies of non-Christians and Christians alike were being vaccinated. What triggered the position taken by the population towards that so called epidemic? The media. The media has power to affect one's decisions. In that same period the Lord spoke to me about the deception of this so called epidemic and I spoke to the congregation that I spiritually oversee and told them under the anointing of the Holy Spirit that no one should take the swine flu vaccine and that no one would get affected by that publicized epidemic. The Lord even mentioned that another news item would take hold of the mainstream media and the so-called epidemic would be forgotten. A couple of months later an earthquake in Haiti changed the attention of world media and all news of the swine flu epidemic systematically died off. Were there people affected by this virus? Most probably, but the overemphasizing of that epidemic was clearly a dictated propaganda.

In January 2010, the earthquake that hit Haiti shifted the faith of the population onto something else because of media and communication. What you read and listen to through the media has the power to affect you. Media is truly a powerful kingdom. It can shift and change the way society thinks or acts on any given issue. If you listen to the news and they tell you that there is a bomb in your city right now, do not leave your house, 99% of the people will not leave their house, even if you had an important meeting. But if a couple of hours later, you hear breaking news that it was a false alert and that everyone could go back to their regular activities, everyone would get back to his regular chores. Surely you would be frustrated about your missed appointment but you would obey and get right back to your normal activities. Therefore, media and communication have power. They have power to affect the faith and belief system of a nation. Media will affect your faith, because faith comes from what we hear. It is a biblical fact.

The Bible says in Romans 10: 17,

> *"So then, faith comes by hearing, and hearing by the Word of God."*

The Word of God has the capacity to channel our faith towards the principles of God. But the media and communications through what one hears and reads also have the capacity to affect someone's faith toward the principles that it conveys.

GOVERNMENT & POLITICS

The kingdom of Government and Politics influences the laws dictating how a society and its structures function. People who are positioned in government regulate the guidelines, the rules and the laws. We cannot underestimate the influence of government and politics. If the government legislates that from now on people should cross a street on the red light and that they should refrain from crossing on the green light, although that system was opposite for years, people under the jurisdiction of that government would have to submit to the changes. While some people or coalitions would be able to fight or resist the ruling, ultimately the laws adopted by an established governmental board affect the functional behavior of its subjects. This is why it is so important that the choices a population makes of who is elected to office to run the judicial and governmental systems of a country or any established entity. For they have delegated power from their subjects to implement laws and changes. The power of attorney given by a population to its political and governmental decision-makers over a nation can either help prosper or destroy the social and economic status of the nation. There are countries that have been destroyed economically and socially within a decade because of mercenaries and fools in governmental offices. This kingdom has overwhelming importance because it can affect all the other kingdoms of influence. The government can affect how religion is being implemented in a nation, the structure of families, the level of information that the media has authority to release, how arts and entertainment can function and how the economic systems in business will function. This is understandable since decisional authority of leaders over the different systems of society will affect them. Hence the devil is very strategic in positioning his agents in government because of the decisional power they have in implementing laws and structures to help advance his agenda and kingdom. No wonder in the quest of the Lord to unfold His will in the ages, He raised a great man of power like King David, King Solomon and many other servants in a government position of leadership. Unfortunately, for centuries the church has been blinded by spiritual ignorance. Due to religious teachings it has failed to raise a significant level, of ministers in the kingdom of government. The devil must have had a ball listening to preachers telling the people of God that all politicians are liars and are going to hell and that a good Christian should not aspire to be in government. What deception from the enemy! The devil knows that the more the Body of Christ is absent from the kingdom of government, the easier it is for him to influence the legislations that will promote his kingdom. Government and politics are instrumental in the effect it has on the other kingdoms, the general state and direction of a nation.

BUSINESS AND ECONOMY

Business and Economy is the seventh kingdom that has major implications and influence on a nation. It influences the finances of a society and decides how a nation is being financed. The economy of a society will affect the provision and assets of that society and nation. It decides what is produced and what is consumed. The business kingdom is the financer of all the other kingdoms of influence. The religion, family, education, arts & entertainment, media and government are all financed through the business kingdom. This makes the leaders of this kingdom very influential. Very often in a corrupted system the governmental kingdom that seems to be instrumental in giving the legislation and laws that govern the right functioning of a nation is manipulated and influenced by the wealthy businesspeople of that nation. For this reason, strong demonic principalities and powers oversee that kingdom of influence because of the way it is able to direct and affect the position taken by the other systems in society. The enemy knows that if he can control the financing of the systems of a nation, he can control that nation.

We have elaborated on the different kingdoms that influence a nation. The problem with the present state of the Body of Christ is that it has been involved measurably in the kingdoms of influence but only has very limited impact. Even in the kingdom of religion, generally speaking, the church has not been able to have truly significant impact in the nations of the world. Surely we have been able to bring salvation to many but have come short in having the type of impact enabling us to significantly advance the kingdom of God and its purpose in the world. Unfortunately, the people of God have been competing themselves in the religion kingdom with too many desiring to be ministering on the pulpit. A great majority of saints are dreaming and drooling to be preachers, praise and worship leaders and head deacons and deaconesses in the church. How tragic to see the number of fights in churches on who is going to be the next pastor. Everybody is battling for the pulpit but oblivious to the fact that there are six other kingdoms that we absolutely have to take over in order to advance the kingdom of God in the world.

You might not have been called to be a great preacher, but you could be great in media, you might not be called to be a deacon in the church but you could affect the arts and entertainment. You might not have the grace to be a great athlete but you could affect education or you could affect family. Some saints in the Body of Christ are called to be great in business. Others are called to step into the field of government and politics to change laws and legislation and establish kingdom principles to transform our society. The major issue is that we need to stop thinking that we are called just to be great in church. Some saints are misled into thinking that their ministry is in church. Their gifts are dormant because they were never called to primarily minister in church but outside of church. They were supposed to be identified, trained, mandated and sent out in another kingdom of influence to manifest the plan of God on earth. Therefore many are sitting on the pews with so much grace, so much capacity and potential and yet are inactive in the perfect will of

God for their lives because their focus and aspiration have been ignorantly turned toward church ministry when they were called to have societal ministry. How tragic to see believers waiting to minister as a dancer once in a while in church when they were supposed to change the entertainment kingdom for God. There are clearly Christians who are called to change Hollywood. The school systems are waiting to be affected by the principles of God. How the educational systems train and teach students who are yearning for changes that are destined to come from a mandated child of God to that sphere of influence. The way the educational systems train and teach students needs reform. They are unconsciously yearning for changes that will come from a mandated *kingdomizer* of God to that sphere of influence. God is waiting for an available servant whom He can send out on television with the grace that will attract the attention of viewers and release the virtues of God through his appointed profession. For a long time, religious preachers have deceived the people of God in believing that they could not be a lawyer or a politician, because politicians and lawyers are supposedly crooks. The devil is a liar; we need to have people stepping into law, into government, into arts & entertainment and all the other kingdoms of influence.

The time has come for the Body of Christ to penetrate the seven kingdoms of influence of a nation and affect them with the principles of the kingdom to advance the will of God on earth. You are not a medical doctor or nurse only to take care of the sick in the hospital but you need to be impacted by the power of God to be an empowering force to heal the sick, find solutions for diseases, to affect the hospital system for the glory of God. It is one thing to be a professional, but something else to be one shifting your sphere of influence for the Lord Jesus Christ by the power of the principles of the kingdom. You have a hair salon, that is great but you are not just there to do hair. There is something that is in you and on you, the power of the Holy Ghost. His presence is there to use you to touch the lives of those you are rending service too. There is a level of grace and anointing and revelation that will permit us to shift our workplace. Imagine doing somebody's hair and being fully conscious and aware of the fact that you are sent out in that sector of activity to advance the kingdom of God. As you are doing the hair, instead of just wondering, you let the Lord use you by a word of knowledge to know exactly the need of that person and minister to their situation. And as you are styling their hair, the power of God starts speaking about what is going on in that person's life. That is why as a hair stylist you are called to have communication skills to minister to your clients. Through these skills, God can use you not only to style their hair but also transform lives by the truth from the Word of God and the power of the Holy Spirit simply by letting the Lord direct you to the need of that person. You are not mandated to gossip about who is doing what with whom or who is mingling with somebody else's wife or boyfriend but you are an agent of God, called to leave a lasting impact on every client that steps into your salon. In fact, you do not even have to mention the name of Jesus initially, but just let God lead you to the psychological problem, the relational problem or social issue that the person may have and minister to them with the love of God. All of a sudden you will get clients coming with suicide thoughts completely set free, depressed clients healed, completely discouraged clients encouraged. You would start hearing client testimonies saying, "Every time I put my feet in that salon, something shifts in my life, something good happens in my being." That is because you are not just a hair stylist but you have understood that you have been sent out by God to that sphere of influence to advance His kingdom on earth. For this reason every saint of God needs to understand that they are called to be positioned to impact. You are relevant, you are important. You are not just in the government office to speak technicalities. You are not a lawyer just to mingle in the business of law. You are not an accountant just to talk numbers; you are not an engineer just to talk about engineering. There is a reason why God has put you where He has put you! Until you understand your role as a kingdom enforcer, you will continue to have two lives, the one in the office with office terminology and the one in church with the church terminology and you will have limited impact in the quest of having dominion in the world.

THE PRINCIPALITIES IN THE 7 KINGDOMS

EPHESIANS 6: 12

"For we wrestle not against flesh and blood, but against principalities, against powers, against the rulers of the darkness of this world, against spiritual wickedness in high places."

In the quest of God's divine mandate to rule and reign on earth, it is vitally important to know the ruling principalities that are affecting the different kingdoms of influence. Notice that Ephesians 6: 12 says that there are spiritual opposing forces fighting for influence and rule on earth. They are spiritual being that are imposing their control illegally. All power has been given to our Lord Jesus Christ who has commissioned us to make disciples of all nations and advance the kingdom on earth. We therefore need to understand that any type of opposition we face in our quest to redeem the kingdoms of influence will not come just from human whims but also from the controlling principalities that have been assigned by the devil to control that specific kingdom of influence.

Satan does not want to lose his grip on earth and mankind living in it. He has assigned different principalities and rulers to control the seven kingdoms of influence in the nations to keep his illegal grip on mankind and the world in order to make an ultimate attempt to quench his appetite for dominion. Therefore, every kingdom of influence has demonic forces fitted to its characteristics to try to enforce the rule of Satan. It is now the responsibility of the identified, trained, mandated and sent out church of Jesus Christ to position itself with the power of the Holy Spirit and the strategic wisdom of God to redeem the kingdoms of influence and bring salvation to man. What are the different principalities and powers affecting the seven kingdoms of influence?

PRINCIPALITIES AND POWERS IN THE KINGDOM OF RELIGION AND SPIRITUALITY

The spirit of religiousness, doubt, unbelief and confusion are strongly operating in the kingdom of religion and spirituality. These spirits are mandated to render the task of bringing the salvation of Jesus Christ to the people of the nations difficult. Unbelief and confusion have become rampant with the number of religions and the various spiritual solicitations that are thrown at the people in our communities. How does one really know the truth when so many religions are spreading their doctrine and beliefs? This massive outpouring of spiritual information clogs the mind and the spirit, so that when a person finally encounters the truth it makes it difficult to accept the salvation of Jesus Christ that can set him free! It is clearly a demonic agenda the rising of different false religions to appeal to the different type of character traits of mankind. Rosicrucian, freemasonry, secret societies, humanistic and spiritism will solicit the more intellectual and educated type; some others will be more attracted to white magic, palm reading, astrology and even others to satanism, blood sacrifice and all heavy witchcraft. There are people who are already indoctrinated and tied up in one of the major religions, Islam, Buddhism and Judaism. But the sects of different nature can also tie you up that spring up periodically throughout the globe. Through all those different religions, occultism and spiritualism, the enemy has worked overtime to create a web that will trap man from knowing the Way, the Truth and Life, the Savior of humanity, Jesus Christ. Therefore the enemy wants to release the spirit of doubt, of unbelief, irreligiousness and confusion to the point of bringing man to the place of not wanting to adhere and connect to any religion. If they open themselves the enemy makes them feel that all religions are the same. Making man believe that whatever he does to enhance his spirituality is fine. It is just his prerogative. But know that where sin abound the grace of God over-abounds. In all that mess created by the master of chaos, there is power in the Word of God and in the gospel of the kingdom of God to uproot the seed of deceit from a sinner's heart and translate him into the kingdom of light with the salvation in our Lord Jesus Christ.

PRINCIPALITIES AND POWERS IN THE KINGDOM OF FAMILY

In this 21ˢᵗ century there is a strong principality pushing the homosexual agenda to affect the kingdom of family. The spirit of Jezebel bringing forth disrespect and disorder in the principle of authority in the family is also running rampant in the kingdom of family. Both rulers are severely affecting the functional bases of the family. Homosexuality and the different spirits behind it are defiantly challenging the foundational divine process by God of man's creation through the relationship of a man and a woman. God's biological reproduction of mankind is done through marriage and intimacy between a man and a woman. In God's divine plan, a family is comprised of a man and a woman with their children. The demonic spirits pushing the homosexual agenda are redefining a family to two adults and children. That agenda is inculcating that a family can be of two fathers or two mothers with children. This social position teaming up with the demonic influences of other kingdoms of influence is gaining strength in our societies especially in the western world.

The spirit of Jezebel is no less working to set disorder and disrespect in the core of the families.

Ephesians 5: 22-25 and 6: 1-3 says,

> "Wives, submit yourselves unto your own husbands, as unto the Lord. For the husband is the head of the wife, even as Christ is the head of the church: and he is the Savior of the Body. Therefore as the church is subject unto Christ, so let the wives be to their own husbands in everything. Husbands, love your wives, even as Christ also loved the church, and gave himself for it... Children,

obey your parents in the Lord: for this is right. Honor thy father and mother; that it may be well with thee, and thou mayest live long on the earth."

In the biblical family structure, the father is the spiritual head of the family. He is called to give spiritual leadership to his family, to set the proper example in helping his family strive toward its divine purpose. The husband is called to be the first responsible in God's divine family structure for the success, growth and fulfillment of his household. The wife, partner to her husband, is called to submit to his leadership and authority for the purpose of the will of God in the couple and household. This does not make her an inferior being since her grace and gifting are to be teamed up with her husband for their family's success and fulfillment. The children are called to obey their parents according to the Lord, which attracts the blessing of God over their lives and long life. The spirit of Jezebel and the demons working under its reign have heavily attacked godly structure. Many families are dysfunctional and deprived of any kind of divine order. Respect and submission to the spiritual authority of the father and the role of the mother have been severely violated in the family unit. Many wives have no respect for the spiritual authority of their husbands. They refuse to acknowledge the leadership and authority of their husbands over them and their family. On the other hand many husbands are patronizing, dominating and abusing their authority over their wives. Many kids can speak however they want to their parents. Nowadays it is not uncommon to see kids in public disrespecting their parents. I still remember waiting in line to pay at the cash in a store with my mother and witnessing a kid disrespecting his mother by telling her to shut up. I was around 12 years old and was severely shocked by such a public display of disrespect. I could not even imagine myself in a nightmare telling my mother such a thing. Unfortunately, such an occurrence is not an exception in our 21st century society, especially in North America.

PROVERBS 22: 6
"Train up a child in the way he should go: and when he is old, he will not depart from It."

PROVERBS 22: 15
"Foolishness is bound in the heart of a child; but the rod of correction shall drive it."

PROVERBS 23: 13-14
"Withhold not correction from the child: for if thou beatest him with the rod, he shall not die. Thou shalt beat him with the rod, and shalt deliver his soul from hell."

Another common occurrence in this generation is children calling their parents by their first name. "Hey, Janet! Hey, John! I want to go see the ballgame." The familiarity displayed by calling parents by their first name has become one of many subtle things used by the devil to disrespect God's principle of respecting parents. It can clearly be attributed to the work of Jezebel depositing her seed of disrespect and the lack of honor in the relationship of the children with their parents. How disturbing to see young boys controlling their parents, deciding what they want to eat, controlling them in the household environment. I just cannot imagine our Lord Jesus rebuking or disrespecting His parents. How fitting that the Word of God ask us to be imitators of our Lord. Let it be known that I am not supporting dictatorial and controlling parents, but it is important and godly for the parents to give proper leadership to their children and instill godly values of respect, honor and obedience. It is clearly godly to want to bless our kids with the best; giving them as much as we possibly can that would make them happy. Nevertheless it is not acceptable to have disorder in the family nucleus which is the common denominator of a society. Unfortunately we have reached a point where the devil has affected the family to a point where there is no more order. The wife can tell her husband off, the husband can tell his wife to shut her mouth and have shouting matches in the presence of their kids. There is no more order, because disorder, disrespect and disobedience fuelled by the spirit of Jezebel are affecting the nations in the kingdom of family.

Sadly enough, the homosexual agenda has also affected the foundation of the family unit. One of the strategic plans of the enemy is to use the other kingdoms of influence to implement his plan. In entertainment, more and more movies are geared toward the acceptance of homosexuality as a social emancipation. Additionally, in education the knowledge being given from elementary school to the students is acceptance and understanding of homosexual traits. It is taught that homosexuality is a normal human behavior and that some people are born with these traits. Therefore, at a very young age the kids are learning that it is ok to be a homosexual; some will be heterosexual and others homosexual. Therefore, the enemy is using the workings of different kingdoms to advance his agenda. As sons of God, it is imperative to know that we are called to love the homosexual as any other sinner. In fact, the Lord's love is equal to all sinners; what He dislikes is the sin not the sinner. We are called as sons of God to be sent out in the world to bring salvation to all sinners including homosexuals. The reality of our generation is the fact that many sexual sins will affect the people of this 21st century. Homosexuals, transvestites, people with multiple divorces will be touched by the salvation of Jesus Christ. The church needs to be prepared for this harvest of souls. The people of God cannot let themselves be so religious to the point of being ostracized by these souls but rather be trained to thoroughly minister to the newborn in Christ independently of his background and sexual affiliation. As Jesus prayed for us not to be taken out of the world but be preserved from the wickedness and sinful world, this will be the challenge. Therefore, the kingdom of family is dealing with homosexuality and the spirit of Jezebel is seeking to plant disorder in the core of family unit.

PRINCIPALITIES AND POWERS
IN THE KINGDOM OF EDUCATION

In the kingdom of education and science, humanism is largely affecting education to dilute to the point of eliminating the notion of God. There's an inclusion on godliness in education. Education is teaching the students to be tolerant, to accept the different cultural and social choices. It is well known that today's educational system promotes different religious views that are supposed to be all right. It emphasizes the fact that the religious views are function to its subject. People are taught to know how to respect and accept the various differences as orthodox. We do not want to talk about God, because there are so many gods, so we need to respect all the gods. So if a person comes and starts saying that he believes that a toy is his god, then it is ok to accept his belief as long as he can express his position. Everybody has a god. Everyone can have their own god. There are different gods - you just need to have one. In fact, the educational system wants to avoid talking about God altogether. Therefore, godliness is subjective in its essence. It can be defined in many ways. Biblical values and principles are no more accepted as a foundational value to the system of the western world, even though the foundation of American and Canadian civilization was biblically founded. Principles and values are being questioned and set aside, gearing the doctrinal taught in the schools more toward accommodation and acceptance of different values and views. Therefore, the scientific beliefs have fuelled the belief of the non-existence of God, shown by the scientific big bang theory and the theory of evolution. These theories are just samples of different scientific theories and philosophies that are clearly against many biblical principles. Education is strictly gearing the scholars toward different inclusive theories and the principle of reasonable accommodation to differences. Although education and science have been major factors in man's mandate to subdue the earth, ungodliness has also been funneled through education and science. Therefore, some erroneous beliefs of the power of man to accomplish what he wills have been released through education and science. The people of God will have to bring restoration to the kingdom of education to reform the beliefs inculcated to our society through the education kingdom. Biblical principles and godly wisdom will have to be brought in education and science to expose heretic philosophical positions. In that perspective, saints will have to penetrate the kingdom of education to bring reform to that system and maximize the capacity of education and sciences to subdue the earth through its implemented findings.

PRINCIPALITIES AND POWERS IN THE KINGDOM OF ARTS AND ENTERTAINMENT

Many spirits are rampant in the kingdom of arts and entertainment. The lust and love of self is in fact very present. People in the entertainment industry will struggle with covetousness, the love of self, silver and sex that are commonly called the 3S syndrome. Many will be dominated by the love of self, the love of money and sexual sins. Pride will be a major issue in this kingdom. It is all about me, being exposed, being the superstar, the wanted and desired one. Did they talk about me? Did they enjoy my show, my movie? Therefore many are living a lie of showing a personality that is not theirs. Because of that double identity, depression, drug abuse and alcohol has become a downfall for many. Those who are called in the kingdom of entertainment will have to be ready to take dominion over these spirits with the power of the Holy Spirit and their sanctified life.

How unfortunate to see children of the kingdom of God entering the entertainment business and being overtaken by the principalities ruling that sector. We are seeing preacher's kids used as a mockery by the demons working overtime to stain the reputation of the church. A daughter of a pastor won the notorious honor of the least dressed in an award event. The demons said because she comes from the church; let us make sure we expose her in the area of impurity. The entertainment media did not lose the opportunity to assault the church by making sure it spread the news that a daughter of a pastor was under the spirit of seduction and uncleanness. But that is the world of arts and entertainment: sexuality, impurity and nudity are commonalities. One's body does not mean anything anymore. Blinded by the spirit of impurity, entertainers can do anything with anyone to get a position in a movie, to sign a record deal or have some type of exposure in the industry. Some have been forced to participate in homosexual relationships to be accepted and to receive their musical or movie deals. Others need to be connected to secret societies to have an edge. Unfortunately, some have sold their bodies and souls to the devil for breakthrough in the industry of entertainment. This is why some are badly wounded in their self-esteem, as they are psychologically and emotionally affected. Some drug addictions and alcohol abuse are sometimes the means taken to alleviate the pressure of doing what needs to be done for the price of glory and success. The spirit of leviathan that releases pride and overexuding of oneself is also active in that kingdom. Living in the illusion of grandeur, glamour, popularity and greatness, one can easily fall in pride. That feeling of actually thinking you are greater than what you actually are - seeing oneself as being superior to what one actually is. The Spirit of pride can lead to jealousy, hatred and even to murder. It is imperative for the Body of Christ to raise up the sent ones who will be able to bring a reform in the industry of arts and entertainment.

PRINCIPALITIES AND POWERS IN THE KINGDOM OF MEDIA

Media is the kingdom that is called to affect a societies' faith through the information released. The enemy wanting societies' faith to be turned toward his beliefs, will want to establish principalities and powers of lies in that sector. Media is very often overwhelmed with lies and half-truths. The spirit of sensationalism is very strong in that sector. The desire to always want to exaggerate information is ever present. The media has come to a point of not accepting simple facts or truths if it is not catchy enough to captivate the attention of the viewer. Giving the truth and nothing but the truth has become unpopular for fear of not being attractive and captivating enough to the reader and the audience that is watching. Good news has become boring and unattractive, but bad news of a multiple killing, a rape or the defamation of a public figure is great news. Everything has to be sensational, big... wow! Glamorizing a situation to make it look spectacular and incredible. Media is truly a powerful medium; this is why the devil will work overtime to put his agents to control the information that is given to society. In that fashion he can dictate what type of information is being released. So many good Christian actions or social deeds are not publicized and have no media coverage. Why? Because faith comes from hearing. If the people's faith is awakened by good Christian deeds, they will be inclined to get closer to God or open themselves to the principles of God. Because of this, the enemy will infiltrate the position of power in the kingdom of media to have the upper hand to cover and publicize news that will help him grow his kingdom. The church needs to raise media moguls, influential ministers of media to be able to shift this kingdom to help spread the values and principles of the kingdom of God, spread the gospel of Jesus Christ directly and indirectly to shift the faith of nations for God.

PRINCIPALITIES AND POWERS IN THE KINGDOM OF GOVERNMENT

The major spirits that affect the kingdom of government are corruption and injustice. If you are called into government, you need to expect to be faced with corruption, injustice and unrighteousness.

The word says in Romans 13: 1-2,

> *"Let every soul be subject to the governing authorities. For there is no authority except from God and the authorities that exist are appointed by God. Therefore whoever resists the authority resists the ordinance of God, and those who resist will bring judgment on themselves."*

Clearly the principle of governing authorities is a kingdom principle. God is the author of authority, but when Satan's influence is released on authorities, the principles of God are overtaken by the application of the principles of darkness. Therefore justice is replaced by injustice, the power given to governing authorities is used to corrupt the systems that they are called to supervise and legislate. This is why God is raising in this generation Daniels and Josephs to uphold the banner of godliness and release the wisdom of God in government for the glory of the king of kings.

Psalms 33: 12 says,

> *"Blessed is the nation whose God is the Lord, and the people whom he hath chosen for his own inheritance..."*

When a nation is governed with the fear of God and by applying the principles of the Word of God, the blessings of the kingdom of God becomes the inheritance for that nation. For many centuries the western countries had accepted to have their systems abide by the principles of God and they experienced great peace and prosperity.

1 KINGS 4: 24
*"For he had dominion over all the region on this side of
the river, from Tiphsah even to Gaza, over all the kings
on this side of the river; and he had peace on all sides
round about him."*

Notice that king Solomon who was ruling Israel with
the fear of the Lord and His grace, had dominion and peace
on all sides around him. His nation was not facing constant
opposition and war with other nations. The word "peace" in
Hebrew also has the connotation of prosperity. They are very
closely linked. When a nation is in war it is very difficult for
it to prosper. Prosperity can only come when there is peace in
that nation. Investors will not invest in a nation that has war,
instability and insecurity. Therefore King Solomon who feared
wholeheartedly his Lord was able to prosper the kingdom of
Israel greatly. In contrast, a nation that is governed by leaders
who are ungodly, unrighteous and corrupted will end up
affecting the wealth and the economy of their nation. God is
raising godly government ministers who are called to infiltrate
the kingdom of government to be instrumental in establishing
and in other cases restoring peace, prosperity and security in
the nations they are in.

PRINCIPALITIES AND POWERS
IN THE KINGDOM OF BUSINESS
AND ECONOMY

It is trivial to declare that people are in business to make
money. A business that does not make profit is an irrelevant
enterprise because it does not serve its purpose. The kingdom of
business and economy is called to finance the other 6 kingdoms

of influence. This sector of influence has a major role in the success of the other sectors. The word of God concurs when it says in Ecclesiastes 10: 19; "...Money answereth all things." The devil has soundly understood that. This is why he has released many of his higher-caliber demons in this kingdom to rule it. He knows that if he can control the economy and the businesses in a nation he will be able to release his principles and beliefs and take the nation to hell with him. In that respect, we will discover that strong principalities hold the kingdom of business and economy. It is understood that biblically Mammon is a principality that works in the sector of business.

MATTHEW 6: 24
"No man can serve two masters: for either he will hate the one, and love the other; or else he will hold to the one, and despise the other. Ye cannot serve God and mammon."

The Holy Scriptures speak here of a principality that is so binding that being under his spell can disconnect us from God. Mammon is always mentioned in connection with business and finance. That principality seems very highly ranked in the kingdom of darkness and is affiliated with money. Leviathan who is depicted in the Bible as a sea serpent is also often connected with finance and wealth.

PSALMS 104: 25-28
"So is this great and wide sea, wherein are things creeping innumerable, both small and great beasts. There go the ships: there is that leviathan, whom thou hast made to play therein. These wait all upon thee; that thou mayest give them their meat in due season. That thou givest them they gather: thou openest thine hand, they are filled with good."

The maritime and air transportation are clearly instrumental in global wealth and economy of nations. As we look at the fish market, import and export that goes by the maritime and by air, we can understand the implication the devil would want to have in affecting these areas of global wealth with high-caliber demons.

ECCLESIASTES 9: 16
"Then said I, wisdom is better than strength: nevertheless, the poor man's wisdom is despised, and his words are not heard."

Wealth and riches are also important to advance the agenda of God in releasing His beliefs and principles. The Word says the wisdom of the poor man is despised and his words are not heard. No matter the level of wisdom one can bring, if he is poor it is very hard for him to be heard. You see, wealth gives power to speak. He who has wealth has the capacity to buy airtime, to show his material on television and any media outlet. He who has money can buy land and build bars and topless bars. He who has money can dictate the decisions of governing boards if they are corrupted and therefore infiltrate its dealings. Hence, he who has money has power to teach and to inculcate his beliefs. This is the reason why the devil has been laughing in the ignorance of religious preachers promoting the poor man's gospel. Understand that our God knows that it takes wealth to advance his kingdom. That is why He said in His word "money answereth all things". The time has come for the Church to have proper understanding of kingdom economics and take over the wealth of the nations to advance the kingdom of God. Let us not underestimate the impact of wealth for the work of God and the detrimental effect of poverty in taking over cities and nations for Christ. The kingdom of darkness is laughing at the ignorance of the Body of Christ in that area. It is time to wake up from the false humility of believing piety is linked to poverty.

Hedonism, the love of more, is also a demonic influential factor in the kingdom of business. It is manifested in the insatiable desire to always want more wealth, even at the price of crushing another for it. Unfortunately, there is an unhealthy view in business that is expressed by the more money you have the more money you want, to the point of being obsessed with making more money. This attitude is often accompanied with this fear of losing one's position of power and influence, therefore stress and all sorts of anxiety are accompanied with it. This escalates in making some businesspeople become sharks who can involve any type of illicit activity and corrupted dealings to keep the edge.

Because of the financing capacity of the kingdom of business, the dealings of businesspeople who truly have the capacity to fund the kingdom of darkness involve strong cultic activities. It is important to know that these cultic activities and covenants do not always appear demonic since it is often presented through the channel of secret societies that, at their genesis, seemed harmless demonically and good-willed. It is only as the wealthy entrepreneur or professional goes further in the echelon of these so-called privileged societies that the depth of the occult is clearly and openly displayed. By then, the level of bondage is already so deep that it so much harder for one to disassociate from such gatherings.

Understanding the effect of the demonic realm over the kingdoms is essential for us to take over the spheres of influence in the world. Do not believe that our natural wisdom, education and good contacts can help us have influence and impact. We need the power of God, His wisdom and understanding to have the spiritual dominance in the world. Lacking understanding in the realm of the spirit and its influence over the kingdoms seduces good-willed Christians who have the heart to have an impact but not the tools to do it. Therefore, some enter a particular sector but instead of having an impact in advancing the kingdom of God, they are rather subdued and overtaken by the principalities ruling their sector of influence. So you can enter government and be a counselor, a mayor, a senator or a governor with a clear desire to be a light in the darkness of politics, but still be overshadowed by the principality of corruption or unrighteousness ruling politics and government. You can enter the arts and entertainment and love God with all your heart and feel destined to have an impact for the kingdom of God. But as you are going through the initial process of your career, you can already be taken by the influence of the spirit of lust and Mammon in the music industry. All of a sudden your Christian beliefs and their impact in your life start dwindling, your style of dressing starts changing, your attitude and values start changing. It becomes ok to sleep around and dress with less and less clothing. Songs that you would have never thought you would sing... you start singing, movie scenes that you would have put your hand on fire that you would have never touched, you do. This is the direct effect of the dominating principalities overtaking an unprepared Christian entering the arts and entertainment kingdom. Scholars, who were ready to be used by God but because they lack proper grooming, enter education and sciences and peculiarly enough start compromising their beliefs. Christians in science been having less and less faith in the Word and more and more faith in their brains and in what they know. What statistics say and what experts say become more important than the Word of the Lord. You therefore become an intellectual striving for more and more head knowledge instead of spiritual knowledge. This is why it is important to be properly trained in an apostolic ministry with apostolic authority overseeing your development and giving you sound teaching and wisdom about the spiritual world to prepare you to have an impact in the sector that you are mandated by God to enter.

Some Christians are called to the media but the media will want to affect them with lies and sensationalism. That spirit in the media, that wants to change the truth into something else even if it comes from a well-purposed and sincere person. If you tell them the truth, it is not enough; they want to sensationalize your statement to make it more captivating and attractive to the reader. The spirit of lie, misinformation and exaggeration are there in the media to exaggerate the truth. So as you enter that system, the enemy will want you to be entangled and bound by these spirits in order to exaggerate stories and falsify news information. But I believe that God, as we step into the kingdoms of influence, He will give us revelation to know how to be relevant and at the same time, true to the Word. It is possible and we need to believe it.

A minister sent out by God into the kingdoms who is spiritually keen will want to know exactly what the principalities affecting his kingdom are and team up with other brethren in seeking God for strategies to know how to truly advance God's kingdom in that sector. My question for you is which kingdom of influence are you in? Whatever kingdom you are in you are called to be accountable to God to not just be a spectator there, not to be one who is living just to live. You are called to be accountable and knowledgeable of your kingdom of predilection, to influence and impact it and bring salvation to the people in it for the King of Kings.

So which area are you in? You need to refuse that the principalities of your kingdom of influence affect you. Are you a professional, a lawyer, a dentist? You don't want your intellect to start taking over. Maybe you're a professional athlete; you don't want self to take over. Where are you? You are an engineer, nurse, accountant, computer analyst, you are in media, arts? Do not let the principalities and dominating spirits overtake you. Knowledge is power when it is applied, so act according to the information that you have received concerning the ruling powers in your sphere of influence and advance the kingdom of God.

4

How to Bring Societal Reform?

It is imperative for us to know how we will be able to bring societal reform. Speaking of the state of our world, analyzing and documenting it should not satisfy us, but we need to look at the work of reforming it.

It is imperative in our mandate to reform systems and bring transformation, to know how we will be able to have maximum impact in our sphere of influence. How do we have maximum impact in our kingdom of influence?

BUILDING KINGDOM ENFORCERS

In order for us to be able to have maximum impact in our sphere of influence, we need to have sound kingdom training. I'm specifically talking about a sound training because one can think that the years in a ministry, or because we took some training automatically qualifies us for kingdom impact. Unfortunately that is not completely true.

God has called us to take the kingdoms of this world. Although the assembly of saints is called to praise and worship the Lord, benefit from the power of healing, deliverance and breakthrough, we should not underestimate the importance of being trained for kingdom takeover in the kingdoms of this world. We need to expect to be trained, not only to be good believers in church but Kingdom enforcers outside of church. We need to be thirst for coming and receiving revelation and understanding so that we can enter our sphere of influence and dominate. There must be something inside of us that pushes us to anticipate more than just a good message when we come to church, but a message that exhorts us. Sometimes God can give us a message to encourage us and to exhort us, but we also need to come to be filled, to have depth and revelation for system transformation.

Very often the saints do not like to be trained as much as they like to be edified. We like to be exhorted, we like to jump and shout, and it is good sometimes when we are down to want to jump and shout, but we also need depth. We need depth to face the realities of the marketplace. If you lack depth in your training for societal reformation, it will show up when you are established in your divine position. Understand that it is very easy to sound impressive and anointed within the four walls of a religious church, but flakiness will not cut it in the secular world. Before a governmental issue, social chaos, sinful indulgence in the arts and entertainment industry, the kingdom minister needs to be seasoned and properly trained to have effective impact for the kingdom of God. We will not be able to have significant impact in our secular world without proper training and depth in the things of God. You cannot just yearn for a feel-good message and good edification for healing and deliverance. You need to be drawing on the anointing of your elders for a Word that will challenge you; that will give you strategic knowledge to change the world.

The feel-good messages preached in our religious churches will not be enough for substantial impact in our societal systems, we will need more relevant teaching and training from our leaders in the Body of Christ. The people of God need to know how to articulate the things of God. The Word said that the wise bring souls; there is a wisdom needed to touch the world. In this generation a Jesus scarf and religious terminologies will not be enough to effectively reform our systems. We can no longer raise up pseudo-soldiers who cringe when they are facing the world's issues. The time has come for us to raise up real soldiers, real "Rambos" who will not have to call an apostle to bring a deliverance or will not have to call a prophetess for a prophetic word in somebody's life.

How tragic to have believers hiding from Jehovah Witnesses, intimidated by the arrogance of some black Muslims and confused by some of the heretical knowledge of Mormon doctrines. The time has come for us to be witnesses before we testify. Notice that Acts 1:8 states that we receive power, when the Holy Ghost came us to be first a witness before even testifying. There is a level of witnessing you do by applying the principles of God in your life that will draw the eyes of the non-Christian and his desire to know your God.

JOSHUA 1: 8

*"This Book of the Law shall not depart out of thy mouth,
but thou shalt meditate therein day and night, that thou
mayest observe to do according to all that is written
therein. For then thou shalt make thy way prosperous,
and then thou shalt have good success."*

Although we have Christians in the different kingdoms of the world, we have not been able to have significant impact. We have not been able to reach a point where the level of teaching and training that we have attained allow us to apply the principles of God that we have learned in our sphere of influence. We need to be able to transpose what we have received in church into our work place. If we cannot reach that level, our training is lacking and should be deemed insufficient. In fact, we have many saints who proclaim they are Christians but are more specifically believers. You see a believer received Christ as his Lord and Savior but a Christian is one who does what Jesus did. So very often the word Christian is used very lightly.

ACTS 11: 26
"And when he had found him, he brought him to Antioch. So it was that for a whole year they assembled with the church and taught a great many people. And the disciples were first called Christians in Antioch."

The people of Antioch called the disciples "Christians" for the first time, because they saw the disciples doing the same things Jesus had done. If you have a problem in casting out devils, you can still be a believer, whether if you have been in church for 10 or 25 years. If you have a problem in clearly sharing your faith without being stressed out, you can still be a believer. If you are not able to lay your hands on the sick for them to recover because you need to call your leader to come and pray, then there is a problem. You are still a believer. You are a child and not yet a son. Galatians 4: 3 says that he who is in bondage under the element of the world is a child.

GALATIANS 4: 3

*"Even so we, when we were children, were in bondage
under the elements of the world."*

If you are in your sphere of influence and are still under
the influence of the things of the world, you're still a child.
The epistle to the Galatians clarifies that a child in faith is in
bondage under the element of the world. Therefore, when you
penetrate society and are still under the spell of its spirits,
you are still a child and not yet a son. Understand that a son
has reached a level of maturity. In the Jewish culture, there is
a ceremony that confirms this transition from childhood to
sonship. The child after that passage into sonship becomes
eligible in the decision making process of the family. He
begins to have a say in the decisions of the family and has his
share of influence in the things of the family. In other words,
he is seen as one who has enough maturity to be decisional.
Unfortunately, this is not the case for too many believers who
have been saved for many years. They stagnate in a state of
childhood. In order to have true impact in our society, we
need to receive sound kingdom training, because you will be
facing corruption and you will be facing unrighteousness.
If you are in government, you will be facing those types of
demons. So if you do not have sound depth with both of your
feet solid in the things of God, not just knowing but practicing
the things of God, you will be overtaken by the system and its
principalities. They will overtake you. If you are in media, the
demons of lying, sensationalism and all those different spirits
that are affecting media and communication sector will affect
you. You see, sound foundation is not just saying, "Jesus saved
me." A sound foundation is not only receiving Christ as your
Lord and Savior. We have heard that salvation is the door to

the kingdom but we need more. We need to enter, to know about the power of God, to know about deliverance, to know about faith, to know about warfare, to know about laying hands on the sick, to know about righteousness, to know about real peace. This knowledge has to take us from the level of information to the level of revelation and manifestation. The number of people who have just a cognitive and cerebral understanding of the things of God is staggering. You can know about peace intellectually but not live in peace, if you are lacking in the revelational level of the peace of God. John 8:32 says you should know the truth and the truth shall set you free. This verse literally means that if you have the truth then you have revelation and that will set you free. Therefore if you do not have revelation on peace you can speak about it and still be worried. If you don't have revelation on prosperity you can talk about what God is saying but you will not be experiencing prosperity. Breakthrough goes deeper than the realm of information. You need to reach the level of revelation before ever thinking of seeing the manifestation. When you are able to walk in a level of revelation in the principle of the kingdom, you will be able to be effective wherever you are, in church and equally in your systemic environment.

Jesus did not build believers. Jesus built a disciple-based movement. He did not raise followers but disciples. You see today, we have churches that have followers. They are filled with people following a leader but they are not disciples. If you put them in front of a demon possessed person, they would call "Pastor Power". If you put them in front of an issue, they would call "Prophetess Anointing". If you put them in a situation that is complicated they will have to dial 9-1-1 Pastor. There's a problem with that, because Jesus did not build followers, he built disciples. Now a disciple is he who masters the principles of his master and can apply them. You can have 20,000 people in a church but among the 20,000, there are not five who can cast out a devil. But the Word said in Mark 16: 17, "And these signs shall follow them that believe, in my name shall they cast out devils." If you are a follower you cannot cast out devils, you call your pastor, but if you are a disciple you will face the demon and cast him out of the person. Many churches have built followers. Every time the preacher preaches, they clap. We have the Pope and we have pastors. But Jesus was so different. He understood that to spread the gospel of the kingdom, he needed to build disciples. Today we have built followers to raise our ministries. We have set up websites, Twitter and Facebook accounts to market to man. But Jesus built disciples who knew His revelation and it did not take 25 years. In three years, Jesus had brought so much depth to his disciples that they were able to change their world. Today it is common to find believers being 15 years in the Lord and still unable to bring someone else to Christ. Many years in the Lord and they cannot cast out one devil and unable to lay hands on a sick person to bring recovery. Their leader does it.

I believe that God is raising in this season, a new generation of leaders who will not be seeking self-elevation or self-glory but they will be able to raise a people. An apostolic people identified, trained, mandated and sent out. Every saint will transition from being a believer into a disciple. To have societal reform we need to start raising disciples. Jesus built a disciple-based movement. They were not just another sect but a center of power for societal reformation and transformation. They were a threat to the status quo; they were a moral force in contrast to the immoral society. They were able to stand against immorality of their nation. We are called to raise a disciple-based church. There is a level of exposition of the truth that can only take place after we have established disciples in position. How can we have true breakthrough if we only have babies in the local churches. Some saints can have one little correction and they are ready to break covenant with their local church. Suddenly they hear the "voice of God" that tells them they are called to move to another church, this is not the voice of God, this is the voice of the flesh or the devil! You give them something to do and you have to tell them 60 times. Jesus sent his disciples two by two to preach the gospel after they had only been around him for training for a year and a half. Can you imagine this today, how many churches could literally successfully send out the saints in effective ministry after a year and a half? How can we take the cities that are in the illegal possession of the devil with an immature and untrained church? Some churches are praying for more members but are they able to take care of them? Some churches have a killing ministry. They kill believers in religion. We need to understand that the lack of maturity is impeding the move of God in taking cities. Because if we are babies in the faith, depression will continue to kill people; the spirit of suicide will continue to take the people out of the city. When the saints who have been in the church for years begin to rise up to the task and seek for stability and maturity, we will then be in position to take our cities for Christ. So we have ministers who are suffering from exhaustion because they failed to equip the saints for the work of ministry. Unfortunately, they have raised saints who have grown used to simply coming to church to gratify their needs.

We need disciple-based churches. You cannot be preaching for years and have not been able to raise five sons who can do what you do. If it is so, there is a problem. This is why God is raising in this season true apostles. You see a true apostle is not seen when he preaches, certainly he can preach but proof of his apostleship is seen in the quality of the preaching and ministering by his sons and daughters. It is not about how long you've been in the ministry, but the sons you have raised up and the fruit the ministry has. Because we have been blinded, in some areas of the Body of Christ it is all about the number of years in ministry and the grey beard.

But in Job 32: 7-9, the word says,

> "I said, Days should speak, and multitude of years should teach wisdom. But there is a spirit in man and the inspiration of the Almighty giveth them understanding. Great men are not always wise, neither do the aged understand judgment."

Elihu, under the inspiration of the Holy Spirit was literally saying that it is not about the number of years that you have but the wisdom that the Holy Spirit gives. The wisdom of God is not acquired with the number of years but through our relationship with the Spirit of God. Today, the ministries counting on age for wisdom would never accept Jesus, because He was thirty years old when He started His ministry. The religious churches would have refused him but accepted Eli, the old High Priest. It is time to have Spirit-filled leaders in the Body of Christ, capable of raising disciples to take over the systems of the world.

We need to raise true disciples if we want to have societal reform. Disciples who are groomed to be a witness for the kingdom of God and not rebels who give one exhortation and cast out one devil and think they are ready to have an international ministry, otherwise our society will continue to transform the church. This is what we are seeing in the Christian community: a reformed church. The same things in the world are in the church. Instead of reforming the world, the world is reforming the church.

DISCOVER YOUR KINGDOM IDENTITY

The knowledge and understanding of the kingdoms of influence and the principalities and powers affecting them should lead us to ask ourselves: where should we be positioned in what God wants to do to advance His kingdom on earth? To adequately answer this question, it is imperative for us to know our kingdom identity. People of God for the longest time preachers have been preaching the gospel of salvation, preparing believers for heaven. The problem with that is the fact that Jesus never called us to preach the gospel of salvation but the gospel of the kingdom. Don't close your mind yet, I will give clarity. The gospel of the kingdom gives revelation to the Body of Christ in order to have dominion on earth. Now the gospel of salvation is the door. Salvation is the door that opens the kingdom of God to us. Unfortunately, too many preachers have stopped at the preaching of salvation, but we need to speak and preach about the whole Word of God, about the gospel of the kingdom and all the riches that are encompassed in it. The Lord himself preached, "The kingdom is now".

MATTHEW 4: 17

"From that time Jesus began to preach, and to say, repent: for the kingdom of heaven is at hand."

The disciples in Luke 10: 1, 9 speak of the gospel of the kingdom.

> *"After these things, the Lord appointed other seventy also, and sent them two and two before his face into every city and place, whither he himself would come... and say unto them, The kingdom of God is come nigh unto you."*

Philip in Acts 8: 12 speaks and preaches about the gospel of the kingdom.

> *"But when they believed Philip preaching the things concerning the kingdom of God, and the name of Jesus Christ, they were baptized, both men and women."*

Apostle Paul in Acts 28: 30-31 preaches the gospel of the kingdom.

> *"Then Paul dwelt two whole years in his own rented house, and received all who came to him, preaching the kingdom of God..."*

Salvation is the door that gives us access to the kingdom, but unfortunately, a lot of believers have stopped at the door. They have not entered and taken hold of all the principles and the riches that are in the kingdom. There gospel is stuck at Maranatha, Jesus is coming back with the thoughts of living in heaven, when they have not yet benefited from all that the kingdom of God has for them right now on the earth. Because of that diminished revelation of the kingdom, the church is lacking the impact it is called to have on earth today.

But in this season, God is raising up a church that will not just penetrate the front door but will step into all the blessings of the kingdom. The escapist mentality preached by religious preachers has separated the church from the world. In fact, there are churches that encourage their saints to stay in church. Don't mess in and connect with the world. The church is so entrenched and concentrated with going to heaven that we forgot that we are called to dominate on earth, we forgot that we are called to occupy the earth. Understand that the gospel of the kingdom releases the church to be at the center of all culture and societal systems. Church is not just called to be effective and efficient in the four walls of a building called "church", but we need to be in every societal system in the world and be effective. No wonder we lack kingdom impact in the world. We have been busy segregating the Body out of the world and waiting for heaven instead of giving the church wisdom to have dominion on earth.

Matthew 6: 10 says,

> *"Thy kingdom come, Thy will be done in earth, as it is in heaven."*

God rules in heaven but we are called to rule on earth. Jesus established His Kingdom 2000 years ago so that we can rule and reign and advance His Kingdom on earth. He established His kingdom so we can be positioned in this world to impact it. In order for the church to do that, it is imperative that every saint understands his or her kingdom identity. You see, knowing your spiritual identity is fundamental. You need to know who you are in the Lord and your divine mandate on earth. A saint needs to know his spiritual DNA to have any type of maximized impact on earth.

"From whom the whole body fitly joined together and compacted by that which every joint supplieth, according to the effectual working in the measure of every part, maketh increase of the body unto the edifying of itself in love."

Ephesians 4: 16 says that the Body needs to be joined and knitted together by what every joint supplies. It is for this purpose that everyone in the Body of Christ has a grace and a capacity to supply something to the growth of the kingdom of God. Every believer has a distinct capacity, a level of greatness given by the Father that only needs to be discovered.

There is a tremendous downside to not knowing your identity. You see when someone does not know his spiritual identity in the Lord; he can have a tendency of being overwhelmed with the gifts and graces of others. It is like the person spending his time peeking and admiring his neighbor's lawn instead of working on making his own lawn great. Some saints, instead of seeking to master what God gave them and how to maximize it, are jealous of others gifts, which can lead to so many atrocities spiritually and even naturally. Very often the problem with jealousy and competition in the church is often the result of insecurity. The saints do not know who they are. Let me give this simple example. We can have three apostles present in a ministry. All of them have a distinctive grace, they have a particular and specific anointing that the Lord has released on them to be great. Not knowing one's spiritual identity can force one of these ministers to have the tendency of ministering or operating in the likeness of somebody else. This imitating can stop the expression of the greatness and the maximization of one's gifts. Our greatness can only be maximized when we are in our spiritual lane doing what God has called us to do. A spiritual father or a minister you respect and honor can surely be a blessing in the forging of your spiritual identity, but as you reach maturity, you are called to be who God calls you to be in your uniqueness.

Spiritual identity is special in the fact that you cannot choose it, you can only discover it. You cannot choose who God wants you to be. You can only discover it. As you are growing in the Lord, as you are growing in understanding of the things of God and as you are growing in revelation of the principles of God, revelation should be imparted to you of whom you are. You see you cannot choose to be a pastor, an apostle, a praise and worship leader, a lawyer, an accountant or even a dentist. You can only discover that specific gift that is in you. It is important for you to know that. Some people go to school to become, but you cannot go to school to become, you can only go to school to ameliorate the gift you already have. Some people think that because they went to a school of theology they are a pastor, because I went to law school I am a lawyer. You can have ten lawyers who graduated from law school but there are only two true lawyers, the ones who are gifted, who have the grace and are called from their mother's womb to become lawyers. That is why one can go to school for a long time to be a teacher and never be able to teach. You have the diploma but you fail to be an efficient teacher because school cannot define you, school can only refine you. School can only refine the grace that you already have, school does not have the capacity to define you.

God is the distributor of gifts. From the day that we were in our mother's womb, God gave us all the necessary gifts we needed to fulfill our destiny. Jeremiah was a prophet from the time he was in his mother's womb.

JEREMIAH 1: 5

"Before I formed thee in the belly I knew thee; and before thou camest forth out of the womb I sanctified thee, and I ordained thee a prophet unto the nations."

In the same fashion, when God created you in your mother's womb, you already had all the gifts and all the graces to become who you are called to be, you can only discover it. You can only discover that you are called to be a renowned musician. You can only discover that you are an accountant. You can only discover that you have been chosen to shift government. You can only discover that you will be the one to change Hollywood. School cannot define you, school can only refine you, it can only make you better. This is why it is so important not to be satisfied with the natural manifestation of your gift, you need to maximize it. You can sing but singing lessons will make you great, you can preach and know some verses but you still need to study and show yourself approved.

It is preponderant to seek God for direction pertaining to your call and mandate in life, knowing that school can only refine and not define an individual. That is why some people have been going to school for so long without any significant result in finding their niche. How tragic to have people jumping from one academic program to another. Why?; No clear direction. When you have direction from God and know His plan, you will not be paying exceeding amounts of tuition fees, you will only pay once. Therefore, many owe astronomical amount to governments because they did not go to God. Taking classes that God never told them to take. So many are failing in school. Why? Because they are expecting school to define them. But let it be known that only God can succinctly tell us who we are. He is the creator and has all the answers concerning his creation.

I still remember in 1995, one week after my wife and I were married. I was translating for a minister and he spoke a prophetic word on my life. He said that I had a teaching anointing on my life. And this anointing as it would grow, would lead me to the apostolic call. It would then become a foundation layer for many lives, many churches and many nations. Now the surreal aspect of that word was the fact that I was just a youth leader at that time and I was not even an ordained minister and was not even in full time ministry. The minister, when he found out afterwards about my status, he was not swayed in what he received. He said this: "Well God is going to do it in His time and in His process". Seven years later, this minister came back in my city and I invited him to minister in our ministry. He himself was surprised to see the video of the prophetic word he spoke from God and how it was fulfilled. That clear direction helped me stay focused in the plan of God on my life. I was able to know where God was leading me because of the prophetic word that the Lord confirmed to me so many times in the process of its accomplishment.

God still speaks in the lives of His people. Sometimes church does not need a three points message, it needs prophetic words that can give personal direction to the people of God. The prophetic has the capacity to release saints in their lives and destinies. When the minister spoke in 1995 about God calling me in the apostolic office, I did not even know what the apostolic ministry was all about. But that word was spoken and it ignited something that was already there. Now 17 years later,

14 nations have been touched by the apostolic ministry on my life, without ever having to go soliciting anyone for a speaking engagement. You cannot decide who you are. You discover it! That is why it is so important to go to God and ask him: who am I? What is my grace and what is my identity? That is why some believers are frustrated in life because they are not positioned to impact. When you are in your position, when you are flowing with your grace and your gift, you enjoy waking up and going to work. When you know your spiritual identity and are in your kingdom position, there is joy and happiness. Your working hours are not an issue. There is a drive to get your job done. Have you ever been in a class with a teacher who loves what he is doing and is great at it, and another one who is terrible and cannot wait to finish with the class? Understanding the subjects was nothing short of confusion and chaos. On the other hand, when you were under a gifted and rightly positioned teacher, going through your class, understanding the subject and passing the course was just a breeze.

We need to know our kingdom identity. We cannot expect to have any type of breakthrough in affecting society, if we are positioned in the wrong place. If you are called to be a lawyer and are in medical school, you are in the wrong place. Yes both of them seem to be very prestigious, but true prestige is when you are positioned in your God-given position and are excellent and thriving in it. It is better for you to be a great mechanic than a lousy lawyer. So you need to be in position, knowing your kingdom identity. You need to be in your identity, in your grace. What a blessing to be in a ministry in which every minister is in his God-given ministry. This can be seen where the singer is a gifted and anointed singer, and the preacher an anointed minister of the word. Sometimes, people are sleeping in church with reason... the preacher cannot preach! Some pastors are called to pastor not to take the microphone and preach but take care of the sheep. In the New Testament church, the three ascension gifts that were anointed for preaching and teaching the saints were apostles, prophets and teachers. They have the grace to minister the word to the saints. Pastors were taking more care of the flock and minister in the houses and the evangelists were ministering in the world to bring souls to the church. Unfortunately the religious church has put everything in the role of the pastor but some of them just do not have the dynamism and charisma for weekly Sunday preaching and teaching. Sometimes, the saints were sleeping, not because they were tired but because they were overcome by boredom from the effect of an anoint-less minister. Remember that Bible school does not raise preachers, it raises theologians. The preacher is gifted from his mother's womb; Bible school can only better equip him to use his gift. My son started playing the keyboard when he was three years old. By the age of 12, he was a music director for his mother in her first concert. Having the grace and the gifting for music, we have put him in music school to refine his gift. Because we have an excellent God; we are also called to be excellent in what we do for Him. The fact that we have a grace does not exempt us from seeking training to reach excellence. So we put him in school to know music not to learn music, to be refined and to be great at it. It is not enough to be in a given position, but we are called to be in our position, using our gifts refined to maximize our impact in our sphere of influence and advance the kingdom of God.

The Church needs to know its identity. Six kingdoms are waiting to be impacted by the Church of Jesus Christ.

We cannot be impactful only in the kingdom of religion and spirituality. The kingdoms are waiting for saints who know their identity, who know that they are called. For the longest time the religious church emphasized one call: the pastoral call. But each and everyone in the Body of Christ have a calling. This is what makes an apostolic church so different from a pastoral church. In the pastoral church everyone is cheerleading the pastor and his family to their glorious destiny. But in the apostolic church, the apostolic leader and his leadership raise an apostolic people identified, trained, mandated, and sent out in their grace. The apostolic leader is not the only one who has an anointing in his position, but he is challenging each and every one not just to clap and shout at the end of the service, but to be identified, trained, mandated and sent out in their grace and in their gifts. In an apostolic church you cannot just come, sit down, applaud, shout and dance, but you are there to be identified, trained mandated and sent out. The apostolic church is raising people who are sent out to change and transform every societal system of the world. We need to release the saints in every kingdom of influence. But in order to be effective in the kingdoms they need to know their identity.

THE PROCESS TO YOUR SUCCESS

The knowledge of our kingdom identity is not the ticket to our divine mandate, but a door that leads us to the process of success. You see some saints make the mistake of thinking that just because they know they have such and such gift, validates that they are ready for their kingdom purpose. Henceforth, people come short of their destiny not necessarily because they are not in their position but because they just did not go through the necessary process to propel them in their success.

Truly, God has called us to be kings in the different kingdoms of influence, but we need to know that there is a process to kingship. There is a process to greatness. There is a process to be kings and queens in our spheres of influence.

INTANGIBLES OF THE SPIRIT

Very often what qualifies us to be a king in our sector of influence in society is the capacity to succeed in the intangibles of the spirit. What are the intangibles of the sprit? The intangibles of the spirit are certain experiences or situations you have been through that you have not thought to be relevant to put in your resume as a prerequisite to be great. Seemingly inconclusive and irrelevant for you, these were thought to have no bearing on your ascension to kingship. Nevertheless, these experiences acquired in your process, that you might not have put on your resume, end up qualifying you to be king. Understand that there are certain things you need to learn and there are other things you need to process, before you can be great as an actor, a politician or a manager. We have learned that different kingdoms have different principalities that are ruling them. If you are not properly trained and groomed, you could step into the right kingdom and still be a casualty in your God-given sphere of influence. Instead of shifting your world, the wicked in your world sways and shifts you into darkness. We can clearly see this example in the arts and entertainment. Many musical artists have entered the kingdom of arts without the proper preparation and training. They went in but they were not ready, they did not go through the process to prepare them for success. Instead of advancing the kingdom of God by their strategic positioning, they have become agents converted by the enemy to advance the agenda of darkness. Many singers start in the church. They practice their singing voices in the choir of the local house but end up in the musical industry a disgrace and a subject of shame for the Body of Christ. Because of the way they conduct themselves and the music they convey to society. The gift is not the problem. Being in the wrong position is not the issue, but there is a proper equipping that was not given to them because they failed to go through the process.

Notice, that I said go through the process. It is one thing to start a process, but it is necessary to go through the process. This is why we should take heed not to haste and be impatient when we are in our process with God. Sometimes we can have the tendency to be our own master and decide when we have passed through our process. We need to remember that man proposes but God disposes.

PROVERBS 16: 9

"A man's heart deviseth his way: but the Lord directeth his steps."

The word admonishes the fact that although we can have our idea and our strategy, we need to let God still be God in directing our steps in the fulfillment of our destiny. He needs to be the one grading and qualifying our process.

There are certain things you have to go through, before you can be positioned to impact. Being positioned in society is not necessarily a gauge in having kingdom impact. In fact the church does not lack professionals, it does not lack human resources positioned in society. What we do lack are the ones who are positioned and recognize the purpose of their positioning, and who are equipped to really advance the kingdom of God in their workplace. A great percentage of saints live a double life, their life in the church setting and their life in their workplace. They have not been trained to translate the principles of the kingdom into their field to advance God's will on earth. Therefore you can be positioned but not have an impact, because you did not go through the proper equipping and grooming process to make you effective as a kingdom enforcer for God. You can be saying to yourself: I know my identity; I know I am called to be a lawyer or an accountant but why is it that I do not have success in being an effective kingdomizer? Often times, it is because you have not gone through the process to success.

Understand that the process is not just school. Academic knowledge can be part of the process, but it is not the only element of a process. There are other things we need to learn as we go through our process. David did not know that managing the small family business would be the stepping-stone to the throne of his nation. Joseph did not know that prison was the preparation to the palace. Do you think that Joseph, who had breakfast in prison, knew that the same day he would be dining in the palace? He did not know. Prison was a process. Many values were acquired in prison. This is why you should not underestimate the prisons of your life. Do not underestimate the process that God wants to do in different areas in your life. How weird is it to have people preaching with so much power and anointing and be so arrogant and cold and show no character of Christ. That is why I told the saints of our local house that it is not how powerful you are on the pulpit but how powerful you are when you step down from the pulpit. I want to see your character, the way you conduct yourself, the way you speak and your humility.

I sat with some "big names" amongst the evangelical of this generation, and you would be shocked to know that some that are recognized as anointed preachers extensively lack the character of Christ. Why? They did not go through their full process. They concentrated on training and manifesting the gift and forgot to put as much time and energy into perfecting the character of Christ. Very often the church makes the mistake of running after the gift instead of running after the character and the gift of Christ. So you step into the position with the gift but you have not gone through the process in perfecting the character and you die before your time. So the wicked of the different spheres of influence have infiltrated the subjects of the kingdom of God and taken them out of their divine destiny. They are dying and have no impact, because they have not gone through the process.

Joseph had the most valuable teaching of his life in the pit and in the prison, not in the palace. Sometimes God is dealing with your personality, with your impatience. God is dealing with your punctuality, with your knowing how to keep your word. But you say hey! I have a master's degree, I have a doctorate and I will transform politics. No you will not, because the intangibles were not touched in your process. When God is dealing with humility, with jealousy and how to relate with people, you should not dodge it. Let the Lord deal in depth with your character. In our quest in understanding the dynamic of being positioned to impact in society, we underestimate the importance of going through our process.

There is a class that we give in our training institute called ministerial protocol. In fact, that course was given to me by the Holy Spirit out of the many discrepancies I have seen in ethics and protocol in ministries. Mind you, these lapses in protocol are not just in the smaller ministries. In many larger ministries, I have personally encountered people who were flagrantly missing protocol. Some without knocking at my door come in before they were asked to. Many people sit in a courtesy chair before they were invited to. This is a lack of protocol. Opportunities are lost because of lack of protocol. Hence, we can concentrate on the most obvious and more apparent principles and lose out because of our lack of refinement in our character. If God is calling you to eat with kings, you need to know how to eat in a formal setting.

You cannot afford to eat with your finger acting as a knife for you. You cannot permit yourself to wipe your mouth with your hands. Having great power to cast out devils will not cut it. These ethics are also important to have, in order to make it in certain areas of influence. You know the tangibles, but do you know the intangibles? You know the tangibles; you know how to do the technicality of the work or of your ministry, but do you know the intangibles that can be the difference makers that lead you to greatness in your sphere of influence? There are things that God will take care of, teach you and process in the closet, out of public scrutiny. You see in God's goodness, He gives us an appointed time to fix some character traits and issues in a more private setting. Why? If we have to be exposed while struggling with those mishaps, it would bring reproach to Him and His kingdom.

I still remember the shock I had of witnessing a renowned preacher pocking his nose on television as he was ministering the word. You see this type of unfortunate mishap is probably the result of a lack of training on proper protocol, in how to conduct oneself in ministry. But sometimes, because we think we know the technicalities, we forget that there are others things we need to learn. When you are in front of people, you might do things that you are in the habit of doing at home but now you are in public. So you need to be groomed, and we are groomed in the prison. Joseph learned humility when he thought that all his whole family would bow down to him, everybody left him and he found himself in prison. So he had to learn to be humble. When they came back, he knew how to treat them, because the Lord had worked on his character. Do you know what it is to be great too fast and start thinking that you're the center of the world? Nebuchadnezzar thought he was the center of the universe and the Lord gave him seven years of eating grass. This was to make him understand that it is neither by might nor by power but it is by my spirit. That is the process. Don't forget the process. You know where you are going. You believe in the call. You know exactly where God wants to use you but you have to go through the process.

Sometimes there are certain doors that do not open because you are not ready. You want to see certain things in your ministry, but you are not ready. Sometimes you need to sit at a seasoned minister's feet to learn. It might seem easier to read books and sound prolific from another minister's lines, but it will catch up to you. There is one thing one cannot imitate and that is true anointing. In order to sit and patiently learn, one needs humility. Humility is very hard to manifest after one's ordination, if it was not nurtured before. Glory, honor and some level of fruit have a way of bringing out the worst of he who did not have a process of humility. In fact, humility is never fully mastered - it needs to be sought in every season of a minister's life. Because the big promotion, the big break in the entertainment world, the business that grows in a flash, being the youngest director of high school in your region can bring out pride that you did not know you had. Let wisdom channel you to go through the process. Isaiah 55: 9 says that the thoughts of God are not the thoughts of man. The ways of God are not the ways of man.

ISAIAH 55: 9

"For as the heavens are higher than the earth, so are my ways higher than your ways, and my thoughts than your thoughts."

Sometimes you expect to rule in the palace, but God wants you to rule in the prison. Accept to rule in the prison, accept to rule where and when nobody sees you. Accept to rule when no one comes to acknowledge your presence. I remember when the Lord spoke to me about being called into the ministry. It took all my energy to go and face my pastor, who was also my father-in-law, with what the Lord had showed me in my dream. After explaining my dream to him with fear and trembling he told me, "I know you are called for ministry. I want you now to start in the maintenance ministry." I said, "Maintenance?" He said, "Yes!" He mentioned that I was called to touch every department of the ministry and I should start with maintenance. So I started cleaning bathrooms. I was then promoted to buff the floor of the whole sanctuary and shovel the snow at the entrance of the church. And then, I started working with the kids, with the youth, I worked with the women, then administration, then ushering and so on. As I look back at my process, surely it is not the way I had planned it but truly the Lord knows best. The steps He impressed my pastor to make me go through helped me groom to the apostolic ministry. His ways are not our ways but His ways are best. Many important lessons and traits of the character of Christ were worked in my life in these times of "out of the spotlight ministry".

You might be called to change the entertainment industry or affect the education system, but you have to go through the process. What is it that God wants to fix, even if you have your degree, what is it that God wants to change? Know how to go through the process and know that the ways of God are not your ways. You might have planned your whole action plan to greatness, but in the midst of all that, God can drop you in a little job even if you were called to be a great boss, in order to mold your character for greatness. In that little job, do not be frustrated, it is just a detour to tweak and fix something in your character. It is a parenthesis necessary to refine your raw talent to prepare you for greatness.

Joseph's prison time was a catalyst for his time in the spotlight. When his time came to shine, he was ready. The day Pharaoh gave him the title of second in command in the whole land; Joseph was ready because he had gone through the process. You know your identity, but you need to go through the process. The lack of faithfulness in the small things will disqualify you in the big ones. If you cannot master the small you will have difficulty ruling in the bigger stage. Luke 16: 10 says that God will want to see your faithfulness in smaller rounds of dominion before giving you your full ownership and stewardship.

LUKE 16: 10

"He who is faithful in that which is least is faithful also
in much: and he who is unjust in the least is unjust also
in much."

So, there are certain things God wants to see how you can rule in smaller spheres, how you can do it with just a little group, before becoming a great leader. Luke 16: 10 says that if you are faithful in small things you will be faithful in greater things. Sometimes you want the greater things, the big position. I know that God called you for the bigger things in life but your performance in the smaller things in life will propel you to your full grown potential.

I remember when I preached my first message on a Sunday morning. I was still a youth leader when a ministry called upon me to minister in their main service on Sunday. I mean for me as a youth leader, it was a major opening. So I fasted, I prayed with my wife, we fasted and in my prayer I was seeing myself ministering to a 15,000 gathering. I therefore expected a major crowd in that engagement. As I arrived, I was expecting a bigger church, but I said, "If it is full there can still be a good 350..." So I arrived there and I sat, and I think that there were maybe 30 people. I was sitting up there on the platform disappointed about my dream turn out. All of a sudden the Lord spoke to me and told me this; "if you can bless them and preach to them like you would preach to a larger crowd of people, I will give you the larger crowd." Believe me, after I heard that from the Lord, I gave those 30 people everything I had. I preached myself out! Now as I look back, I am so grateful to God for that opportunity. I was faithful in small things and the Lord opened the bigger things.

But sometimes we want the big break or the big call, the big firm or the big opportunity. I don't want to be just a counselor I want to be president. I want to be the politician but God wants you to start in the politician's office. David was called to be king but his first job in the palace was as a musician to King Saul. You can be right now playing music in your own palace. You can be teaching in your own school or working in a city that will be yours as a mayor. That is the process; do not underestimate the small spheres of dominion.

What has God called you to do that you have refused to do because you had found it insignificant and not worth it? Do not be impatient in your process. It took the Lord 30 years of anonymity before the three years of greatness. What would you have told God? I am God; this is too long let's shorten this to five years. I am God, why do I have to stay 30 years as a carpenter connecting with people for 30 years and just have greatness for three years. But the greatness found in those last three years still affects humanity today. So do not undermine your process. You can be going through stuff and ask yourself when you will get your breakthrough. God is just tweaking some things; it is just your season of anonymity. Sometimes you might find it is too long. The break is taking too long. That opening is taking too long. I received the word but I have not seen it yet. Instead of thinking about the break, think about why it is not there yet, what do I need to shift or change so that I can be ready when my breakthrough comes?

Bishop TD Jakes preached for years in storefront churches and no one saw him. It took one message and his ministry shifted. You could be a great lawyer and have very few clients, just having enough to function and pay your bills. You might be saying: I did so well in law school. I do not know what is going on. I gave them 250% of myself and they won their cases. Where is the flock of clients? It takes just one case, one contact, and one connection to change the tide. It takes one question answered, solving a dilemma; one strategy that turns the business around and you are propelled in your place of greatness. Because you were patient in going through the process and doing what you are called to do.

I do not think that Esther knew that a beauty contest would lead her to become queen. She just participated in a beauty contest. She would have never known that this contest would be the door for her to become queen and save the whole Jewish nation. She went through the process. Do you think that Rahab, once a professional hooker, knew that she would be part of royal lineage to King Jesus? Do not underestimate what you have been through in your life, do not underestimate dirt because many times jewels are found in dirt. You have been through so many things in your life that people see you as dirt. But it was a process. Stones do not start out as precious; when you see the stone you see dirt. Everybody saw Rahab as a "nobody", but God had royal lineage planned for her. Therefore, do not underestimate what you are in life and what you have done in life because when the blood of Jesus comes to clean and purge you, you are a new person set in process for success. Maybe your grace is your nails or even your voice. Some actors are on television but you do not see them, you just hear them. They are now millionaires because they understood that their grace was their voice. Michael Buffer made a famous catchphrase "Let's get ready to rumble!" It has generated him over 400 million dollars. It does not matter what your identity is and what God gave you, what is important is to accept it, hold it, care for it, and love it. Believe in what you have and love what you have. Do not underestimate the gifts that the Lord has given you and go to your process. It will take you to success.

POSITIONED AS KINGS

In the Lord's master plan for us to advance his Kingdom on earth, He will position us as kings and queens in position of influence. It is imperative to understand that wherever God positions us we are called to dominate. We are called to be the head and not the tail. Clarity needs to be given to certain slogans that the church has been religiously using. We have been saying that we are the head and not the tail and that we should be first and never last. Unfortunately, we have been using those terms in the four walls of the church. However, the fullness of the revelation of being the head and not the tail should manifest in our God-given position in the kingdom of influence. In whichever kingdom you are positioned you are called to be Kings and Queens. You are called in the area you are at, in your sphere of influence to be a King. If you are not a King where you are, if you are not a Queen where you are, you are in the wrong place. Wherever you are called to be in your godly position, you are called to be first. There is tremendous grace and potential inside of you and wherever God places you, he places you there to be king. He places you there to be the head and not the tail, to be first and not last. Unfortunately, too many believers who have received Jesus Christ as their Lord and Savior do not really feel as Kings.

You are called to be kings and queens in the fullness of your gifting and graces to be excellent. In fact, God makes us go through our process to reach a level of excellence in our character and gifting that will make a difference in our circle. We will not be impactful in the sector that we are in, if we are not excellent. The word of God speaking about Daniel and his friends said this in Daniel 1: 20 that in all matters of wisdom and understanding about which the king examined them, he found them ten times better than everybody else. Ten times better than all the others that were with them.

DANIEL 1: 20
"And in all matters of wisdom and understanding, that the king enquired of them, he found them 10 times better than all the magicians and astrologers that were in all his realm."

In order for the Body of Christ to change the world, it will have to be excellent in what it does and where it is in the spheres of influence. We will not be able to do it any other way in this 21st century that is so geared towards excellence. You can be a good teacher but they will go for the excellent one. You can be a good lawyer, but people will look for the one that is excellent. What a blessing to be in the Lord and have the Spirit of excellence who will lead us to all greatness. It will not be enough to be professional we need to strive for excellence. In this generation, we need to raise the bar of excellence in what we do. It is not enough to be a director, we need to be an excellent director, it is not enough to be an accountant, we need to be an excellent one. Whether you are a teacher, a technician, an agent, a mechanic or a governor, excellence will be a prerequisite to impact your societal system for Christ.

You need to strive for excellence. The way you present yourself needs to be excellent. The way you talk has to be excellent, the way you conduct yourself has to be excellent. Excellence will not pass unnoticed.

You see everybody would want to connect with a winner. There is not a person that would not want to connect with a superstar in his or her field; for this purpose excellence becomes so preponderant in our quest in impacting our spheres. Everyone wants to be connected to someone who is great in his profession. You see, when you are excellent, people will want to know who you are. People will want to be connected to you. When you are excellent in your government office, people will want to know why it is that you are so great in what you do. They will enquire to know your secret. They will seek to know why you are 10 times better than your colleagues. I believe God wants the Body of Christ to flow in the 10 times better anointing. But that anointing will come for a purpose, advancing the kingdom of God in the system of the world.

You see Daniel was in a hostile environment that was not very easy. He was not with his family, he was not with the Jews, he was in a land that did not believe in God; they believed in many gods. But he stayed consecrated and purposely continued to grow his spirituality. He in fact chose not to eat the delicacies and drink the drinks of the King. He set himself apart with his friends and the word said that they graduated from the higher learning school of Babylon 10 times better than the rest. What was their advantage? The Holy Ghost, the Spirit of knowledge and wisdom. The Body of Christ needs to start maximizing the advantage it has.

You are not called to be a common professional in your particular field. You need to be seeking God to have an edge in your sphere of influence. Your prayer should be, "Lord give me power, give me capacity to be the head and not the tail, give me wisdom and grace to be 10 times better than the others. Permit me to excel and be noticed, give me favor to advance your kingdom." Our Lord is not a respecter of person but of principle. Imagine if you step into your sphere of activity with that 10 times better anointing. You would not have to chase and beg for a promotion, the promotion would be chasing you. Sometimes we are asking God for a promotion, we are asking God for a breakthrough when we should be asking to receive the 10 times better anointing to out-compete the competition. How can one be promoted if one is mediocre? How can one be promoted if one is in the bottom of the pack in production? As we are rightly positioned and master what we do, we become candidates for excellence and greatness.

Understand that it is not arrogant to strive to be the best in what you do. It is not pretentious to want to be the best. In fact, you need to decree it. Life and death is in the power of your decrees. Saying, "Lord, you know I am a piece of dry wood. I am nothing. I am completely ignorant but because of your love, please God have mercy on me", has nothing spiritual about it. These types of religious decrees just hide a false humility and ignorance. There is nothing wrong in you saying: Lord I thank you because I am the best. Father when I take the microphone to sing, I thank you in advance because my voice will be angelic and touch everyone's heart. No matter what position you have and your field of predilection you need to speak greatness in you craft. You should not be shooting for second or third string but first, and excellent in what you do. Wherever you are, whatever you do, strive to be the best.

The word said that when the king took the time to analyze the level of all his students of Babylon, he looked at Daniel and his three companions' resume and they overwhelmingly surpassed the rest. Even if he was racist, even if he was sexist, he could not overlook the excellence of the young Jews. There is nothing that can wipe out discrimination and prejudice in this competitive world better than excellence and greatness. Therefore, as a Christian we need to stop talking about having a hard time from the devil and tap into the anointing of excellence that the Holy Spirit gives and take over our sphere of influence. There is no devil in hell that can stop a kingdom enforcer flowing in the 10 times better anointing. In fact, your company will not care about your accent or cultural background when you can bring a level of productivity that exceeds your counterparts and competition. Rather, they will be seeking out special breeds like you. This henceforth becomes a door to lobby for your Christian companions for an open door as Daniel did for Shadrach, Meshach and Abednego.

Know we need to understand the reason why we have to be excellent is because God has called us to be positioned as kings. We need to understand that the reason we can aspire for excellence is because it is the will of God for our kingdom mandate. 1 Peter 2: 9 says that we are a chosen generation, a royal priesthood.

1 PETER 2: 9
"But ye are a chosen generation, a royal priesthood, an holy nation, a peculiar people; that ye should shew forth the praises of him who hath called you out of darkness into his marvelous light."

REVELATION 1: 6
"And hath made us kings and priests unto God and his Father; to him be glory and dominion for ever and ever. Amen."

God is calling you to be king in the kingdoms. One of the major mistakes of the church is to believe that we can change systems from the bottom up. Very often we have been going after the people that are in the lower echelons of society. We have been praying for people who are in drugs, we have been praying for people who are itinerant, who are having issues and problems. And there is nothing wrong with that. It is good, but the church cannot be filled only with people who are part of the lowest echelon of society. Understand that it is very hard to change a sector when you are in its lowest echelon. You see it is very hard for a clerk to change the policies of a company he works in. On the other hand it is much easier for a Chief executive officer to change the policies, philosophy and work ethic of the company in which he works. That is why in this season God is positioning kingdom enforcers in decisional positions in their companies. God is calling the church to raise men and women equipped for the upper echelon of the societal systems. We just cannot have everybody from the Body of Christ working in the lower echelons. We will not change education, arts and entertainment and the corporate world without ministers positioned in position of power. It is time to invade the upper echelon of our societal systems. The time has come for the church to become kings in its societal systems. We need to have elites in those different spheres. We cannot affect government if we have everybody working as an assistant secretary in the government. We need to have some who are positioned as mayors, positioned as MP's. We need to penetrate the upper echelon in education, we need to be placed on the board of education and be decisional in advancing the kingdom of God.

Imagine if we start having Christian ministers established as corporate tycoons in the 40 billion dollar cosmetic industry (solely in America), instead of only having a beauty salon. People of God, we need to raise the bar of what we are aspiring to. Stop aspiring to just make it. I graduated and I have a job in my field and it is ok. A job is good but you need to be a ruler. You need to be a king in your societal system.

KING IN THE KING'S COURT

Although some saints are called to be kings, some others are called to be king in the king's court. Understand that not every Christian will be a king in the upper echelon of an industry. It would be unethical to expect every Christian to be in decisional positions in the higher echelons of the systems of the world. Some have that grace and that call and need to be challenged to reach it. But some others are called to be kings in the king's court. You see some of you will become kings, heading certain kingdoms, but some of you will become kings in the king's court.

ESTHER 5: 1

"Now it came to pass on the third day, that Esther put on her royal apparel, and stood in the inner court of the king's house, over against the king's house: and the king sat upon his royal throne in the royal house, over against the gate of the house."

You see Esther was not ruling the kingdom but had access to the one who was ruling. She had access to the king. Being in the king's court, she had power to affect the king. Therefore, you might not have the top position but God can strategically position you as a great assistant. People of God, if everybody were Batman, who would be Robin? You see some of us might not be called to be Batman but we can be Robin. And if you are an excellent Robin you can affect Batman. Sometimes God will position his agent in a supporting role to radically affect the one who is in charge of the company for kingdom advancement.

Very often the president of a company or a nation will have somebody out of the public eye who has a resounding impact on his decision. Mrs. Condoleezza Rice reached a high level of influence in the President's decisions, George Bush Senior and Junior. How did that happen? Because of her unique knowledge of Russian culture, she was selected to a position in the close circle of Mr. Bush's father. She did such an astounding job that she was later solicited and taken by Mr. Bush son, in his terms as President of the United States. Her greatness made her become queen in the king's court. She was not the commander in chief (as they call the President of the United States), but she was an influential force to the president. Her excellence elevated her in the position of National security advisor in one of the greatest crises in the history of her nation, the 9/11 crises.

Therefore you might not be king heading your department, but still be king in the king's court and in that capacity influence the person having the influence to reform things. Esther was the queen and because of her understanding of protocol and respect, she was able to win the heart of the King where the ex-queen was enabled and destitute. She was excellent. Some saints certainly will not be king in the upper echelons of their sphere in society but will be able, with the power of the Holy Spirit, to position themselves in the king's court as kings to influence key players for societal transformation. If you are not called as a king, get in the king's court.

Whether we are positioned as kings or kings in the king's court, we are purposed to have influence. Since influence is instrumental in bringing changes in any system. Our kingship will set us up for influence and our influence will position us for societal transformation.

TWO KINDS OF INFLUENTIAL AUTHORITY

The Greek word for authority is *exousia*. It literally means the legal right to exercise. Authority speaks of the ability of having an impact on the position and decision of something or someone. There are two kinds of authority that I would want to emphasize. There is an authority that is translated through the position one has and there is another that is exuded by the influence that someone has. You see influence has the power to affect the direction that the authority in position takes. The one who has power of influence will affect the power of position. There are people who have authority because of their position. As a CEO, you have the authority of position. If you speak, the whole company has to listen. But the one who has the authority of influence can affect the CEO who has the authority due to his position. Therefore, do not underestimate your ruling power in the king's court. You might not be able to rule with the authority of position, but you can rule with the power of influence. The key for reformation is to bring the applied principles of God through the two types of authority in order to godly affect our systems. Working for the purpose of God, our worry should not be to strive for one or the other type of authority but to be in our rightful godly position to fulfill our mandate of having dominion on earth. If you are not president you can be vice-president, if you are not manager you can be assistant-manager, if you are not CEO you can be the executive assistant of the CEO and be powerfully used by God to bring transformation in your area of activity.

If we are just professionals, it is not enough. We will not be able to shift things in the systems just because we have a bachelor's degree and are working. It is not because you are making good money that the kingdom of God will advance. It is not enough that you are a professional and that you are a good technician. It is important to know how you can advance the kingdom of God where you are. You can be a great professional and yet still live a life of a nominal non-impactful Christian. Every Sunday you are just happy that you made another Sunday not completely overtaken by the spirit of the world. You see it is not enough to just make it to Sunday and appreciate the presence of God that cleans and renews you for another week. Your mandate is to come to church to be equipped so that you can step in your pulpit, which is in your sphere of influence. Henceforth, you cannot step into your sphere of influence and just be blessed that it has not been able to pollute you. You are called to significantly shift it for the kingdom of God. If you cannot bring the principles into your position as a professional you will not advance the kingdom. You will be maybe a good tither because sometimes even that you do not do but you will not accomplish our mandate of dominion in our world. You might be at the least a good tither but still come short of your kingdom dominion mandate. Stepping in the king's court is one thing but being influential in accomplishing our destiny is another. It is not enough to get to the king's court and be a great assistant or be a great person of influence or going into the sphere and the sector of society and be the supervisor and the president if you are unable to manifest the kingdom of God.

It is imperative for you to step into your workplace on Monday with the mindset that I am a king, I am the supervisor, I am the executive in place or I am the executive assistant, the secretary that is in position to upgrade the business, change lives, heal the broken heart and advance the kingdom of God. Apostle Paul said that he entered the city and the city went upside down. It can seem preposterous when you are in a big hospital to think that you can change the system of that hospital for God, as you watch and see the amount of atheists, freemasons, witches and the rigidity of its structure. Most definitely, this situation may seem a daunting task that seems virtually impossible, but know that what is impossible for man is possible for God. Our Lord strives in manifesting the greatness of his power in such a situation, knowing that He would get all the glory. For such a reason, it is so important to have depth in the things of God. Daniel and his friends were in a similar situation. In fact, his situation was worse since they were slaves with no social rights but they were still able to bring a whole heathen nation to believe in their God. They were able to use their influence being in the king's court to affect the king's reality and social position.

UNDERSTANDING THE MILLENIAL GENERATION

To be able to strategically bring societal transformation in the kingdoms of influence, we need to know and understand the generation we are living in. Every generation has its realities and intricacies. It is imperative to have knowledge of the inherent generation, in order to bring transformational change in the systems of a specific society. This generation is very different from the previous generations. In fact, this generation is called the millennial generation. Unfortunately, a good number of evangelical Christians who want to advance the kingdom of God in their society have no clue about the realities of this generation. Let us not be caught up in a religious whirlwind, forgetting the realities of the society we are living in. In that respect, we absolutely need to know the generation and the way it lives. What is important for this generation? What are the beliefs of this generation? What singularizes this generation from previous generations? These questions are important because our God will advance his kingdom through a people in tuned with the heartbeat of its generation. You cannot change a generation that you do not know. For this reason, Apostle Paul said that he was "a Hebrew with the Hebrews". That did not mean that he penetrated their sins, that meant that he knew them. He knew the Hebrew culture and how to deal with that culture. That did not mean that he participated in the whims and their sins, it simply meant that he knew their culture and their realities. He knew how to intermingle with them in order to bring the gospel of Jesus Christ. He knew how to deal with the Hebrews and how to deal with the Greeks. Certain strategies would function with the Greek culture but would not function with the Hebrew culture. Apostle Paul was conscientious and knowledgeable in that respect. Henceforth, we cannot affect our millennial generation if we do not know it.

HERO FOCUSED GENERATION

This generation is a generation that is hero-focused. It is seeking heroes, superstars and compelling examples. That is why people in this generation are always looking for a hero. Independently of the political views of America, why did many Americans vote for Mr. Obama in his first term? Mr. Obama exuded the allure of a hero for that nation. He spoke well. He was very articulate. He was well spoken and articulate. He was well dressed, well presented and had tremendous charisma. He released hope to an American culture that was badly bruised by its failing economy, unpopular wars and past terrorist attacks that were not healed. When they looked at Mr. McCain, although they may or may not agree with his policies, they might not have seen the prototype picture of the hero-like look, the superman type look to resurrect the American image. When they looked at Mr. McCain, the Americans could not recognize in him the prototype picture of the hero-like figure they were looking for in that specific period of the nation's social and economic reality. Were his policies better than Mr. Obama's? It could be debatable but unfortunately for him, his personality and presentation were lacking. Many public figures, reporters and political analysts said of Mr. Obama that he was bringing a refreshing look to the American culture and politics. Why? because in this generation people are looking for heroes. This generation is looking for someone it can connect to. Therefore some are connecting to Lady Gaga, Rihanna, Jay-Z, Marilyn Manson and Oprah Winfrey. You might not like them, but people are connecting to them according to their liking. Because of the quest to identify to a public figure, a large number of advocates of good morality and Christians are connected to Tim Tebow, the professional American football player in his rise as a star for the football team. The popularity of Tim is not necessarily because of his greatness on the football field, although he had his moments, but because of what he represented. He personified faith, hope to some and dedication and perseverance for others in the way he related his evangelical faith as a player.

OUTWARD APPEARANCE GENERATION

This generation is also looking for the outward appearance. The style, the look, the name brands are very important for this generation. For this reason people are looking to wear "Nike, Gucci, Louis Vuitton, Versace, Rolex", even if it's a fake model. In fact, the industry of replicas is booming because of the hunger this generation has for name brands. Even if they have to fake it until they make it or even if they have to fake it and never make it, people in this generation are running after name brands for the outward appearance. That is why people will sleep in front of the Mac store in the cold to be among the first to have a new iPhone even if the old one still works fine. This is the type of generation that we are in. Knowing this, the Christian community needs to step up and have other types of Tim Tebow's in order for us to give this generation other types of heroes to identify itself to. Imagine if we start merchandising a popular brand or raising icons in the different societal systems with the proper persona and look that can attract this generation. One of the reasons Jesus had such an impact on his generation was because of the popularity that the manifestation of the power of God attracted to him. That might seem unfitting for the religious preacher or theologian but he was a Superstar figure in his generation.

Mark 1: 45 says,

> "...However, he went out and began to proclaim it freely, and to spread the matter, so that Jesus could no longer openly enter the city, but was outside in deserted places; and they came to Him from every direction."

Jesus had such a reputation from the miracles, signs and wonders of his ministry that he was unable to enter the city because of the commotion and flocking that he generated. He had to stay in desert place and people would come to him from everywhere. Our popularity in the systems of this world will strategically position us to advance the kingdom of God. It is therefore not carnal for a Christian to think of raising a new innovative brand. It is not ungodly for a Christian to start a new line of clothing. All these endeavors can be precursors to touch our generation in search of heroes with which to identify themselves.

HOMOSEXUAL MOVEMENT

This generation will have to reckon with the rise of the homosexual movement. This movement has changed the landscape of our social behavior and lifestyle. We therefore need to be ready to know how to cope with this new social reality. We cannot shun this reality but rather face it and be able to know how to wisely express our views with love and be able to bring salvation and ministry to this little percentage of a social system that was yet able to raise awareness of their identity. Our mandate is not to ostracize them; we cannot belittle and degrade them but rather love them and be an instrument of God to bring salvation to them like any other sinner who needs to receive Jesus. Understand that we are called to love the sinner, not the sin. Let us put emphasis on the sinner in order to help him overcome his sinful position or sin. It is crucial to know that if we cannot even identify to this society, if you cannot identify with the way our society is functioning, we are in trouble. We will not be able to have any type of impact in this society. In order for us to have impact in a given society we need to first of all be able to identify with it. We need to know its realities, issues and challenges.

HYPER-SEXUALIZATION

Our systems are affected by hyper-sexualization. There is sexuality everywhere in the systems we are in. An actress can be called to do a commercial on salt or shoes, and for no purposeful reason be sumptuously dressed. The woman has become a sexual object to feed sexual desires through the seductive spirit to attract men to buy things by attracting their attention. In fact, in this generation not only women but also more and more men have also become sexual objects. More emphasis is put on the man with the muscular frame and the 'skinny model look' like if this look was the only attractive look to the human eye. Unfortunately this media attraction and pop culture attraction to these physical types has put tremendous pressure on this generation to force itself to look like these public figures. Very often, these same models, actors and public figures can barely stay in that fashion for the picture or commercial. Very often they even need graphic manipulation to ameliorate their look. Some others literally jeopardize their life to try to stay in that specific physical frame. But because we are living in a generation of replica and of lies, not enough people bother with that truth, what matters is to close our eyes to this reality and let us try unwisely to get there. And for this reason, health centers are capitalizing and people are paying large amounts to be part of a gym that they end up going just once in a while in quest of the top model look that will keep on evading them, while costing them a ludicrous amount in the process. Hyper-sexualization and its ramifications are severely affecting this generation. Even the movies that have been rated G for the general audience have scenes that are clearly seductive and sexual in their nature.

The trendsetters in arts and entertainment are selling the sexual look; they are selling the image of seduction and sexual impurity. The less clothing you are wearing the more you will sell. The more unclean you are, the more popular you will be. It is important for the Body of Christ to understand the demonic agenda behind hyper-sexualization. It is nothing else but the devil and his kingdom of darkness coming against the principles of purity, sanctity and holiness embedded in the culture of the kingdom of God. Hyper-sexualization has been given as a choice to our society but we need to give them another choice. We need to raise other type of attractive stars, who are successful in what they do but are advocating virginity until marriage, purity, cleanness, holiness, sanctity but yet still attractive, fun, interesting and appealing to our contemporary society. We need to know our systems.

DIGITAL AGE

We are in a digital age. Things are done much quicker. Technology has taken over – smartphones, Facebook, Twitter, Blu-ray, etc. Internet use has completely changed the social, cultural and professional interaction of society. Unfortunately, a large majority of churches have been sleepwalking. Many churches and ministries still do not have functional websites or do not have a website at all, forgetting that we are in a technological and informational generation. We are in a world that functions so fast and so quickly. We need to adapt ourselves to this generation to be able to impact it. Social networks have changed the way society communicates: texting, tweeting, facebooking. So Christians need to know how to upgrade. Even in business, technology has changed the way we do business: market globalization. Companies have access to a worldwide clientele. If you are called to impact the kingdom of business and only have a storefront, you are in disadvantage in this digital world. You will have to structure, to capitalize in the global market by having an online store. When you are aware of the way the systems function today, the Holy Spirit can now give you insight to be relevant, effective and efficient in this generation.

Understand that not very long from now we will not be functioning with paper books any longer. We are going to have e-books. So if you are not present in the digital world, how will you be relevant? We are in a generation where the systems are constantly upgrading. The church needs to be educated in order to shift the way the saints function, the way they do church and the strategies used to affect society. Jesus would have never crossed the Atlantic on a boat in this generation. He would have taken the plane. He would have used this cutting edge technology to have a maximized impact just like he did in his time. In his generation, he used a boat and preached in it from the seashore to use the waves to help make his voice travel to be able to speak to a larger amount of people. In the same optic, he would stand on top of a hill to speak to be able to affect a greater amount of people with his sermons. Unfortunately, some flaky and religious disciples are using the Lord's techniques in our day and age, instead of tapping in our new technology to affect a greater amount of people. We will not be able to be great in our spheres of influence if we don't know how to maximize its prevalent technology. Let it be known, that we will not be able to have significant impact in our world if we don't master its specificities, its social views and technological realities.

KNOWING THE SYSTEMS

Having mastered the understanding of the generation we live in, the Body of Christ has the responsibility of seeking to know the systems that it is called to impact and transform. Whether you are in arts & entertainment, family, education or any other kingdom, if you are called to impact it you need to know the system. You can't impact a system that you haven't mastered. To have substantial impact in a system that we are positioned in, we need to have knowledge of its realities.

ACTS 7: 22
*"And Moses was learned in all the wisdom of the
Egyptians, and was mighty in words and in deeds."*

Moses was able to face the Egyptians because he knew
them. He was learned in all the wisdom of the Egyptians. He
knew their language, he knew their structure and he knew
their culture. He knew their systems. How can you bring
reform in the educational system when you don't know its
functionality and realities? In order to affect that system, you
need to know the issues plaguing that specific system.

It is one thing to know our millennial generation but we
need to also know the system that we are in. If you are in a
certain system, whether you're in education, entertainment,
business or government you need to be in tune with what is
going on in that specific system. You need to know the key
players, the realities, the issues and challenges of your system.
How can you be called to affect a system and not even be aware
of its dominant figures, key players and trendsetters? How can
you even aspire to become influential in a sector if you don't
even know the ones that are influencing that system and why
they are influential? Who are the leaders in your sphere of
influence? What is going on in the system you are in? You need
to adequately know the realities in your workplace. Who's
who, how it functions, the issues and challenges, to know
and master every important detail in it. You need to know the
language, the terminology, and the ideology of your sphere of
influence. You need to study and show yourself approved in
the knowledge of the functionalities of your workplace and
societal system. Don't just say that I know the Holy Spirit and
the Holy Spirit will make me become impactful in my area.
This is just religious lunacy. The Holy Spirit can only use what

you know. If the Holy Spirit would give you more than the effort you're giving, everybody would have mastered the word without studying it. But the Holy Spirit uses what you know, He guides you, He doesn't do it for you. Therefore you need to do your homework concerning your societal system.

The lawyer needs to know the reforms in the legal system and master it. The hair stylist needs to have a head start on the competition and know the new products and what works best. The teacher needs to know the education reforms and how he can position himself to be impactful for the kingdom of God. The kingdom enforcers positioned in their area of predilection needs to be up to date, learned and strategic to advance the plan of God. We have to know our systems. Now understand, we are not there to accept everything in the system, but we still need to know the system. If we know the system, God will give us revelation to know how to affect it. Our efficient and proficient training cannot be maximized in a system that we don't know.

ENTERING THE SYSTEMS

The knowledge that we have of our societal system is called to prepare us to enter fully in that system. What do I mean by that? You see some people just go to their workplace and do what they have to do and leave. You will never be able to affect a system that you are running away from. You are not called to run away from your system but run to your system. You can be in the world and never be in that world. You hate it, you pray against it; you curse it all the time. Some people after a day of work get to their church and literally crush their workplace. My workplace is full of devils! The boss is satan incarnated! My co-worker is truly a witch. I hate their faces. Praise the Lord I am finally in the presence of the saved and sanctified! So you are constantly negative and downcasting the system you are in. Hence, you can be in a societal system that you are totally absent from. A system that you are ineffective in changing and shifting because you just can't transition and transform a system that you have no passion and love for. The same way you need to love a sinner to take him away from his sins, you need to have compassion for a system you want to change. We just can't affect a system that we are absent from.

Look what the Lord told the disciple in Luke 10: 3,

> *"Go your way: behold, I send you out as lambs among wolves."*

By nature a lamb is not inclined to gravitate around wolves. Why? Because wolves eat lambs, why would a lamb desire to gravitate around the one that wants it for dinner? But the Lord said I send you as lambs among the wolves. He knows that your system will be a hostile environment if still under the power of the prince of darkness, but nevertheless, the Lord still sends us there. Henceforth, believers by nature should not be inclined to be around non-believers and in a heathen environment, but it's still your mandate. How terrible to have Christians only connecting and having interaction with other Christians and even boast about it saying, "All my friends are Christians, I only connect with believers! I don't talk to people from the world. All my friends are full of the Holy Ghost!" And even quote a scripture out of context to support their ignorance. "The word says there's no relationship between the believer and unbeliever!" If everybody you know is light around you, when will your light shine? You see you cannot shine as light in a place that is already lit. Light can only shine in darkness. In fact some Christians have no fruit and do not shine because they are not seeking to be in the presence of someone that is in darkness. If everybody around you is saved, whom will you bring to salvation? Now on top of the fact that you only interact with the saved and sanctified, you curse and downcast the system you are in and which has souls crying for salvation. How tragic to be in that state and feel justified as a great Christian on your way to heaven. But our Lord Jesus said, "I send you out as lambs among wolves".

Notice that the Lord said he sends us out. We are not called to be great in the four walls of a church building. We are not called to be great among believers, we are sent out. We are sent in the world, in the societal systems as lambs among wolves to advance his Kingdom. We will never be able to advance the kingdom of God if we are not sent out. In fact this is what apostolic is all about, identifying, training, mandating and sending out a people of God to advance the kingdom of God in the world. Therefore our mandate is to enter the kingdoms of this world and gravitate around non-believers to transform them with the gospel of Jesus Christ.

I know that might sound strange for the religious Christian but it's time for you to mingle with the nonbelievers, to upgrade your opportunity to impact them for God. I know we have heard the word, never mingle with Non-Christians because they are going to hell. There are even songs that some believers and churches sing that say "I can't wait to leave the earth and to go, to go, to heaven!" Surely the Holy Ghost did not inspire these songs. If Jesus sends us among wolves how can we only want to gravitate only among lambs? If we are only thinking about reaching heaven, who will be reaching the unsaved in the world? The Lord Jesus died for the world not for a little percentage of believers. He wants to save the world not just bless a saved church.

Another verse that has been damaged contextually is Matthew 28: 19 that says,

> *"Go therefore and make disciples of all the nations, baptizing them in the name of the Father and of the Son and of the Holy Spirit."*

Mark 16: 15 continues and says,

> *"And He said to them: Go into all the world and preach the gospel to every creature."*

Did you notice that both of these verses said, "Go"? They never said to come? We tell people come to church but Jesus said go in the world. Instead of weekly penetrating the world with a determination to change it, we want to force the world to come to church on Sunday. But Jesus never said come to church, Jesus said, "Go!" The Body of Christ needs to have a holy desire to penetrate the systems of this world for reformation and transformation because Jesus said to go!

Matthew 28: 19 that says,

> *"Go therefore and make disciples of all the nations, baptizing them in the name of the Father and of the Son and of the Holy Spirit."*

There is something very particular about the word nations in this verse. This word in Greek speaks of a group of people who have the same mindset partaking of a specific society, a certain culture or a certain sector of activity. Therefore that verse can literally be translated by, "Go in your sphere of activity and disciple it." If you're a lawyer, the firm where you work with the people who work in it have commonalities of education, mindset and area of interests. The word of God is saying to penetrate it and because of your commonalities to your environment you become conducive to bring kingdom impact and societal reformation in your workplace. Why, because it is much easier for a lawyer to touch another lawyer than a non-lawyer, due to the commonalities. The points of affinities with our work environment can better help us relate to the people we meet every working day. It is easier for a nurse to touch another nurse because of the knowledge of what she's dealing with. When people do common things, they are more inclined to listen to one another. Since one can feel more understood by the other. You don't have to go far to affect a nation or even affect your nation. Start by affecting your sector of activity that has commonalities with you. How tedious to want to affect a foreign nation when you have a close one every week that you can radically change for Jesus.

This revelation should lead you to pray for the boss that you think is the incarnated satan or the co-worker who is a witch, since they are in your nation, your area of commonality. In fact some saints never prayed for their workplace, because they hate their guts, they hate the system that they are involved in, not understanding that they have been there for 15 years to transform that system with the principles of the Kingdom. If you're in a sector of activity that has not experienced kingdom reform, it's literally your fault, because it is impossible for light to penetrate darkness and not enlighten it. You are God's agent of reformation. If you do nothing about the grip of darkness on your sector of activity, who will? It is time to truly enter the systems we are in. Concretely making our system our sphere of ministry, praying, fasting and meditating the word of God with the backdrop of our system in our spirit to seek revelation to transform it. When we start praying, we start fasting, we start releasing peace on our system, we start releasing blessings upon our system, when we start caring for the people in our system change will start happening. Our sphere of influence will start shifting according to our decrees and prayers by the power of the Holy Ghost. Issues will start being taken care of, challenges will find solutions for kingdom breakthrough, because death and life are in the power of the tongue, what we decree, we will see the fruit thereof.

Imagine when you start praying and you start releasing the power of God on your colleagues in your workplace. When you start breaking the powers of darkness affecting the structure, the policies and the functioning of your sphere of influence. When you start coming against the spirit of doubt, disbelief and false religion, imagine the impact you will have on the penetration of the gospel in your system and the people involved in it. We are able to influence the spiritual atmosphere of our workplace by our prayers. The truth of the matter is we are not affecting our systems because we have not truly entered them. We're visitors in the systems, running away from the systems to stay in the confines and comfort of a local church and church services. When in fact, we are called to be passionate about the people in our workplace and the system we are connected to. The erroneous mindset of the religious church towards the world has to be demystified. The Church needs to start loving the world; start thinking about how to change the world. This is the prayer of our Lord Jesus Christ pertaining to the world.

JOHN 17: 15

"I do not pray that You should take them out of the world, but that You should keep them from the evil one."

Jesus never prayed for you to be out of your societal system but the church did. How many religious prayers were vociferated to sectorize saints in the confinements of a local house. Do you know that there are countries that have countless days of fasting and praying? They tell you to even sleep in the church in the revivals of 50 days. If you are staying in church every day fasting and praying when will you change the world? We have made the believers so comfortable in a local house that we forgot that our mandate was to change the world not the church. We forgot that we have been saved and are expected to be identified, trained and mandated to be sent out in the world to affect it with the gospel of the Kingdom. People of God we are saved to be edified and trained in church to go in the world! Jesus said, "I have not prayed to take them out of the world, but that you should keep them from the evil one". We need to be in the world, we need to be active in our spheres of activity to reform them but equipped enough in the things of God not to be affected by the evil one.

Stop being afraid of the world. Connect with it! If you're so super spiritual that you cannot have a full sentence without hallelujah and are unable to affect your society, you are non-productive for the kingdom. The Church desperately needs to be thought on how to function in the secular world, how to wisely mingle with the people of the world and be affective in our mandate of transformation.

KNOWING HOW TO COMMUNICATE IN THE SYSTEMS

The Saint that has genuinely accepted to enter its system needs to furthermore learn how to communicate in his system. It is very hard to affect a system that you can't communicate with. It is imperative for the ministers that are established in a particular system, to know how to communicate and relate with the people in that sphere of influence. There are terminologies that are understandable in the evangelical setting but are completely inappropriate in the secular setting. You cannot be saying amen after everything a colleague in your workplace says that you agree with. After you have completed a group assignment and received a positive mark from the board of governors of the multinational corporation you work for, you cannot jump and shout and speak in other tongues in the conference room. Our mandate is to positively affect not reject the world. So when you penetrate the societal systems, you need to be able to talk their language, to be relatable to them. If you can't properly relate to your environment, you will not be able to have a lasting impact in their lives. There are terminologies that are just fine in the Christian context but uncalled for in the secular context. It's not because you are fake, it is just wisdom. If you don't say: "Glory Hallelujah" for the whole day, it does not mean you have backslidden or are a lesser believer. The evangelical terminologies can be an obstacle sometimes for people to know God. I have heard non-believers stigmatizing Christians of being too forceful with their beliefs and their whole Christian culture. Instead of pushing our evangelical terminologies and culture down the throat of the non-believers we should be determined to show them the goodness, abundance and love of God in the way we act, function and relate with them. When we start communicating forgiveness to our fellow students and workplace colleagues we would be surprised to see the life transforming results. We need to know how to effectively communicate with the secular world, and that will take effort. Laziness will fight against the believer who wants to make the effort to learn how to effectively communicate with its world. Learning something that we don't know, that we are not comfortable with is never easy. This is the reason why saints like to stay in the cuddly environment of the church setting, because they feel secure there since it is a known environment. But in order to have an impact in the system we have entered, we need to come out of our comfort zone and learn how to communicate effectively with our system.

INTERACTING WITH THE SYSTEM

LUKE 15: 1-2

"Then all the tax collectors and the sinners drew near to Him to hear Him. And the Pharisees and scribes complained, saying, this Man receives sinners and eats with them."

You never had dinner with that fouled mouth colleague in your workplace, but Jesus would. The reason why the tax collectors and the sinners drew near Jesus is because He was relatable. Jesus interacted with tax collectors because he knew a truth. He had a wisdom that he understood that much of the Body of Christ has not yet understood. What is that truth? I need to interact with them. Jesus understood that in order to touch tax collectors and sinners he needed to be relatable to them. He understood that when He would start to relate and interact with them, they would become open to be touched by him.

Therefore the reason why they drew near him, to hear him, is because he had previously eaten with them and they had grown fond of him. Have you ever done something with a sinner to open his heart to the gospel that you carry? Well Jesus was the tax collectors and sinners' friend and the religious were complaining. Any time you will be doing the true work of God with the wisdom from above; don't be surprised if the religious rise up against you. It won't be the sinner that will be bothered but the religious believers and leaders will certainly be. But the true kingdom enforcers who understand the mandate will not be deter. Very often, the reason that believers are afraid to mingle with non-believers is by fear of being polluted and influence by them. But understand that darkness cannot affect light, light only can have an evident impact on darkness. This fear will be nullified by the proper kingdom training of the Christians. The devils that affect the world will not be able to affect the well-trained Christian but the power of God and the life of God that sips off joy, peace, success, humility, kindness and love are called to radically affect the non-believer that is around you. Tax collectors and sinners, Jesus ate with. He went to the restaurant with the sinners. Jesus ate with them, shared with them, enquired on how they were doing and this opened their hearts to come to listen to the gospel he was preaching.

I had the opportunity to bring various secular colleagues to Christ. The people in the world are real people with feelings just like believers. If we know how to interact with them and manifest the principles of God instead of firstly talking about them, they will be touched. This was Jesus' way of doing ministry. Unfortunately, many have erred away from the strategy of Christ to their own selfish and fruitless religious ways. The Lord penetrated the non-believers' circle and ate with them. In that process, He was able to affect them. They started enquiring on where he was preaching and felt compelled to go and hear the truth that set them free. There are some people who seem very bad and far from God in your environment, but as you start interacting with them, you would be surprised to see the miraculous transformation the Holy Spirit can perform through you. Stop shunning your system and the needy people in them, in order to impact them we need to interact with them.

SOLVING THE ISSUES OF THE SYSTEMS

The systems of our nations are desperately crying for help. Creation is waiting for the manifestations of the sons of God. As we position ourselves in the systems of our nations, we are called to solve the issues that are affecting them. For the longest time the power of God was used for healing and deliverance among the Body of Christ but the time has come to release the power of God for societal transformation. Our heartfelt question should be how are we going to strategically solve the issues of our systems?

HOW ARE WE GOING TO CHANGE THE PROBLEMS OF THE SYSTEMS?

1 CHRONICLES 12: 23, 32
"Now these were the numbers of the divisions that were equipped for war, and came to David at Hebron to turn over the kingdom of Saul to him... from Issachar men who understood the times and knew what Israel should do..."

The sons of Issachar were the least in number of those who came to help David take the kingdom from Saul. But they had something very special about them. The word says that they understood the times and they knew what Israel should do. So literally, they were able to understand the season, the culture, the realities of their times and were able to give to David solutions in how to be a conqueror. They were able to give him strategies to know how to take the kingdom of Saul. They brought solutions to Israel. They understood the times and knew what Israel should do. Therefore they had divine wisdom and strategy to execute things. Although they were few in number, their wisdom and strategic understanding made them special, because they brought solutions. They had what I call the anointing to solve.

That same anointing that was on the sons of Issachar is greatly needed in this generation. That special anointing that is enabling the kingdom enforcers to solve the issues of their Kingdom of influence. You desperately need to seek for the anointing to solve, that special anointing to bring solutions to the needs and to solve the issues in your societal systems. That grace will give you keys to know how to affect your area and sphere of influence. The anointing to solve is this God-given revelation to step into your work place and shift it with the principles of the Kingdom of God. Contextually we can take an example of a Son of God sent out as a lawyer in the realm of legal law. You have been working in an important case with many colleagues of the firm and have been encountering difficulties to properly unfold the enigma of that case. Everyone is trying to find the strategy and the solution for the case. This is a case that has never been seen in the judicial system in your nation before. And the partners are overwhelmed by the intricacy of the case, having no precedents. Imagine the impact on your firm and the judicial sphere when the anointing to solve permits you to solve the case and leave an indelible mark on the judicial system. This is the dimension of strategic systemic breakthrough that the Holy Spirit wants to release in this generation. As we open our spirits to be used by God as Daniel had made himself available with his companions to solve the dilemma of Nebucadnesar, the anointing to solve will bring tremendous societal transformation. God had given Daniel a ten times better anointing on the rest of his peers. This is our portion in the Lord and as we tap into that grace we will be able to demonstrate the anointing to solve. We serve the God of all wisdom and knowledge. It is his will to show this generation His manifold wisdom through the church.

I believe in this season the people of God will need to arise with the power to solve, to bring changes, to bring new ideas. Bezalel received grace from God; he received the spirit of creativity.

The Word of God says in Exodus 31: 1-4,

> "Then the Lord spoke to Moses, saying: See, I have called by name Bezalel the son of Uri, the son of Hur, of the tribe of Judah. And I have filled him with the Spirit of God, in wisdom, in understanding, in knowledge, and in all manner of workmanship, to design artistic works, to work in gold, in silver, in bronze."

He was able to do things with great awe. The Lord had given him the Spirit of God in wisdom, in understanding, in knowledge to design. His grace was supernatural. It was given by God. In this season God is releasing the anointing to perform, to design, to innovate, to transform and to solve different situations and different realities in the societal systems. You just cannot be in your workplace simply for an act of presence but you want to be positioned with the power to solve. The anointing to shift, the anointing to fix, the anointing to restore, the anointing to transform and change things in your systems.

We will not have any real impact in our systems without solutions. What will put a line of demarcation between the Black Muslim, the Mormon and the Jehovah witness who are working with you in the same department in the company where you work... the anointing to solve? What will give you the edge on the Newager and Buddhist in your sphere of influence... the anointing to solve. Daniel and his companion were in a hostile environment. They were taken far away from their families and their culture. They were surrounded by pagans and idolaters of different gods. But the insight given by the Holy Spirit was able to set them in a class of their own because they were able to solve the issue of the king. When you begin to solve the issues of your system, you will be put in a class of your own. And as the anointing to solve strategically put you in a position of elevation, you will then be in a position to advance the kingdom of the true God of Abraham, Isaac and Jacob. You see the power of God has a way of showing forth the uniqueness of Jehovah God. When we are able to take care of the needs of our workplace with the higher wisdom of God, our social environment will not have a choice but to acknowledge the goodness of God and to recognize his wholeness.

How tragic to have more professionals who are religious Christians in the marketplace then ministers who are professionals, able to shift their workplace with the anointing to fix, to restore, to upgrade and to change. Separation needs to take place between the kingdom enforcers in the kingdoms and the nonbelievers who are struggling to succeed with their own strength and intellect.

It will take us more than just the simple fact of stating we are believers in order for us to bring societal reform. Apostle Paul in 1 Corinthians 3, speaks of being a master builder; an architect. An apostle has the capacity to receive divine download of wisdom to give strategy, to know what can be done to fulfill the Great Commission. That apostolic anointing will be instrumental to affect our generation. Daniel made people know his God. Daniel had pre-eminence because he had the anointing to solve. Joseph was promoted because he had the anointing to solve. Joseph was not promoted just because he was Christian, Joseph was not promoted just because he had his Jesus tie but Joseph was promoted because he stepped into an arena and he showed forth the anointing and the power to solve. Because of the power to solve he had breakfast in prison but ate supper in the palace. When you have the power to solve, you cannot stay in the prison forever. The prison will have to free you from its bondage to let you step in your divine regal destiny. You've been waiting for a long time for the promotion. Know that the promotion will not come only because you pray unless you let your prayer lead you to the appointed revelation and knowledge to make a difference in your professional assignment.

Understand that the life of prayer of a kingdom enforcer is very different from the religious 'praying without cease' believer. You see the minister who knows his mandate to advance the things of God will have a much more strategic prayer life. He will not only pray for his family and for money. He will have a burden for the company where he works. He will be seeking God for insight in how to shift things in his workplace and have spiritual clarity on how to solve the issues of the workplace. He wills for God to give him the keys for his sector, innovative projects, new inventive ideas for the benefit of his sector of influence. These types of prayers will release you in a whole different sphere of connection with God, because such cries to Him implies a burden to advance his Kingdom in this world. Daniel and his companions prayed for a need in their kingdom of government. They did not fast for a raise or to get married with some nice girls. They prayed for a societal issue and God answered from heaven. I believe that as we get more tuned with the mind of Christ, the burden of our Savior and Lord, our prayers will be answered with a greater ease. Too often as James 4: 3 states our prayers are not answered because it is for our own carnal desires and not for the will nor the advancement of the kingdom of God. Daniel interceded for a need in his societal system, God clearly answered. The answer the Lord gave Daniel, little did he know was going to be the door to his unexpected sudden promotion. When we begin to concentrate on the issues of our world and our society that are concerned to the God of heaven and of the earth, God will also take notice and take care of our terrestrial needs. Don't look for the promotion but look for the solution needed in your workplace. The faster you bring solutions the faster you will experiment promotion. As you call upon the Lord for system solutions, as you pray and fast for the needs of your workplace environment, certainly Jehovah will show Himself the provider. He did it for Joseph and his professional career made a leap in a couple of hours that he would have never expected. God can shift things in a blink of an eye, if you dare call for the manifestation of the anointing to solve for your system. That anointing did not only open doors to the palace for Joseph but that same anointing gave him renown as he was able to solve the economical system of his government. What a blessing, when a Son of God set himself up for the promotion from God. We are able to be without worry. You see the same God who gives you the promotion, He is more than able as you continue to be consecrated to Him and determined to advance His Kingdom, to continue to give you wisdom to fulfill your professional mandate with greatness. It is the blessing of the Lord that makes rich and make it follow without any sorrow (Proverbs 10: 22). If God has set you in position, He has the power to keep you in position with the power to solve.

HOW WILL THE ANOINTING TO SOLVE MANIFEST?

EPHESIANS 3: 10
"To the intent that now the manifold wisdom of God might be made known by the church to the principalities and powers in the heavenly places."

There is wisdom that God wants to reveal to the world through the church. We cannot content ourselves in being churchgoers we need to release the manifold wisdom of God in the systems of the world. That wisdom is called to affect not only the natural realm but also the spiritual realm. In fact the wisdom we are called to bring forth in the world will, first of all, affect the realm of the spirit where the principalities and powers that are illegally dominating the societal systems are established. This impact in the realm of the spirit will have for repercussion a clear manifestation in the realm of the natural. There's wisdom in that we are called to bring to shift the heavenly and the world. The manifold wisdom of God is called to be revealed by the church and through the church. That manifold wisdom was instrumental in raising Daniel and Joseph in system relevance. It is not Joseph's academic degree that made him national treasurer; Daniel did not become prime minister because of his studies in Babylon. He knew the wisdom and the systems of Babylon but that did not make him Prime Minister. It's the manifold wisdom of God that opened the prime ministerial position for him. The word said in Proverbs 18: 16, "The gift of man will make room". The gifting of God in your life is the channel through which God will open doors for you in front of the kings of this world. The anointing of solution will be channeled through you, through the gifting of God in your life. It is not enough to be positioned in systems but you need the wisdom of God to work through you in those systems. The time has come for us to receive downloads of the wisdom of God to impact the kingdoms of society. I call that spiritual technology. Spiritual technology is the spiritual process and methods, the know-how of the spirit to transform and impact our society. We cannot expect to shift our systems with only our intellectual capacities. God needs to give us the wisdom so that we can know how to do things in our sphere. You need spiritual technology for your system. You need practical wisdom of God to affect your sphere of influence. We need the technology of God to advance his Kingdom. We need the manifold wisdom of God to have significant impact in our society that He may take the glory. When you understand that, you will no longer have self-centered prayers but you will have kingdom-centered prayers. It is not that I think that it is easy to be a Daniel but our God is the same yesterday, today and forever more. If he did it for Daniel we can put ourselves in a position that He may use us likewise in our generation. So if you are wondering how am I suppose to interpret a dream that the king didn't even know and give him understanding of that dream? Well you might not be in that same situation but one thing is certain God is able through spiritual technology, to use you to bring forth solutions for your system. There is a strategy, an idea, and a solution that God wants to anoint you with to give you prominence in your domain for kingdom greatness. You can be facing what seems to be an impossible task at hand in your workplace. This was exactly the situation of Daniel. The king of Babylon had a dream that he forgot and he wanted somebody to remind him the dream and secondly to interpret the dream. You know how daunting of a task that must have been. That ultimatum was followed with a death threat, its either the magicians and wise men of Babylon solve the enigma or they would be put to death. In that terrible situation, Daniel needed to be more than a preacher with a good wise word. He needed revelation from God. He needed fellowship with the Holy Ghost. Theology in such a case would be irrelevant. Intellectual gymnastics and diplomacy would not be enough.

The word said in Daniel 2: 16 and 18,

> "So Daniel went in and asked the king to give him time, that he might tell the king the interpretation. Then Daniel went to his house, and made the decision known to Hananiah, Mishael, and Azariah, his companions, that they might seek mercies from the God of heaven concerning this secret, so that Daniel and his companions might not perish with the rest of the wise men of Babylon."

Daniel went in and asks the king to give him time, that he might tell the king the interpretation. Then Daniel went to his house and made the decision known to Hananiah, Mishael, and Azariah, his companions. In that type of situation you cannot afford to have carnal prayer partners, you truly need to have those who can touch and agree with you to touch the throne of God. Unfortunately a shocking number of born-again believers, deacons and even ministers have a lethargic prayer life. Daniel's challenge was one for the ages and he needed true solid spiritual friends. So he went to his companions to seek intercession and said there's a little issue here, the king does not remember his dream and second of all he wants us to interpret it. So here's Daniel a governmental official facing an issue in his workplace calling for the support of his minister buddies in the same system. They have a common purpose, solving the issue raised in their system. This is not self-centered this is kingdom-centered. In such an ordeal, we are shifting from praying for our personal need to a societal need. Understanding that if we can solve the situation of our system, we can positively affect the people in our sphere of influence for the Kingdom of God. Surely arts and entertainment have issues, education has issues, media has issues and government has issues. Instead of focusing and monopolizing your time to pray for your personal needs. Praying for yourself, your family, for a car or a house, we need to address the needs of the societal systems. It is time for us to manifest Matthew 6: 33, "But seek first the kingdom of God and His righteousness, and all these things shall be added to you." The blessing of this verse comes with Kingdom-centered prayers. Kingdom solutions come with kingdom-centered prayers. Daniel and his companions did just that. They set time apart to seek God for their system's issue. These prayers are needed and will shift things in our societal systems.

The mindset of the Body of Christ needs to change. Before we can ever think of finding solutions for our sectors of activity, we need to put time on them. We need to pray for the solutions needed in our workplace. We might have prayed for a particular person in our workplace but have we been putting time in prayer for the system we're in? You see there's a strategy to the how we will change the world. We cannot just penetrate the world. We need to desire to change it. We need to desire to shift it for God, in order to do that we need the manifold wisdom of God. How will the anointing to solve manifest?

ACTION FOR SOLUTION

When we speak of solutions, we need wisdom. The manifold wisdom of God is necessary to bring forth solutions. There are actions that God can call us to make for solutions. What Daniel did? He solved an enigma. He solved a secret. Therefore wisdom was given to him to give solution to a dream. But there are other types of solutions that can come from actions.

Joseph was used with a specific action. A specific action, a divine action plan was given to him to affect the economical system of Egypt. When God revealed to him the future agricultural issue of Egypt, Joseph also received the way to solve it. In fact this is what will set us apart in the marketplace. It is one thing to analyze the future status and issues of a system but it is a whole different level to accurately give the solution to solve it. In order for you to impact your sphere of influence it might take you to build a specific project, a structured action plan that needs to be implemented in the system for a needed change.

GENESIS 41: 33-37
"Now therefore, let Pharaoh select a discerning and wise
man, and set him over the land of Egypt... And let them
gather all the food of those good years... Then that food
shall be as a reserve for the land for the seven years of
famine... So the advice was good in the eyes of Pharaoh..."

Literally, the solution was good in the eyes of Pharaoh. God wants to give the sons of the kingdom action plans. His desire is to give us plans, reveal to us programs to solve the social issues of our generation. Because solving issues in a system gives prominence and importance to an individual. If an educator minister seeks and receives solutions to the educational system, he will become prominent and important for that system. You see prominence and importance in a system will bring the people in the system to listen to what you have to say. Your thoughts and ideas on a specific issue will matter. It is in that fashion that we can use the principles of the Kingdom in our action plans and work policies. Through the principles of God we can shift the mindset through the programs we are inspired by God to bring forth. We truly need the anointing to solve to bring changes in the societal systems, the anointing to put together programs to impact our sectors of activity. How do we do it?

IDENTIFICATION OF SYSTEM ISSUES

We need to first of all, identify the issues or needs of our societal system. Before God can give you divine wisdom to solve, you need to know the issues. For example, the high rate of high school dropout is an issue. Be it known that the needs of the society should be the burden of the churches. We should expect the world to run to us for solutions to the issues of society. Unfortunately in many areas in the world the church is completely absent and a non-factor in the social issues of his society which is ludicrous since we are the carriers of the truth that is called to set the world free. We have the anointing of God. We are supposed to be the light of the world and the salt that gives it flavor. It is no longer time for the church to hide from its responsibility toward the state of its world. The state of the world is a direct reflection of the state of the church. When the church is impactful its society is impacted. Therefore we need to start by identifying the problems of our system.

CORPORATE CONNECTION FROM SAME SYSTEM KINGDOMISERS

We then need to connect with the brethren in Christ who are in our system to deliberate on the issues of our sphere of influence. The deliberation should lead to strong and revelational intercessory prayer for the issues of the sector. These types of prayers will be very powerful and insightful because it is the will of God to take care of the issues of our world. How different these types of prayers are to the egotistical prayer that most believers regularly do. Most of the time the believers only pray for their personal needs. Praying for a spouse, a child, a house, a car, a promotion or a family member. It is not that God is not willing to take care of our personal needs but his desire is for us to seek first the Kingdom of God and all those things shall be added to us. As prayer is raised by faith to God he will prophetically begin to speak on the different issues in our field and give us solutions for transformation. This dimension of breakthrough can only be reached by the coming together of the kingdomizers from the same system. Understand that there is a level of societal transformation that can only happen through corporate implication. There will be no superheroes able to fix societal issues by themselves. It will take corporations. For this reason the devil has been working overtime through the years to severely hit the body of Christ with division. The enemy knows that it will be absolutely impossible for us to have major impact in the systems of the world if we are divided. Wisdom is necessary to save a system and the souls that are in them and advance the Kingdom of God on earth. We have so much talent in the Body of Christ. When we start putting these talents and these gifts together in a system, taking away religious mindsets that are hindering the work of God and start using strategy to change systems, we will not have place to put saved people. For creation is waiting for the manifestation of the Sons of God. God did not only raise you to be a professional, to just have your little salary, your beautiful car and your house. But God is calling you to have the wisdom like Daniel to receive revelation to know how to come together and find programs for societal transformation. What can we put together as we come and we sit and we pray? In order for Daniel to take care of the issues of the governmental system that he worked in, he called upon his companions who were with him in that system. It took corporate connection from the kingdomizers from the same system.

STRATEGIC ACTION PLAN

The third step is strategic action plan. We will be called to establish a dynamic plan. Through the wisdom given by God through prayer and insight, we will be able to establish a plan, a dynamic program to solve the issues based on the principles of God.

The time has come for the manifold wisdom to be manifested through the kingdom enforcers to establish nonreligious programs to deal with the problems of our societal systems.

Psalms 138: 2 says,

> "I will worship toward Your holy temple, And praise Your name For Your loving kindness and Your truth; For You have magnified Your word above all Your name."

Our Lord God magnifies His principles above His name. He is careful with the application of His principles. For the longest time we have been magnifying His name above His principles. People have been using His name, declaring His name but have been walking far away from his principles. It is time for a turnaround!! We can magnify His principles above His name. This truth is very instrumental for societal reformation for social transformation. By the understanding of this powerful word of God, we can affect our society with the application of the principles of God without primarily mentioning the name of the Lord. If we can establish the principles of the Kingdom in our societal systems we have made a great step in making them acknowledge the God of these principles. You see it is quite easier to make someone recognize the author of a truth that he abides by then to make someone apply the principles of an author.

The devil has been using this strategy for a long time. His name is very often absent in the systems but his principles are very present. We can see corruption, sexual impurities, jealousy, hatred, murders and destruction clearly visible in the systems. A lot of believers have testified their allegiance to Jesus Christ but still fall short of applying his truths.

Knowing this the Lord declares in John 14: 15,

"If you love me, keep my commandments."

The greatest sign of loving the Lord is our observance of His commandments. Therefore by establishing strategic action plans and programs in our societal systems through the wisdom of the Holy Spirit to fix the sector's issue, we are literally infusing our system with the principle of God without even saying the name of Jesus. All of a sudden, we begin to shift the mindset of our sector. The people in our systems begin to abide by the will of God and therefore put themselves in a position to receive the God of the principles that they abide by. Given salvation to a soul that has been abiding in the principles of God is much easier than trying to bring salvation to a soul that has been profoundly gripped and under the spell of the principles of the kingdom of darkness.

God will give you programs that will take care of issues in society. This will usher in your prominence and your positioning in the forefront of your system as one who is recognized as a problem solver. You see every professional every director and every CEO wants to be connected with an employee who can bring solution in the company or institution. The minister therefore becomes a voice that is able to release and infuse the principles of God by the ability of the Holy Spirit. People of God, we are talented but we leave it in the four walls of a church building. It has to change! When the anointing to solve begins to manifest we will have the results like Daniel and Esther. Look at the result of the anointing to solve in Daniel 6: 26. Due to the way God used him in his sphere to affect government, the king will say, "I make a decree that in every dominion of my kingdom man must tremble and fear before the god of Daniel". This is the end result. The end result of affecting and transforming the systems of nations is to reach the level where the nations recognize the Lord God whom we serve. Therefore the result of the solutions that Daniel brought, through the power of the Holy Spirit, was the decree made by the King to acknowledge the greatness of Jehovah God. Imagine how solving a major economical issue in your nation could open an incredible door to make known the Almighty God that you serve. This type of breakthrough could have such an impact in the government that the President or Prime Minister could be forced to openly acknowledge God and the principles of the Kingdom. Well that is exactly what the Lord accomplished through prophet Daniel. The Lord gave wisdom through the anointing of solution to solve his system's issue, and without initially mentioning the name of Lord, His sector acknowledged the God that he served. The fruit spoke for him, can you imagine the level of impact we will have in our nation when we start fixing the issues of violence, fixing the issues of lack of respect and lack of submission, fixing the issues of families, fixing the issues of government. Imagine today if the president of the USA, would have a Joseph coming forth with the solutions of the economic chaos of his nation. What do you think would happen? It would be certainly hard to undermine the source of such solution. He would certainly give a position to such a person and henceforth pave the way to acknowledge the true source of true sustainable societal solution; the Almighty God.

POWER TO CHANGE NATIONS

Power will also be needed to change the nations. If intelligence could change nations, many nations should have been changed already. We have intellectuals, we have people who have graduated, we have sociologists, psychologists, we have all the "ists", but we still have issues with man. And as the Body of Christ we cannot use the same tools they have. We will not be able to take the nation without the power of God.

Acts 1: 8 says:

> *"But you shall receive power, after that the Holy Ghost is come upon you: and you shall be witnesses unto me both in Jerusalem, in all Judea, and in Samaria, and unto the uttermost part of the earth."*

The word of God states in that verse that we shall receive power. The word power literally means capacity and supernatural enablement. Notice that it did not say that you shall receive gifts but power. Understand that without power your gifts will not bring systemic dominance. Zechariah 4: 6 says that it is not by might nor by power but by the Spirit of God. The Holy Spirit is necessary for societal reformation. You can have all the intellectual capacity or talent you want but to be able to overtake the principalities reigning over the systems it will take power of God! No wonder believers have been in systems so long and have no influential impact. You need the power of God. You need supernatural enablement to shift the systems of this world. The capacity, the enablement, the strategy given by the Holy Spirit will be instrumental for the disciples to become witnesses for God.

Notice that the word says, "You shall be a witnesses to me." You can do a lot of things in the name of the Lord and yet still be fruitless for the kingdom. But to be a witness for God you need his supernatural enablement. For the longest time, the Church has passed by its divine destiny. The power we receive by the Holy Spirit was called to be ministered in the world not in a building called church. The purpose of the power of God was to be instrumental in helping us regain dominion of the earth. The power of God was for global influence. I know we use the power of God for healing, deliverance and to prophesy in the church. And that is all good but comes short of the fullness of its purpose. In church, ministry is the initial stage of the power of God and global influence is its full purpose. The church is the agent of change that is called to kingdomize the world and advance the kingdom of God in the world.

We don't just have the power to change lives but we also have the power to change systems. You see we have been engaging in changing lives. But the devil is saying, continue to take them individually and I will continue to rule the systems and take them globally.

Notice that the word did not say that you will be witnesses in the church, but rather that you will be witnesses in your city, state and your country. For example living in the city of Montreal in the province of Quebec in Canada. The saint cannot only be a churchgoer enjoying Sunday service with a good praise and worship and a good message for his soul. Every saint in that church is called to be a witness in his city of Montreal, province and nation. The Lord never said that we received power to come in a building that we call church. But He said that we will receive power, the Holy Ghost will come upon us and we will be witnesses in Jerusalem. The power is for the work place, not for the church place. We have taught people that the power of God is for the church. We release power in the church, but we are primarily called to release the power of God in the world. The power of God needs to be released in our streets, neighborhoods, workplaces and systems. To take our nations we will need wisdom but we will also need God's power. This generation needs to see the power of God through the wisdom of God. There's wisdom that God will gives us for this generation. That's why as a leader we have the responsibility to ask God how we are going to do it and shift this generation. We need power for the work place, power to take away stress, power for depression, power to take away anxiety, power for solution.

DANIEL 2: 47-48

"The king answered and unto Daniel, and said: Of a truth it is, that your God is a God of gods, and a Lord of kings, and a revealer of secrets, seeing thou couldest reveal this secret. Then the king made Daniel a great man, and gave him any great gifts, and made him ruler over the whole province of Babylon and chief of the governors over all the wise men of Babylon."

We need to use the power wisely. Power of God will raise you in prominence. When you use the power to fix the situation in your accounting firm, when you use the power to take care of the situation in the administrative work you are doing and when you use the power to change things in the school, they will recognize you. All of you who have received the Lord as Savior that power is in you to fix things. It's time for us to change the nations with the power of God.

For this purpose God is raising Apostles in this generation. True Apostles who will not only exhort the people of God to do things but will be able to show them strategically how to do it. The Body of Christ needs to raise its standard to step up from only seeking to know what to do to the level of knowing how to do it. We need to have the spiritual technology of God for supernatural wisdom in the how to bring forth transformation in the systems. God will give us wisdom for programs for social transformation. The programs will not just be geared solely on having a job and a salary. Sometimes programs are sometimes uniquely geared on having government subsidies for job creation, to have a salary without any substantial fruit or lasting impact on the community. Our Kingdom purpose is to have programs geared toward societal reformation for social transformation. Programs that bring solutions to the issues of our society and strategically help advance the Kingdom of God on earth. God will cause our anointed solutions to have so much impact that it will move people in higher echelon of society, the kings and queens of the systems to want to be connected and participate in the results. Understand that if you have success in the area you are in, where God has positioned you to impact, the people in high places will look for you. They will find you and want to associate with you. This will henceforth open the door for their salvation because influence is an important key to change the mindset and spiritual position of a person.

Because of the impact of Esther in government, the word says in Esther 8: 17, in the second part of the verse,

> *"The many of the people of the land became Jews"*
> *Because of Esther's influence many people decided to*
> *become Jews."*

Because of the influence of Esther, the Babylonians became Jews. A nation that previously was getting ready to eliminate the Jewish nation was now becoming Jew by multitude. The attitude, the conduct and the piousness of Esther in her system brought massive conversions. She was so successful as a Queen that she brought the people to change their religion. This is exactly what the Lord intends to do through us in this generation. Because of the impact we are called to have in the systems of our communities, people will desire to receive our Lord and Savior Jesus Christ, the author of our applied wisdom in our sphere of influence.

The revelation of Psalms 138: 2 has been instrumental in the implementation of The A.C.T.I.O.N. Vision that the Lord gave me to advance his kingdom in the world. We acquired a nonreligious building: the A.C.T.I.O.N. Center that is a platform for many organization that have for mandate the advancement of the kingdom of God in the societal systems of our nation and in the world. The A.C.T.I.O.N. Center is not a church but a multifaceted building. The church, the spiritual entity which is PQL (French for Liberating Word) has the general assemblies and various meetings in the Center. When Jesus Christ prophesied in Matthew 16: 18, He was not prophesying about a physical building but a spiritual building. 1 Peter 2: 5 is clear about that when it says, "You also, as living stones, are being built up a spiritual house, a holy priesthood, to offer up spiritual sacrifices acceptable to God through Jesus Christ." The church is a spiritual house that can therefore meet anywhere. So, PQL Ministry the spiritual entity of our A.C.T.I.O.N. Vision has its assemblies of the saints in the auditorium of the A.C.T.I.O.N. Center. The auditorium is also available for different other purposes and activities geared to be conducive to Kingdom advancement by the revenues it generates or the Kingdom activities it holds. We strategically advance the plan of God by having kingdom enforcers trained in the ministry that are spiritual sons and daughters heading the different entities that are established in the Center for the shifting of society. This divinely given strategy has diversified the way we are advancing the Kingdom of God. We are implementing the will of God not only through the assemblies of the saints but by using the organizations to affect the different kingdoms of society. This divine model has already been reproduced in different parts of the world; Chili, USA, Barbados and Brazil by the apostolic impartation of A.C.T.I.O.N. Network. The Body of Christ has been receiving theoretical understanding of the kingdoms of influence in the last couple of years but I truly believe that the time of implementation has come. The Body of Christ needs to come out of its comfort zone in just being theoretical and analytical and enter a more active and applicable state. That spiritual state would force churches to find actions plans that work and are practical for the advancing of the kingdom of God in their respective regions. Speaking on social transformation is one thing that unfortunately felt short of having substantial evidence of societal reform that truly brings social transformation. I believe the time has come for us to step out of theoretical talk to true kingdom transformation in our nations. We will not be able to have true success by copying patterns. Different regions will have different needs but the revelation given in this book will give foundational truths necessary to go through the phase of understanding societal reformation and implementing solutions to bring social transformation.

Printed in the United States
By Bookmasters